ESOL: A Critical Guide

s to

SEP

Also published in
Oxford Handbooks for Language Teachers

The Oxford ESOL Handbook
Philida Schellekens

Teaching American English Pronunciation
Peter Avery and Susan Ehrlich

Success in English Teaching
Paul Davies and Eric Pearse

Doing Second Language Research
James Dean Brown and Theodore S. Rodgers

Teaching Business English
Mark Ellis and Christine Johnson

Intercultural Business Communication
Robert Gibson

Teaching and Learning in the Language Classroom
Tricia Hedge

Teaching Second Language Reading
Thom Hudson

Teaching English Overseas: An Introduction
Sandra Lee McKay

Teaching English as an International Language
Sandra Lee McKay

How Languages are Learned (3rd edition)
Patsy M. Lightbown and Nina Spada

Communication in the Language Classroom
Tony Lynch

Teaching Young Language Learners
Annamaria Pinter

Doing Task-based Teaching
Jane Willis and Dave Willis

Explaining English Grammar
George Yule

ESOL: A Critical Guide

Melanie Cooke
James Simpson

OXFORD
UNIVERSITY PRESS

OXFORD
UNIVERSITY PRESS

Great Clarendon Street, Oxford OX2 6DP

Oxford University Press is a department of the University of Oxford.
It furthers the University's objective of excellence in research, scholarship,
and education by publishing worldwide in

Oxford New York

Auckland Cape Town Dar es Salaam Hong Kong Karachi
Kuala Lumpur Madrid Melbourne Mexico City Nairobi
New Delhi Shanghai Taipei Toronto

With offices in

Argentina Austria Brazil Chile Czech Republic France Greece
Guatemala Hungary Italy Japan Poland Portugal Singapore
South Korea Switzerland Thailand Turkey Ukraine Vietnam

OXFORD and OXFORD ENGLISH are registered trade marks of
Oxford University Press in the UK and in certain other countries

© Oxford University Press 2008

The moral rights of the authors have been asserted

Database right Oxford University Press (maker)

First published 2008

2012 2011 2010 2009 2008
10 9 8 7 6 5 4 3 2 1

2 006 002 180

ISBN: 978 0 19 442267 3

Printed in China

CONTENTS

Acknowledgements   ix

Introduction   xi

1 ESOL in the world   1
   Introduction   1
   English in the world   3
   ESOL around the world   4
   ESOL in England, Wales, and Northern Ireland   5
      ESOL as a 'Skill for Life'   6
      ESOL, policy, and politics   8
      Citizenship and language   9
      The current picture: ESOL and the economy   11
   Conclusion   11
   Further reading   12

2 A world of difference: being an adult ESOL learner   13
   Introduction   13
   Diversity and heterogeneity   15
      Languages   15
      Educational background and literacy levels   17
      Gender   17
      Family relations and intergenerational language issues   18
      Experiences of immigration, settlement, and asylum   20
      Asylum   20
   Aspirations and obstacles   21
      Employment   21
   The range of ESOL settings   24
      Community and constraints   25
   Conclusion   26
   Further reading   27

3 The challenges of ESOL practice   29
   Introduction   29
   Who are ESOL teachers?   30
   The challenges of ESOL practice   32

Student diversity and student needs 32
Students' changing needs and attitudes 33
Diversity and group learning 35
Affective benefits of group work 36
The challenges of audit culture: centralization and accountability 38
Meeting the challenges 39
Professional identity 39
Approaches to language teaching in ESOL 41
Teaching methods 41
Methods and principled pragmatism 44
Conclusion 46
Further reading 46

4 **The content of ESOL lessons** 49

Introduction 49
The tensions of lesson content 49
From home-produced materials to the global textbook 50
Adult ESOL in England, Wales, and Northern Ireland:
    curriculum and materials 54
Student-generated content 57
Taboo subjects 60
The playful side of language learning 61
Conclusion: principled pragmatism in lesson content 63
Further reading 64

5 **Oral communication** 67

Introduction 67
Oral communication outside classrooms 68
Speaking in ESOL classrooms 73
Opening up and closing down 74
Encouraging learners to talk 76
Tackling real world challenges in the ESOL classroom 78
Testing oral communication in ESOL 82
Conclusion 88
Further reading 89

6 **ESOL, literacy, and literacies** 91

Introduction 91
ESOL students with basic literacy needs 92
Teaching basic literacy to ESOL students 94
Expert language literacy or English literacy? 96
Literacy theories in conflict: basic skills and literacy practices 98
Literacy as a basic skill 98

Literacy practices   100
Functional literacy and employability   104
   Literacy and employability   105
A critical take on literacy   110
Conclusion   112
Further reading   113

7 **ESOL and electronic literacy practices**   115
Introduction   115
Reading online: multimodality and web literacy   116
   Multimodality   116
   Web literacy: reading in virtual space   118
   Multitasking and polyfocal attention   119
Computer-mediated communication (CMC)   122
   ESOL students' use of email and messenger out of class:
   two examples   122
ESOL, ICTs, and globalization   124
Inequality and the information poor   127
Conclusion: electronic literacy and communicative competence   131
Further reading   132

8 **Learning about teaching**   133
Introduction   133
   Standardized teaching qualifications   134
   Developing professional vision   134
Observation in ESOL   135
Critical issues in observation for evaluation   137
   The difficulty of observing teacher behaviour   137
   Inspections encourage prescription   138
   Peer observation for teacher development   140
   Peer observation: the pitfalls   141
   Doing peer observation   141
Teachers engaging with research   142
   The theory/practice 'gap'   142
   Research and practice: a mutual dialogue   143
   Research as 'common sense'   144
Exploratory teaching and action research   147
   The features of action research   148
   The stages of action research   149
Conclusion   152
Further reading   153

Appendix: overseas contexts   155
Bibliography   167
Index   181

ACKNOWLEDGEMENTS

Our greatest debt of thanks is owed to the many students and teachers of ESOL who we have worked with and talked to, whose classes we have observed, and without whom there would be no book.

Our special thanks go to Celia Roberts and Mike Baynham, whose support of our work has been unstinting. Many other people have shared with us their insights and knowledge, among them Elsa Auerbach, Anne Burns, Patrick Bushell, John Callaghan, Mary Clayton, Sue Hackett, Michael Hepworth, Jennifer MacDougall, James McGoldrick, Bonnie Norton, Sheila Rosenberg, Catherine Wallace, Stephen Woulds.

Other colleagues read early drafts and chapters, and made valuable suggestions for improvements. We'd like to thank in particular David Block, Karen Dudley, Helen Sunderland, David Thornton.

Finally we would like to thank our families and friends for their encouragement during the writing of this book.

The authors and publisher are grateful to those who have given permission to reproduce the following extracts and adaptations of copyright material: Page 19 © National Extension College. Page 16 *Effective Teaching and Learning: ESOL* by Baynham, M., Roberts, C. et al. NRDC: London 2007 © Crown Copyright 2007. Reproduced under the terms of the Click-Use Licence. Page 78 Dialogue from *Skills for Life ESOL Learning Materials*, Entry 1. Reproduced by kind permission of The Quality Improvement Agency for Lifelong Learning © 2003 www.qia.org.uk. Page 79 Dialogue from *Skills for Life ESOL Learning Materials*, Entry 2. Reproduced by kind permission of The Quality Improvement Agency for Lifelong Learning © 2003 www.qia.org.uk. Page 80 Dialogue from *Talk on Trial – Job Interviews, Language and Ethnicity* by Celia Roberts and Sarah Campbell © Crown Copyright 2006. Reproduced under the terms of the Click-Use Licence.

Sources: Page 45 *TESOL Quarterly* 28/1, 1994. Page 135 ELT Journal Volume 57/2, April 2003. Page 139 *Reflect*, Issue 4, October 2005.

The publishers would like to thank the following for their kind permission to reproduce photographs:

Alamy Images pp 15 (classroom/Bill Bachman), 19 (students with computer/ Janine Wiedel Photolibrary), 75 (group of students/Ian Shaw); Getty Images pp 10 (Citizenship ceremony/Ian Jones/AFP), 71 (cleaner/Reza Estakhrian/ Stone+); Matt Salusbury p 40 (ESOL demonstration).

INTRODUCTION

ESOL: A Critical Guide is an introduction to English for Speakers of Other Languages (ESOL). ESOL refers to the English that is taught to and learnt by adult migrants to English-dominant countries, and is the common term for this branch of English Language Teaching in Britain and Ireland. In some countries, notably Canada, the United States, and Australia, it is known as ESL: English as a Second Language. The aim of the book is to provide readers with an up-to-date broad understanding of ESOL pedagogy in its social, political, and economic contexts, with a particular focus on research undertaken in England.

The teaching of English to adults suffers from a proliferation of acronyms, which are sometimes contradictory and overlapping. This is because English Language Teaching (ELT) is a broad and complex field. While this book has relevance to all areas of ELT, it is not principally concerned with EFL, English as a Foreign Language, which is taught and learnt in parts of the world which are not English-dominant. Nor is it about the Englishes used in countries where English holds some official or formal status, such as India or Singapore, but where the majority of the population do not have English as their first or expert language.

Global society in the post-colonial age is characterized by international flows of people, many of whom come to English-dominant countries with a need to learn English. There are over one million such people of working age in the UK alone, and about one third of these are currently taking ESOL classes. They come from a hugely diverse range of geographical, social, and economic backgrounds, and include asylum seekers and refugees, people from more settled communities, so-called economic migrants escaping poverty in their home countries, people joining their spouses and family members, and—in the UK and Eire—EU nationals, especially from countries which joined the EU more recently. The book considers this diversity, and engages with the challenges and issues it presents.

Migration and asylum, citizenship, social exclusion, the economy, and globalization all bear upon ESOL, a field which is passionately contested by practitioners and policy makers alike. Given this atmosphere, people connected with ESOL—readers of this book—will not be working in an apolitical sphere. This book does not shrink away from discussing contentious aspects of ESOL. For example, we examine how imposed structures such as a national curriculum for ESOL and an obligatory testing regime can have negative as well as positive effects on teaching and learning in ESOL classrooms. We also address the question of how far the content of ESOL lessons should be oriented towards 'survival' English or preparation for work. We promote the notion that teachers and students can question prevailing ideologies by developing a critical consciousness. ESOL teachers and students frequently find themselves at odds with public ways of talking and writing which associate migrants with the supposed negative effects of immigration and with threats to social cohesion. Finding ways of using language to counter such positions is a constant challenge.

This book is populated by the voices of real ESOL students and teachers, from interviews and transcripts of classroom interaction drawn from a number of ESOL research projects we worked on between 2003 and 2007. These were instigated by the National Research and Development Centre for adult literacy and numeracy (NRDC) and include: the ESOL Case Studies Project (published as *ESOL—Case Studies of Provision, Learners' Needs and Resources*, Roberts, *et al.* 2004); the ESOL Effective Practice Project (published as *Effective Teaching and Learning: ESOL*, Baynham and Roberts, *et al.* 2007); the Turning Talk into Learning Project (published as *Developing Adult Teaching and Learning: Practitioner Guides–ESOL*, Cooke and Roberts 2007a and *Reflection and Action in ESOL Classrooms*, Cooke and Roberts 2007b); and the Placement Practices Project (published as *The Right Course?* Simpson, *et al.* 2008).

Outline

The book starts with an overview of ESOL in the world, with particular attention to England, Wales, and Northern Ireland. Chapter 2 directs its focus to ESOL students and their contexts of learning. The next two chapters, 3 and 4, discuss the 'how' and the 'what' of ESOL teaching: the approaches of ESOL teachers and the content of ESOL lessons. Chapter 5 is about oral communication, particularly characteristic of ESOL classrooms, and Chapter 6 is concerned with the teaching of literacy in ESOL classes. Chapter 7 extends the topic of literacy to encompass electronic literacy and ESOL, communication using new technology. The final chapter, 'Learning about teaching', describes how teachers can develop through engaging with research. Finally, an appendix contains summaries of ESOL in policy and in practice in other English-dominant countries around the world.

The book contains reflective activities within each chapter, included with the aim of enabling readers to relate what is said in the book to their own contexts, be they teaching, training, management, inspection, or policy. For trainers, the activities can be expanded and adapted as desired. The book also contains suggestions for further reading at the end of each chapter.

1 ESOL IN THE WORLD

I don't know how the teachers made me hear what they said. They built me, I was just like a stone. They knocked my head and they made me hear. At the beginning I was hearing nothing, just sitting there then leaving.
Eritrean woman, Leeds

Introduction

- It is 7 am in Manchester. A group of men, recruited from Poland as bus drivers, are sitting in a classroom in their depot. They are waiting for their teacher to arrive for an English class before they start their first shift of the week.
- It is 9 am at a primary school in East London. A group of Bangladeshi women bring their children to school before gathering in the parents' centre for their twice-weekly English language and literacy class.
- It is 9 am in a room at the local Buddhist temple in Leeds. A group of elderly Hong Kong Chinese men and women, resident for many years in the UK, are having their weekly English class.
- It is 9 am at a large secondary school in a poor suburb of outer London. A class of teenagers—recent arrivals from Africa, Asia, Europe, and South America—prepare for their day at school.
- It is 11 am in Bradford. A group of men and women seeking political asylum are in their English and ICT class at a community centre on the outskirts of the city. Some of their children are in the crèche next door. Most of the students are still waiting for a decision from the Government about their claims for asylum, and many have been sent to this part of the UK under a programme of 'dispersal' of asylum seekers from the capital.
- It is 5 pm at an educational charity in central London. A group of overseas nurses are studying on an intensive language training course as part of their preparation for work in English hospitals.
- It is 8 pm at a large college in outer London. Students from Africa, Asia, and the Caribbean study English and Maths on a course which they hope will equip them with the qualifications they need to get into a British university. Further along the corridor, another group of migrants, hoping soon to find work, practise for job interviews and learn to write CVs.

These snapshots from the research informing this book illustrate some of the settings in which migrants might be found learning English, and some of the aims they might have in doing so. They demonstrate too that, taken as a whole, students of English for Speakers of Other Languages (ESOL) are an extremely complex and diverse group. This diversity has important implications for practice and policy and is one of the major themes of this book.

The roots of the diversity of ESOL students lie in the processes of globalization, post-colonialism, and mass migration. Globalization refers to the extent to which the world is structured at an international level and to the ever-increasing interconnectedness in the social, political, economic, cultural, and technological spheres of life. One of the features of globalization is the increased movement of people from one country to another, although this is not by any means a new phenomenon. It is estimated that around one in 35 people in the world are migrants, and the reasons for their migration are varied, as our snapshots suggest—included here are people from ex-colonial settings, people who have come to the UK because of the shortage of labour in certain sectors such as health and transport, and people who have migrated to be with their families. In addition, many students in ESOL classes are forced migrants or refugees escaping war, civil unrest, poverty, fear of persecution, and economic deprivation. While most refugees stay relatively near their home countries—among the 'top ten' host countries for refugees are Sudan, Tanzania, Pakistan, Iran, and China—migration to more peaceful and prosperous countries continues to grow, despite attempts by the governments of some of those countries to curtail it.

The processes of globalization and migration help to shape the make-up of towns and cities in English-dominant countries. Much of the work we refer to in this book has been done in London, which in terms of language and ESOL needs, has much in common with global cities in other English-dominant countries. Earlier sociological definitions of immigrant 'groups' and ethnic minority 'communities' fall short of describing the global flows in cities such as London, which Vertovec (2006) has labelled 'super-diverse'. We also refer to research undertaken in the industrial towns and cities of northern England. Here the picture is varied: in some cities the dynamic diversity echoes that of global cities such as London, while other towns reflect earlier migration patterns of people from the ex-colonies forming established ethnic minority communities. In such a dynamic field, this picture is one which will continue to change—one recent change, for example, is high numbers of workers from Eastern Europe requiring classes in parts of rural England where there was no demand before. Of all the dimensions of English Language Teaching (ELT), then, ESOL has a particularly close link to the consequences of migration and globalization, processes which have brought large numbers, and also a huge variety of people, to ESOL classes.

English in the world

An understanding of mass migration and globalization is essential when considering the provision of ESOL classes in English-dominant countries. These phenomena are also helpful for understanding the changes taking place in the English language itself. The spread of English as a global or international language is well-documented, and there have been several attempts to describe English as a world language. Some of these, such as Kachru's (1985) 'circles' model, present a rather fixed notion of English as a world language, and fail to capture the linguistic realities of rapid globalization. For many people learning English today, whether migrants or not, there has been a move away from the simplistic notions of 'native' and 'non-native' speakers of English, or of English as a first or second language (L1 and L2), and an increased association of the language with dynamic and varied use, bilingualism and multilingualism, geographical movement and migration, and new speech communities such as online virtual communities. More recently, academics have begun to examine the rise of English as a Lingua Franca (ELF), looking at issues such as how linguistic features of English develop as the language becomes less closely associated with particular geographical areas or with native speakers (Jenkins 2000; Seidlhofer 2002). Another issue of interest to ELF researchers is the impact their findings might have on English Language Teaching (ELT) internationally, especially with regards to decisions about which variety to teach (Jenkins 2006).

Other analyses of the spread of English are concerned with questions of power and the distribution of linguistic resources. Robert Phillipson (1992), Alastair Pennycook (1994), and Adrian Holliday (2005) hold a critical stance on English dominance and the linguistic imperialism inherent in the global export of western-dominant ELT. This reflects well-founded anxieties about the role of English in imposing a western-oriented, English-speaking hegemony on the cultural and economic world—although David Graddol (2006), in his account of the global status of the English language, suggests that its dominance should not be taken for granted.

Many writers who adopt a critical position on English as a global language are concerned with minority language maintenance in the face of the global spread of English. ESOL, however, has a different concern, that of the right of newcomers to an English-dominant country to learn English. Migrants to English-speaking countries have two basic rights connected to language. First, they should be allowed to maintain the languages they grew up speaking, even as they and their families settle in a new country. And second, they have an entitlement to learn the language of their new country, to learn to communicate in English. Certain sectors of the media and some politicians present this second right as an obligation, and even imply reluctance on the part of some migrants to learn the language at all.

In fact, the majority of migrants to English-speaking countries do want to learn English, but face barriers of access to appropriate high quality tuition. Discussion of such barriers, and of attempts to overcome them, is another thread running through this book.

ESOL around the world

ESOL is understood differently around the world. There is great variety in policy and provision in different English-dominant countries, a variety which is caused by many factors: whether the country is historically one of immigration or emigration; whether political and social structures are in place to enable and assist newcomers in settling in their new country; whether there is a history of coordinated language support for new non-English-speaking arrivals; who the new arrivals actually are; and how those patterns change over time.

Some countries have long experience of publicly funded ESOL and others less so, which is reflected to a certain extent by the level of development of curriculum and provision. The Appendix of this book includes brief outlines of six English-dominant countries and their approaches to ESOL policy: Australia, Canada, Ireland, New Zealand, Scotland, and the USA. These sketches show how each country has dealt with inward migration and the factors they need to consider when planning policy with regards to the provision of language tuition. One factor is the question of funding, that is where the money will come from, how much will be available for language classes, who will be eligible for them, and for how long. Some countries stipulate that funding will be available only for certain groups of migrants, for example permanent residents. Others, such as Australia, have a set number of hours for which migrants are eligible for free classes. Some countries organize funding centrally on a national level, while in others it devolves to a provincial or local level. Another decision to be made is whether or not to adopt a curriculum nationally, and upon which theoretical principles that curriculum should be based.

Other points in common around the world of ESOL include its frequent alignment with adult basic literacy, bureaucratization in the name of accountability and transparency, and a growing focus on workplace needs. A phenomenon in many countries in the West is a tightening of the relationship between language, immigration, citizenship, and national security, seen most clearly in the rise of language and citizenship testing. In fact, how host countries plan and provide for newcomers is often a sign of prevailing attitudes to immigration in general, and sometimes to broader issues such as race, ethnicity, and class. As Bonny Norton (2006: 96) writes, 'While adult ESOL language learners may strive to make a productive contribution to their new societies, unless the host community is receptive to their arrival, they will struggle to fulfil their potential.'

ESOL in England, Wales, and Northern Ireland

Although many of the concerns of this book are pertinent to all ESOL settings, most of the research we draw on has been carried out in England; the rest of this chapter therefore presents a brief outline of the broader social and political contexts which form the backdrop to the rest of the book.

Britain has a long history of inward (as well as outward) migration and a corresponding long history of ESOL. Britain's history of immigration dates back to pre-Roman times and intensified in the late nineteenth and twentieth centuries as a result of British colonial and post-colonial policy, the upheavals caused by two world wars and other conflicts, and more recently by the processes of globalization and the growth of the European Union. In her book on the history of ESOL in the UK, Sheila Rosenberg (2007) tells how an evolving ESOL profession has responded to patterns of migration over the years. Some of the important moments in migration and ESOL history are: Jewish settlement in London's East End at the end of the nineteenth century; the creation of refugees by the Spanish Civil War and Nazi Europe in the 1930s and 1940s; migration from the Indian sub-continent in the 1960s and beyond, and the succeeding groups of refugees from Latin America, Uganda, Cambodia, and Vietnam. In recent years, ESOL classes have seen students arriving periodically from places such as Kosovo, Somalia, Sudan, Congo, Iraq, and Afghanistan, as the political and economic situations in these countries force people to uproot and leave their homes. More recently, tougher asylum laws and curbs on non-European immigration, along with the expansion of the European Union, have shifted the focus of attention to migrants from Eastern European countries such as Poland, the Czech Republic, and Hungary, as represented by the first snapshot at the beginning of this chapter.

The evolution of ESOL as a sphere of language education mirrors to some extent the various stances taken by successive governments to new arrivals, as well as broader trends in government and education. The first large-scale growth in the field happened from the 1950s onwards, in an attempt to respond to the needs of large numbers of non-English-speaking people who immigrated in the post-war period. At first the response was ad hoc and organized on a voluntary basis, often taking place in people's homes, and was expressly targeted at women—usually Asian—as men were expected to acquire English at work.

The prevailing ideology of the post-war period was that immigrants should try to assimilate into British culture: one of the major steps towards this assimilation would be to learn English. In the late 1970s and early 1980s the field of English as a Second Language (ESL), as it was then known, became more organized and better funded, and in some areas ESL began to be taught in colleges or in workplaces. Materials, which previously had focused on 'survival' English began to better reflect the realities of life as experienced by ethnic minority immigrants.

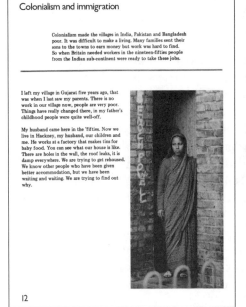

ESOL publications from the 1970s: Asian Women Speak Out *(1979)*
English for Driving *(1977)*

New qualifications were created and a national professional body (now called NATECLA), was set up to support teachers around the country. At the same time, some ESL practitioners adapted their practice according to prevailing notions of cultural pluralism and anti-racism, in a response to the realities in immigrants' lives of unemployment and racism. To try to offset the discrimination and disadvantage faced by many ethnic minority bilingual adults, particularly in employment, courses such as 'linked-skill courses' appeared, which taught English alongside a practical skill, followed later by courses which led to specific vocational training qualifications and language support for students on mainstream courses. In current ESOL provision and practice there are strands visible from these earlier phases of the development of the field, a theme which we return to in later chapters.

ESOL as a 'Skill for Life'

By the 1990s ESL had become known as ESOL—English for Speakers of Other Languages—reflecting the reality of multilingualism among Britain's English language learners. Despite the efforts of teachers in the sector, as well as some attention from local and central government at different times, during the 1990s adult ESOL provision in the UK, in common with adult literacy and numeracy provision, was largely neglected in policy circles. In some urban centres with large migrant populations the provision was well organized, but in many other areas the model persisted of ad hoc teaching and learning in community groups, homes, and workplaces, with volunteer or part-time teachers who were often untrained.

A major watershed came at the turn of the twenty-first century with the decision to bring the fragmented field of ESOL under centralized control, linked to a more general overhaul of the provision of adult literacy and numeracy. Influenced by findings from the International Adult Literacy Survey, Sir Claus Moser's report to the Government, *A Fresh Start* (DfES 1999), recommended the launching of a national strategy in England, Northern Ireland, and Wales (provision in Scotland was organized separately) to reduce the number of adults with low levels of basic skills. The response of the Government was to put in place a strategy known as Skills for Life. The language needs of bilingual students did not receive much attention in the Moser report, and ESOL was not originally included as a 'skill for life'. After some lobbying, ESOL was incorporated into the literacy and numeracy policy, thus yoking ESOL and literacy formally together, mirroring a long established trend in the USA and a more recent one in Australia.

The aligning of ESOL with literacy is not without its detractors, especially those who believe that ESOL has less theoretical common ground with literacy than with the fields of second language acquisition and applied linguistics, but those who wished to avoid ESOL being sidelined once again by policymakers recognized that this was the compromise that had to be made. The assimilation of ESOL into Skills for Life brought with it the creation of a statutory national curriculum (DfES 2001) along with a new teacher training framework, and the establishment of a research centre, created to provide a research base with which to inform the new policy.

Initially the Skills for Life policy invested heavily in ESOL, though Government commitment to funding ESOL provision in general is not consistent and demand for classes outstrips supply in most areas. Many teachers broadly welcomed the long overdue injection of cash into their sector, as well as the fact that they were being taken seriously as a field for the first time. But bringing ESOL under centralized control and regulation has involved contentious clashes in cultures. As John Callaghan writes, in the context of his study of ESOL teachers' professional identities (2006: 30):

> *Whilst Government initiatives have brought in welcome resources, they have … laid a heavy bureaucratic burden on teachers, one which many see as being driven by auditing purposes and economic motives related to global competitiveness rather than the facilitation of language learning or the meeting of learners' needs.*

The bureaucratization of ESOL is largely responsible for current tensions between ESOL practitioners on the one hand and government agencies, particularly inspectorates, on the other, and is a theme of Chapter 3. On a pedagogic, as well as an ideological level, a further critical issue in ESOL is the model of language adopted by the curriculum, a direct result of its origins in a skills-based literacy curriculum. Language in the literacy curriculum (and subsequently the ESOL curriculum) is broken down into word/sentence/text, in contrast to the whole text- and genre-based view of language taken in, for example, the Australian curriculum. With Standard English as its model, and its failure to respond to the multilingual reality of much of modern Britain, the curriculum also contributes to a general monolinguist attitude in education and society more broadly. We revisit this issue when we discuss ESOL and literacy in Chapters 6 and 7.

ESOL, policy, and politics

As well as the changes wrought by Skills for Life, the ESOL sector has found itself at the centre of bigger political debates concerning citizenship, cohesion, integration, and national security. The response to post-colonialism and globalization by governments—in the UK and elsewhere—is sometimes contradictory: they must attract inward investment by offering skilled low-wage labour while also appealing to certain sections of the electorate by being seen to be 'tough' on asylum and immigration. In many communities, alongside persistent older forms of racial and ethnic discrimination, new forms have appeared—namely an increase in the demonization of Muslim communities since 11 September 2001 and the vilification of asylum seekers and refugees. Some ethnic minority communities have been blamed for 'self-segregating' and causing a lack of cohesion in towns and cities. In such discourse, there is often a focus on the English language skills of migrant groups. Politicians and the media have gradually conflated an inability to use English with a breakdown in cohesion and even with national security. In a press conference given shortly after the terrorist attacks in London on 7 July 2005, the then Prime Minister Tony Blair announced measures to combat Islamic extremism. Among them was a reference to long-term UK residents who do not speak English. This is despite the perpetrators of the London bombings all having been born in England and being native speakers of English. At the time Tony Blair said:

> *There are people who are isolated in their own communities who have been here for 20 years and still do not speak English. That worries me because there is a separateness that may be unhealthy.*

This speech echoes earlier comments made in 2001 when street disturbances erupted between Asian and white youths in some towns in the north of England. Despite the fact that most of the young men involved were British-born, lack of English language amongst their (overwhelmingly law-abiding) parents became a focal point for politicians during the search for underlying causes of the disturbances. Later, in 2005, Margaret Hodge, then Minister for Work and Pensions, took the issue further by suggesting that immigrants shirk their duties by failing to learn English:

> *We have to make the learning of English an unavoidable must ... Immigrants have to see language acquisition as an essential part of the contract they enter into when they settle in Britain. People should not opt out of their obligations on the back of multiculturalism.*

The notion that people do not *want* to learn English quickly became a 'common sense' one, accepted by politicians and the broader public. By the following year (June 2006), Gordon Brown, then Chancellor of the Exchequer, had adopted a more authoritarian stance:

> *People who come into this country, who are part of our community, should play by the rules ... I think learning English is part of that. I think that understanding British history is part of that ... I would insist on large numbers of people who have refused to learn our language that they must do so* [sic].

Government discussion and policy, backed by discourse of this kind, is characterized by the creation of various commissions, investigations, and legislation on the social cohesion of communities and integration of 'minorities', with a heavy focus on the English language. A major plank in this policy has been the implementation of ceremonies for new British citizens and the introduction of a citizenship test, which finally brought together ESOL and immigration policy for the first time.

Citizenship and language

Citizenship and language tests are now the norm in most countries in Europe as well as in the English-dominant countries we mentioned earlier in the chapter. Testing new arrivals to the United States for basic literacy and 'intelligence' has been practised since the great waves of migration to the Americas in the nineteenth and early twentieth centuries, and a test of language and knowledge about the history, legal, and political systems of the country has long been part of US legislation. In more recent times this has been emulated by other countries such as the UK, Australia, and many EU states. Some tests are more onerous than others—reflecting political attitudes within nation states towards inward migration—but all of them are justified by an ideology which places language at the centre of national identity and which emphasizes the duties and responsibilities of new citizens.

In the UK the Nationality, Immigration, and Asylum Act of 2002 required UK residents seeking British citizenship to show formally 'a sufficient knowledge of English, Welsh or Scottish Gaelic and about life in the UK' and to take a citizenship oath and a pledge at a civic ceremony. In 2007 this requirement was extended to include people requesting permanent residence in the UK. The test is a multiple-choice test taken on a computer and based on the publication *Life in the UK: A Journey to Citizenship*. Those applicants who use English as an expert language, or those who are speakers of other languages who have reached the appropriate level of English, are encouraged to study the guide and take the test. Those who have not reached the level of English necessary to take the test, or who do not have the required level of literacy, must enrol on an approved course of English language in a citizenship context. Thus, teachers of ESOL became teachers of citizenship almost overnight. Some teachers were alarmed to be implementing legislation so tightly connected to immigration policy; some also pointed out that as no extra funding had gone into the provision of ESOL citizenship classes or teacher training, the Government had found a cheap way of getting their cohesion and integration work done. Many teachers and students, however, enjoyed teaching and learning citizenship: the writers of the citizenship materials mainly avoided an assimilationist stance of teaching 'Britishness' and 'our way of life', opting instead for a more neutral focus on 'rights' and benefits.

The relationship between national security, immigration, integration, social cohesion, and language is becoming progressively tighter. In most government reports, and in very much political and media discourse, a great deal of attention is paid to English as the greatest shared resource and the need

A citizenship ceremony

for everyone to be able to speak it to integrate fully in their communities. The contradictions in policy are evident, however: the same government that stressed the importance of English for integration was simultaneously responsible for cutting funding for the very ESOL classes that would enable the poorest migrants to meet this requirement.

The current picture: ESOL and the economy

In recent years there has been increasing private sector involvement in ESOL. This tendency is associated with a strengthening of links in policy between learning in the adult education sector and business. Colleges are increasingly expected to market themselves and teach their courses in workplaces. ESOL departments in colleges are expected to provide work-related courses and to cooperate closely with local employers. This, coupled with Government initiatives which are encouraging employers to fund their workforce's literacy, numeracy, and ESOL studies, has led some to believe that adult education is in fact undergoing a slow wholesale privatization. Private sector investment in the education and training of adults, be it in infrastructure, in materials and methods, or in direct funding of courses, brings with it an obligation, implicit or explicit, to orient learning and teaching towards work and employment. Yet with regard to ESOL, this has led to confusion between the broader aim of English language education and the pedagogic focus. While many (though not all) ESOL students need to improve their English language skills for employment purposes, it is not at all clear that the way to do this is to concentrate in class on narrow employment-related concerns, and there is little pedagogical justification for ESOL teaching and learning to be entirely needs-driven and vocationally relevant. In Chapter 4 we discuss how factors such as a concern for the economy, social cohesion, and citizenship affect the content of ESOL lessons, and in Chapter 6, on literacy, we see how a particular understanding of literacy corresponds with a drive towards ESOL as language training for employability.

Conclusion

These are interesting times to be studying and writing about the teaching and learning of ESOL. In second language acquisition the turn towards a focus on the social aspects of learning makes ESOL highly relevant to theory as well as vice versa. ESOL is at a junction where cognitive, social, political, and geopolitical concerns intersect. Governments need to attract migrants to service the economy, and populations must be educated and literate enough to compete globally, while at the same time there is a growing concern with fostering social cohesion in local communities. There is thus a strong case to be made that governments have an obligation to provide ESOL classes for migrants, who make a massive social and economic contribution. Oral communication and literacy in English is at the centre of these concerns, thereby extending the task of ESOL teachers way beyond the walls of the classroom or the pages of the textbook. This makes ESOL an exciting field, but one with many challenges, not least that of implementing government policies which are far from clear cut or straightforward. In 1972 the sociologist A. H. Halsey cautioned that we should avoid treating 'education as the waste paper basket of social policy—a repository for dealing with social problems where solutions are uncertain or where there is a disinclination to wrestle with them seriously' (1972: 8). Because of the position of ESOL at the crossroads of policy, theory, and practice, ESOL teachers find themselves having to respond to constantly changing outside pressures. This book aims to show how they respond, but also how they might resist such pressures.

Further reading

English and globalization

These books all engage with the position of English and ELT at a time of globalization. Block and Cameron's edited collection considers issues raised by globalization for language teaching and language learning. The possible future trajectory of English as a global language is laid out in Graddol's British Council publication. The collection of papers edited by Lin and Martin examines the juxtaposition of language policies and classroom practices in a variety of contexts worldwide. The politics of English as a global language is the topic of Pennycook's readable critique of the broader implications of the global spread of English, and of Phillipson's influential book.

Block, D. and **D. Cameron** (eds.). 2002. *Globalization and Language Teaching*. London: Routledge.

Graddol, D. 2006. *English Next*. London: The British Council. Available online at http://www.britishcouncil.org/learning-research-englishnext.htm

Lin, A. M. Y. and **P. W. Martin** (eds.). 2005. *Decolonisation, Globalisation: Language-in-Education Policy and Practice*. Clevedon: Multilingual Matters.

Pennycook, A. 1994. *The Cultural Politics of English as an International Language*. Harlow: Longman.

Phillipson, R. 1992. *Linguistic Imperialism*. Oxford: Oxford University Press.

2 A WORLD OF DIFFERENCE: BEING AN ADULT ESOL LEARNER

You can meet a real cross-section of the world here; so many different cultures and people from different parts of the world in one place.
Iranian woman, London

Introduction

The last chapter pointed out that English for Speakers of Other Languages (ESOL) is taught in a wide variety of settings: large super-diverse cities, smaller cities and towns, and more recently, rural areas. The make-up of ESOL classes is also often extremely diverse; students might be refugees, asylum seekers, people from settled communities who may have been in the country for many years, newly-arrived husbands or wives, so-called economic migrants, people who are joining family members, people with work permits, and even some people born in English-dominant countries who spent their childhoods in countries where English is less widely spoken. In other words, learners of ESOL represent a spectrum of people living, often side-by-side, in post-colonial societies in a time of globalization. In this chapter we look at some dimensions of the diversity between students such as national origins, language, educational background, literacy level, immigration status, and employment. There are also significant differences among students from within the same communities, along the lines of gender, age, class, religion, ethnicity, family, social networks, and aspirations for the future, as well as individual differences such as personality, a sense of agency—how an individual takes control over some aspect of his or her life—and motivation to learn.

ACTIVITY 1 ESOL class

Here are some thumbnail sketches of the students present at the beginning of the year in a real lower intermediate ESOL class in London. What are some of the challenges and opportunities such diversity might present to ESOL teachers and syllabus planners?

A Spanish woman in her thirties, who is working for an international voluntary organization and wants to learn English to be able to work in Africa. She has a degree in geography and history and has previously worked in Latin America. She has also worked as a social worker and teacher in Spain. She has been in London for just over a year and before that spent time in Ireland.

A Brazilian woman in her twenties, who is in London because her husband is working there. She previously worked in Brazil as an administrator. The teacher later finds out that she is trying to make a living as an artist. She has been in the UK for seven months.

A Somali asylum seeker in her thirties, who has been in the UK for two years and has not studied English prior to coming to this class. She says she only went to school in Somalia for two years. She speaks Italian as well as Somali.

A French man from Paris aged 55, who has been in the UK for a year and a half. He is in the UK 'for business reasons'; in France he had been a locksmith and a mechanic. At one point he says he has been in prison somewhere in London. He drops out of the course after a few weeks.

A Turkish woman in her twenties who has been in the UK for over 12 years (since she was 14). She attended secondary school in London for two years. She came to London to be with her family and now has a young son. Her spoken English is fluent but she has been placed in this class because of her low level of writing.

A Colombian woman in her thirties who has been in London for seven years and came to the UK as a migrant worker. She works as a cleaner in two different offices.

An Albanian woman in her thirties who has been in the UK for two and a half years. She came here 'for a better life'. She has a university degree and worked in Albania as an 'assistant doctor'.

A refugee in her twenties originally from Chad who spent time in Cameroon and Benin prior to coming to the UK. She speaks French, Arabic, and Karang. She has been in the UK for two and a half years.

A Somali refugee in her thirties who has been in the UK for seven years. She speaks Arabic as well as Somali. She is a full-time parent.

An 18-year-old speaker of Lingala and French from the Congo who has been in the UK for three years. She left school when she was 14 and came to the UK as an asylum seeker.

A Turkish Cypriot woman in her fifties who has been in the UK for 22 years. She came originally because of the war in Cyprus. She left school when she was 12. She is a housewife and has previously studied on an ESOL course at another centre.

A Somali woman who came to the UK three years ago because of the civil war in her home country. She left school at 14. She says she can read and write Arabic as well as Somali. She studied English for one year at another centre.

An Indian woman whose first language is Bengali, who also reads and writes Hindi. She has been in the UK for 18 years having come to join her husband.

She has a BA in Political Science and Bengali and is now working at a crèche in London. She has done a few other courses at the college including childcare, first aid, and interpreting.

A contemporary ESOL class

Diversity and heterogeneity

Languages

An obvious difference between learners of ESOL is the range of languages they speak, which is again a reflection of the extraordinary diversity of contemporary global cities and of ever-changing migration patterns: for example, it is estimated that over 300 languages are spoken by pupils in schools in London. A survey of 489 ESOL students in London and the north of England found that they reported a total of 50 languages spoken as their first language. The top fifteen are shown on the next page.

These figures however do not encapsulate the full complex picture of language use amongst ESOL students. 'Kurdish', for example, encompasses the different varieties spoken in Turkey, Iraq, and Iran. People from Pakistan identify as speakers of either Urdu or Panjabi, languages which share many features, Urdu being seen as the national unifying language in Pakistan, and varieties of Panjabi being spoken mainly in the home. Neither do these figures show, for example, the fact that many of the students are multilingual and multi-literate. Bilingualism or multilingualism, as well as bi- or multi-literacy (including literacy in more than one script) is taken for granted

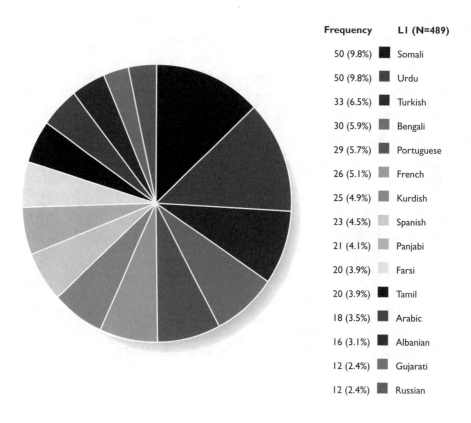

Frequency		LI (N=489)
50 (9.8%)		Somali
50 (9.8%)		Urdu
33 (6.5%)		Turkish
30 (5.9%)		Bengali
29 (5.7%)		Portuguese
26 (5.1%)		French
25 (4.9%)		Kurdish
23 (4.5%)		Spanish
21 (4.1%)		Panjabi
20 (3.9%)		Farsi
20 (3.9%)		Tamil
18 (3.5%)		Arabic
16 (3.1%)		Albanian
12 (2.4%)		Gujarati
12 (2.4%)		Russian

Figure 2.1: First languages of ESOL (adapted from Baynham and Roberts, et al. 2007)

by many ESOL students, so much so that they often fail to mention it on official forms. For example, an Angolan participant in the survey above initially reported that he spoke only Portuguese: when interviewed later he revealed that he is also a user of French, Lingala, and Kicongo. Another typical pattern is that of a student in his late teens who speaks Panjabi with his mother, Pashto with his father, and English with his brothers. ESOL students are often surrounded by many languages and use English as a lingua franca with speakers from diverse backgrounds.

Recording language background is fraught with difficulties as there is no straightforward link between ethnic identity or category, nationality, and language. Many speakers use several languages and 'cross' between them as a matter of course. As the sociolinguist Ben Rampton (1990) points out, learners' stated language backgrounds are often a mix of languages they are expert in, languages they have an affiliation or attachment to, and languages which are part of their inheritance. They may also use non-standard varieties of these languages, and perhaps only their written or spoken forms.

Educational background and literacy levels

Another dimension of diversity amongst ESOL students is their educational background and literacy level. It is not unusual to find in the same class people who have received a university education together with people with very little schooling and therefore with little literacy in their first languages. Reasons for low literacy vary. A student may have suffered interruptions to schooling because of war or other strife. This is the case with some refugees from Kosovo, Congo, Sri Lanka, and Angola amongst other places. Others may come from societies which do not have a strong literate tradition, such as Somalia, or from a tradition which does not prioritize the education of girls. Others still may have been deprived of an education because of poverty. Some of the many issues arising in ESOL literacy education are dealt with in Chapters 6 and 7.

ACTIVITY 2   Language awareness

Think about an ESOL class you are currently teaching or have taught. What different languages do your students speak? How much do you know about their multilingualism and levels of literacy in their other languages? Is it important to know about these language issues of your students? How can you find out more?

Gender

There are often more women than men in ESOL classes, especially those classes held during the day and in community settings. While all the issues we raise in this chapter apply to both men and women, there are some which affect the lives of women in particular. The first is an issue which is relevant to all parents, whether they are ESOL students or not, and concerns the lack of universal access to childcare of a high standard at times which suit parents. This is particularly acute for women wishing to raise young children and attend regular full-time ESOL classes. Some women talk explicitly about not being able to come to class when their children are young. Renata, an Ecuadorian woman living in London, says: 'Maybe if I had studied when I arrived, if the kids hadn't been so little I would speak good English. I always liked studying, yes. It was because of the children.' This means their learning happens in a piecemeal way over a much longer period of time. Women often carry the burden of looking after the health needs of their family members and some are restricted by the demands of their cultures and traditions. Migration and asylum affect women in different ways to men—for example, people-trafficking as part of forced prostitution affects women and girls almost exclusively (Campbell, 2008). A less obvious but still important issue is the changes in family patterns associated with migration. Traditional family patterns go through many changes during and after migration. These are sometimes to the benefit of women but sometimes not. For example, many Somali women migrants are single mothers who have been widowed due to the civil war in Somalia, and are therefore living in situations at odds with the traditional norms of their communities, as well as coping with increased poverty.

Women are also more greatly affected by low literacy in many countries; girls are sometimes less likely to receive an education, which compounds other factors such as interrupted schooling due to war and poverty. As a Turkish woman, Gulnaz, whose story features in Chapter 6, says:

> *They did not send me because there wasn't a secondary school in my village and my mother told my father that I was a girl who can't travel to the town all the time. 'Something will happen to her', she used to say. And my father accepted it. We did not have enough money. We were quite poor.*

ACTIVITY 3   Reflection on gender

What other issues (in class and outside) do you think might affect women ESOL students in a different way from men?

Family relations and intergenerational language issues

Many parents, deprived of an education themselves, are determined to make sure their daughters and sons have more opportunities than they did, and thus pay great attention to their children's education; many children of migrants become successful second generation adults. The subject of intergenerational bilingualism and multilingualism is complex, and there are many variations in the levels of linguistic competence acquired by the children of migrants (see for example Harris 1997, 2006). Parents are often aware that being bilingual is a useful resource, cognitively and socially, but differ in their approaches to it when raising their children. Some believe that they should speak English to their children at home, even though they may not speak it very well themselves: research shows, however, that a child benefits more from the stronger language model of their caregivers' expert language. Other parents speak their expert language with their children at home but might come up against problems when their children go to school and begin to have ambivalent feelings towards their heritage language; sometimes children reject their parents' language altogether. The following comments point to the gap which can develop between the immigrant parent population and their children, both in terms of behaviour and language shift, and how parents experience this:

> *My youngest daughter always talks with her sisters in English at home. I begged her not to speak in English with me because I couldn't understand. Do you know what her response was? She said: 'Mummy, do you know speaking Chinese is stupid!' She is only 4 years old. I explained to her that*

she is Chinese and she needs to learn Chinese, otherwise she will not be able to communicate with me. She said she didn't care. My second daughter was quite willing to talk with me when she was young. She used to talk with me about what happened in school. However, as she grew up, she refused to talk with me. I asked her why she refused to talk to me now, she just said: 'You don't understand'.
Chinese woman, Leeds

Now I want to learn English so that there won't be any problems with the family. Now I feel that the children speak with me and feel comfortable with me. They bring their schoolwork and show me and I take an interest in what kind of homework they get. I try to help them but mostly their mother helps them because she is British-born and knows English very well. I feel that the children are getting a little bit closer to me, previously they used to avoid me, run away from me and used to say that Daddy does not know English. But since I have learnt English and can talk broken English they sit and talk with me and look happy.
Pakistani man, Bradford

Secondary school children

Li Wei's research (2000) on the Chinese population of Newcastle-upon-Tyne found that the children whose parents did not learn English tended to become monolingual English speakers, causing stress for their parents in ways similar to those described in the quotations above. Wei's study suggests that children are more likely to become proficient bilinguals and to maintain their heritage language if their parents also speak both languages well. The data drawn on for this chapter show that one of the main motivations for parents to attend ESOL lessons is cohesion in their own immediate families, especially when their children are growing up. Therefore, adequate funding and provision of English classes for adults is also a long-term investment in the cognitive development, achievement, and well-being of the next generation.

Experiences of immigration, settlement, and asylum

Media and public discourses frequently construct migrants as being somehow to blame for a perceived lack of social cohesion. However, the full picture of migrant experience is complex and there is extreme diversity in ESOL students' relations with their own ethnic and linguistic groups and in terms of networks and access to community support, facilities, and influence. Some people are settled with their families in English-dominant countries and belong to dense social networks. Others may be in the country for a while but without the intention of permanent settlement. Some do not have families in their new countries but have a network of people who originate from their home countries to support them. Others, especially young asylum seekers, neither have families in the new country nor belong to established groups, but have formed communities with others in the hostels and accommodation where they live, and in their English classes. Some people have strong identities as role models or elders in their communities. Immigration status also has a profound impact on motivation, mobility, and the right to work and choose where to live, amongst other things. Steve Vertovec, an anthropologist who studies transnational migration, suggests in his research (2006) that differences in immigration status, and the concomitant differences in rights, entitlements, and constraints, are some of the main features of super-diversity in Britain.

Asylum

ESOL classes are made up of people from all of the situations described above. However, many ESOL students are refugees or asylum seekers waiting for a decision to be made on their claims. These people have particular difficulties to contend with, dealing as they are with the aftermath of war and other strife, as well as with the uncertainty caused by the laws governing immigration and the ever-changing attitude of the Government towards the funding of asylum seeker education. The story of Haxhi below is one of extreme destitution and mental stress, and is quite typical of the experiences that asylum seekers suffer.

CASE STUDY 1   Haxhi

Haxhi is a 28-year-old asylum seeker from Kosovo who lives in Bradford in the north of England, having been moved from Birmingham and rehoused there under the UK government policy of 'dispersal' from areas with large asylum seeker populations to those with smaller ones. His story is an example of someone whose life is almost entirely dictated by the laws governing asylum in the UK. Haxhi and his wife have been waiting for a decision on their asylum claim for five years. They have no right to work, cannot choose where they live, and must survive on a reduced level of state benefits. Along with other asylum seekers in the town, they live in temporary accommodation on a housing estate where they suffer constant racist abuse and harassment; their door and windows have been broken 'many times'. This constraint, enforced poverty, and harassment are causing Haxhi to feel bored, frustrated, and anxious. Worse, however, is his fear that he may be deported, an anxiety which is not eased by the fact that two members of his class have had their asylum applications refused. Haxhi says:

> I don't know what is going to happen. I have a family here and I want a better life for them but it does not depend on me. Today I am here in college and at midnight the police might knock on my door and tell me to leave this country and go back to Kosovo.

Haxhi's story is echoed by many other asylum seekers: there are some classes which are composed entirely of people living with similar levels of fear and stress. Those who have had positive decisions on their asylum applications have gained a higher degree of stability but must still deal with the aftermath of the events which led them to seek asylum in the first place. Some came as young unaccompanied asylum seekers, others have suffered extremes of bereavement, imprisonment, torture, and other mistreatments, and some have no idea of the whereabouts of their close family members.

ACTIVITY 4 Teaching asylum seekers and refugees

How do you think the experiences of refugees might impact on their learning? How might teachers take their experiences into account when planning their teaching?

Aspirations and obstacles

ESOL students are diverse but do have certain things in common. They desire to somehow forge a better life than the one they left behind, or to improve their current situations; they also share the knowledge that learning English is the first step they must take to do this. Thus ESOL students are often very motivated to learn and sometimes frustrated with their progress.

Employment

The mixture of motives and desires that students have towards their target language can usefully be seen as a form of investment. Drawing on her work with adult ESL learners in Canada, Bonny Norton (2000) says that people invest in a language in the understanding that it will give them a wider range of symbolic and material resources. Learners invest in English for many reasons, but one of the most pressing motives is that of employment. ESOL students bring with them a wide array of qualities and attributes which normally they would expect to give them status in society—what the French sociologist Pierre Bourdieu (1986) calls cultural capital. This cultural capital includes previous education, language and literacy, a range of qualifications, skills, knowledge, and prior experience. ESOL communities might include skilled tradespeople such as plumbers and electricians, people who ran their own businesses, and highly qualified professionals, such as doctors, teachers, and accountants. But those migrants who do find work are often employed below their professional level and may remain in this position for years to come, sometimes for the rest of their working lives. Finding that their cultural capital has less value than it had at home can have an impact on their social identity when they move to a new country. It is the case that low-paid jobs in sectors such as cleaning, hospitality, home care, and food processing are almost exclusively done by migrants. Researchers in London (Evans, *et al.* 2005) interviewed over 300 low-paid workers. This study revealed that 49 per cent had tertiary level qualifications; the same survey also showed that 90 per cent of informants were earning less than the recommended living wage for London.

Some people must go through a readjustment period when they realize they might not be able to do in the UK what they had done in their previous lives. They realize that the sheer hard work required to stay afloat economically means they may not fulfil the dreams they had upon arrival in the UK:

> *My intention was that I had hoped to do well in Bangladesh. But now that I am here, I have to think about things differently. After thinking about it differently I realized that it would not be possible to spend five years studying for a degree.*
> Bangladeshi man, London

There are also those who have worked in local industries in their new country and who are now facing unemployment due to a downturn in local economies. This situation can be compounded by a lack of qualifications. Many people know what they wish to do in terms of work but do not have a clear idea what might be required of them in the modern workplace. They also sometimes lack the linguistic and cultural knowledge to negotiate procedures such as job interviews. These can be seen as linguistic gate-keeping processes, either implicitly or explicitly designed to control access. In their research, Roberts and Campbell (2006) have shown that job interviews present a major barrier to second language speakers and contribute to high levels of unemployment amongst linguistic minority people.

Some are highly motivated to continue practising their professions, despite the effort and time required to retrain, but are prohibited from doing so by the laws governing asylum seekers. In the story of Dasha below, we see how waiting for a decision to be made on her application to remain in the UK affects her working life.

CASE STUDY 2 Dasha

Dasha is a highly qualified and experienced nurse from Russia. Despite having worked as a theatre nurse in Afghanistan and Chechnya, and therefore having skills sorely in demand in the health service, as an asylum seeker Dasha is not allowed to work. She works long hours illegally in an amusement arcade in east London, studies English grammar in her spare time, has hidden all her Russian books and videos from herself, and attends an ESOL class every day. She is now trying to gain the level of English she needs to get on to a skills transfer course. Even if her asylum case is successful and she manages to get on the course she wants to, it will have taken Dasha many years since her arrival in London to reach the bottom rung of her profession. This is despite the high levels of investment she has made in her English language studies.

ACTIVITY 5 Aspirations for the future

The following are real examples of the aspirations and desires of ESOL students. What do you think they need to do to achieve their aims? What might be the barriers they face?

Faizal is a 17-year-old asylum seeker who came alone to the UK from Iraq. He finished his secondary education in Iraq and wishes to become a doctor. He is studying on an ESOL course at intermediate level.

Julia, in her thirties, worked as a dental hygienist in Colombia. She would like to do the same job in England. As an asylum seeker she is not permitted to work and has sole responsibility of her young child. She is in a general ESOL class in an outlying suburb of London.

Xun Wang is an unemployed Chinese man in his fifties who has worked for many years in his own takeaway business, which he was obliged to close because of an economic downturn. He is on a welfare-to-work type scheme, which helps him to prepare for interviews and to fill in application forms. His dream is to work repairing computers, which is what he does as a hobby, but he feels that he will not be given a chance to do this job because he has no formal experience.

Mariana is a Colombian refugee in her fifties who works as a cleaner. She wishes to bring one of her grandchildren from Colombia to live with her, but to do this needs to get a better-paid job, because cleaners are 'very very cheap'. She is enrolled on a course which teaches basic survival spoken English, which she attends between her two cleaning jobs. She would like to get a job in a factory.

The range of ESOL settings

The heterogeneity of students in many classes reflects the range of ESOL student backgrounds generally, and is a result of a number of historical, political, social, and economic factors. The implication for teachers is that they have to cater for this range in their lessons. Furthermore the particular ethos or purpose of certain centres where ESOL classes take place gives classes a distinct and unique flavour. In some cases this has an especially marked effect, either for good or ill, on practice. This section looks at the range of settings for ESOL, and how these settings can influence the teaching and learning that goes on there.

In the UK, ESOL classes are offered by a range of providers, among them tertiary education colleges, 16- to 18-year-old classes in schools, voluntary and charity organizations, children's centres, churches and mosques, government welfare-to-work schemes, the military, offenders' institutions, and employers. A similar range of provision is seen in other English-dominant countries (see Appendix). Furthermore, the actual physical surroundings of ESOL classes can vary enormously. Some classes take place in large well-resourced and supported centres while others occur in poorly managed, badly organized, and isolated environments with few teaching and learning facilities. There is a correspondingly wide variation in the range of ESOL classes across a number of further dimensions. Some classes are for women only; some contain only men. Many classes are linguistically and culturally heterogeneous. Intensity of tuition, attendance patterns, teachers' qualifications and experience, and a relative focus in classes on oral or literacy skills are among the other variations. This variety of factors combines to have an effect on the decisions about teaching that the teacher has to make.

ACTIVITY 6   Range and variety of ESOL classes

Here are short descriptions of four different ESOL classes. What are the distinctive characteristics of each one? What challenges do these characteristics present to the class teacher?

Alice's class at Childsbeck is located within a secondary school. As with other classes for 16- to18-year-olds, some students in the class are unaccompanied asylum seekers and some have very low literacy levels, having had interrupted schooling. Lessons, however, take place within a school, and there is an attendant emphasis on behaviour management.

The students in Nasim's class at the Sergeant Street Centre are unemployed ESOL students referred to the class on a government retraining scheme. They are obliged to attend Nasim's lessons for 30 hours a week for 26 weeks, otherwise their benefits are stopped. Funding for the private training provider which Nasim works for depends upon students achieving quantifiable, narrow, and easily assessed learning outcomes.

Liz teaches a mixed level class at the Northfield Hotel in London. The seven students in the class attend their ESOL lessons either before or after their long shifts, as they are not given time off during work, and often miss a lesson because of work demands.

Students at the Wen Hua Centre, all women, attend for the whole of one day a week, and the ESOL lesson, taught by Maureen and Manjit, is just one of the day's activities, which also include cooking, singing, and praying. The centre where lessons take place is a Taoist cultural centre for Chinese women.

Community and constraints

A decision to provide classes in community centres and work places may have honourable motives, as may attempts to provide for so called 'hard to reach' groups. Yet structures to support tutors working in community-based teaching and learning environments are often lacking. Community-based provision is often referred to by teachers as 'outside', 'other', 'off-site', and 'out in the community'. Such terminology reflects the marginalization and isolation which can be felt by teachers and students in community-based classes, even though students may be pleased a class is accessible, and teachers may report that they enjoy teaching it. Furthermore, for students themselves, there are implications of learning in very small centres which might only house one or two ESOL classes. These concern the likelihood of being taught in a mixed level class, and the opportunities for progression. Community-based classes can be close-knit units with a strong co-operative spirit, taught in congenial surroundings by committed and experienced teachers. Yet in some centres teaching conditions are quite difficult.

CASE STUDY 3   Zeta

Zeta's mixed level class takes place in a local community centre and shares the same teaching space with another class whose lessons take place at the same time. The crèche in the room next door is staffed by unqualified assistants, and students' children often come into the classroom. Zeta adopts the role of crèche manager and caretaker as well as ESOL teacher. Zeta describes her classroom as perceived by her manager during a visit:

> She was quite taken aback I think about the conditions that the students were learning in. And we weren't providing the conditions that the college provide. And you know, it was impossible. To look at it from an inspector's point of view, the boards weren't big enough and it wasn't clean enough, and everybody seems to forget about how dirty it is. It's only people who come in from the outside and—I mean I think it's probably as well that people in college have really little idea of what we have to work with.

Such difficult conditions are not eased by a lack of management support in many community centres. ESOL teachers working in any context may have line managers who are not ESOL specialists, and who do not understand the particular needs of ESOL learner populations. But in a remote and isolated community centre there may well be no management structure at all, and there might even be only one ESOL teacher at the site. This situation would not be of such concern if all teachers in community centres were experienced, as Zeta is, and could handle the difficult conditions. Yet in many cases the teachers in community centres tend to be the less experienced. In the face of poor resources, unpredictable attendance patterns, frequent isolation from managerial support of any kind, and the attendant difficulties of running ESOL classes in poorly resourced centres, is it better to have the more, rather than the less experienced teachers working there?

Conclusion

This chapter has described only briefly some of the differences amongst learners of ESOL, for example, language, gender, prior education, professional experience, and immigration status. In the rest of the book we will return in greater depth to these themes of difference and diversity as we take a close look at what happens in the classrooms where these heterogeneous groups or communities come together to learn English, and the challenges—as well as opportunities—this presents for teachers and providers of ESOL.

Given that in some parts of countries such as the UK, the US, Canada, and Australia the foreign-born population outnumbers the local-born population, the points about difference and diversity made in this chapter will be familiar and even obvious to some readers, above all to ESOL teachers in global cities such as London. However, as we shall see in the rest of the book, when it comes to teaching and learning, ESOL students are often treated as one 'group', so responding to their diverse needs, experiences, and aspirations becomes an essential part of the work of the ESOL teacher and a major challenge to curriculum planners. With ever greater demand for ESOL classes and a high level of insistence from governments that migrants learn English for employability and citizenship, the job of ESOL teachers goes way beyond teaching the forms and structure of the English language. In the next chapter we take a look at what happens in ESOL lessons and consider the ways in which teachers approach the challenges and maximize the opportunities offered by the remarkable mixture of people in their classrooms.

Further reading

Asylum

These two papers describe the human consequences of government policies on asylum. The second looks specifically at the experiences of some asylum seekers in an ESOL class in a town in the north of England:

Bloch, A. and **L. Schuster.** 2005. 'At the extremes of exclusion: Deportation, detention and dispersal.' *Ethnic and Racial Studies* 28/3: 491–512.

Hodge, R. 2004. ' "This is not enough for one's life": Perceptions of living and learning English in Blackburn by students seeking asylum and refugee status' in C. Roberts, *et al. English for Speakers of Other Languages (ESOL): Case Studies of Provision, Learners' Needs and Resources.* London: NRDC.

Gender, language, and migration

Norton's book is an in-depth account of the experiences of migration and learning English of five women in Canada. Drawing on post-structuralist and feminist theory, the book shows the impact of their experiences on their changing identities. The other papers look at the issues of migration, adult education, and language learning with a specific focus on gender:

Gordon, D. 2004. ' "I'm tired. You clean and cook." Shifting gender identities and second language socialization.' *TESOL Quarterly* 38/3: 437–57.

Kouritzin, S. 2000. 'Immigrant mothers redefine access to ESL classes: Contradiction and ambivalence.' *Journal of Multilingual and Multicultural Development* 21/1: 14–32.

Norton, B. 2000. *Identity and Language Learning: Gender, Ethnicity and Educational Change.* Harlow: Longman.

Rockhill, K. 1987. 'Gender, language and the politics of literacy.' *British Journal of Sociology of Education* 8/2: 153–67.

Migration and super-diversity

These three papers examine how many towns and cities are becoming 'super' or 'hyper' diverse. They suggest that old categories of race and ethnicity for describing neighbourhoods are no longer accurate.

Kyambi, S. 2005. Beyond Black and White: Mapping New Immigrant Communities. London: Institute of Public Policy Research.

Vertovec, S. 2006. *The Emergence of Super-diversity in Britain.* Oxford: University of Oxford Centre on Migration, Policy, and Society. Working Paper No. 25.

Zetter, R., D. Griffiths, N. Sigona, D. Flynn, T. Pasha, and R. Beynon. 2006. Immigration, Social Cohesion and Social Capital: What are the Links? York: Joseph Rowntree Trust.

3 THE CHALLENGES OF ESOL PRACTICE

A student came to me a couple of weeks ago and she was so proud, she'd been to the doctors on her own for the first time and not had to use an interpreter. I was so thrilled. I'll never forget her telling me that.
ESOL teacher, London

Introduction

This chapter is about what takes place in ESOL classrooms and why. In order to begin to unpick the 'why' of ESOL practice (or more accurately *practices*) we need to look at a complex range of factors, starting with the personal and professional life histories and identities of ESOL teachers and the routes they have taken on their way to their current posts. There are two major—often conflicting—challenges faced by these teachers: first, the challenge of how best to respond to the multiple and varied linguistic and social needs of their students, and second, the challenge of how to meet the institutional and bureaucratic demands made upon teachers by funding and inspection regimes. The sensitivity and flexibility needed to respond to the first of these challenges are not always possible within the rigidity of the systems in which ESOL is often located. In some contexts, ESOL teachers live with a constant tension between their understandings of their subject and their students on one hand, and their perceptions of policy and audit demands on the other. On top of this is the fact that ESOL teachers' work is political, and increasingly so, whether they see it or wish it that way or not. Earlier chapters showed that migrants and their English language skills are frequently placed centre-stage in ongoing debates about integration, social cohesion, and national identity, all of which gives ESOL a profile which is sometimes beyond the original expectations of teachers when they enter the ESOL field, and which in most cases lacks correspondence with the recompense they receive for their work.

Although most ESOL teachers see their main role as teaching language, they are also expected to act as administrators, advice workers, counsellors and mentors, social organizers, literacy brokers, and interpreters. The focus in further and adult education is often on individualization, differentiation, accountability, pastoral care, and the attendant bureaucracy these create, which leads some ESOL teachers to feel that scant attention is paid in their training and professional development to the actual processes of language learning and teaching. For this reason, in the final section of the chapter we discuss approaches and methods in language learning and teaching, to reorient readers to some central concerns in language pedagogy.

Who are ESOL teachers?

ESOL teachers come from a wide range of sociocultural and professional backgrounds. There is a traditional tendency to dichotomize the world of English Language Teaching in the private sector and the world of publicly-funded ESOL as rich/poor, apolitical/political, global/local, and so on, and to regard these worlds as entirely separate. However, the norm in present-day ESOL is that most teachers have worked in more than one setting and often in many settings with many different kinds of students; in fact ESOL teachers collectively are almost as diverse as their students. Some have spent most of their careers in the state sector, while others have come into ESOL teaching having worked in other countries, doing voluntary service overseas (VSO) or its equivalents, or with other kinds of international experience. Some have come from primary or secondary education, or from the university sector, some have taught other subjects and some have entered ESOL as a second career having had quite different jobs for most of their lives. By way of illustration, here are some brief sketches of the professional trajectories of teachers who have been involved in research into ESOL in England in recent years.

SIMA teaches a class for 16- to 18-year-olds at a large college in the outer suburbs of London. She is a British Asian woman who is a speaker of Urdu. She has been teaching for four years, having gone into teaching straight after university. Her training and work have all been undertaken since the introduction of the national curriculum and she has always worked at the same college. She places great emphasis on attendance, discipline, and assessment, which she sees as giving structure to the chaotic lives of her young students, many of whom are unaccompanied asylum seekers and refugees. She is interested in pursuing a career in educational management.

SALIMA teaches at one of the local centres of a college in Leeds. She has been involved in managing ESOL provision and in multicultural education for 18 years. Before that she worked in computing, and as a chiropodist. She came to England from Pakistan in the 1950s, when she was very young, has three expert languages (English, Urdu, and Panjabi), and is currently—and for the first time in her career—teaching a class of predominantly Urdu- and Panjabi-speaking Pakistani women, most of whom are housewives and mothers. Her own life experience has led her to the belief that 'learning and life cannot be separated' and that the purpose of learning is to enable independence and self-reliance in an unpredictable world.

JANE is a teacher at a large college in north London. She originally worked in publishing as a typesetter. She was involved in a political campaign against the first Gulf War and met people from the local Kurdish and Turkish communities. She started helping out the women on the campaign with their English, and decided to study for an ESOL qualification. She has worked at the same local college since then and a few years ago started to train as an ESOL literacy teacher. In her current literacy class there are 15 students, from Somalia (the majority), Turkey, and Eritrea. All are housewives and mothers, and many look after grandchildren. Nearly all have lived in the UK a long time and are part of established ethnic communities, and most do not speak English outside class. Jane places a lot of emphasis on encouraging her students to become independent learners and achieve more autonomy in their lives.

TOM teaches with a charity which provides education for adults at its city centre site in Bradford. ESOL teaching is a second career for Tom. His first was in textiles, in which he has a degree, and he worked in Australia for a number of years. He happened to be in Bangkok at the end of a contract he was working on, and he stayed there, teaching English and computer skills in a primary school for children with special needs. Back in England he worked in textiles again, but could see that the future was uncertain for the textile industry. At the centre where he teaches, he started as a cross-curricular basic skills tutor and at the same time studied for his Certificate in Teaching English as a Foreign Language. The make-up of his current ESOL group changes very frequently, because the centre caters for an ESOL population which is constantly changing.

ANDREA teaches a class of 16- to 19-year-olds in a secondary school sixth form centre. She has taught English as a Foreign Language for 20 years, in Madrid, Rome, and London, and on high-level courses such as an MA in International Relations at the University of Vienna. She has also taught legal and business English in London for ten years. She is a very experienced teacher trainer and writer of textbooks. Many of her current students are young asylum seekers with varying degrees of education and levels of literacy. The school requires the teachers to use materials written to support the ESOL core curriculum as their ESOL syllabus, but Alice feels that these are often unsuitable for young adult learners.

ROSA teaches a class of unemployed ESOL students at a private training centre. She is originally from Slovakia. She trained at university for five years as a teacher of English, and once Slovakia became a member of the EU, was able to validate her qualifications and work as a teacher in the UK. Her students are job seekers and it is very important for them to find work. Rosa is expected to teach them 'job-seeking skills' but also takes a rigorous academic grammar-based approach to language learning. As a successful language learner herself she is able to empathize with her students and understand the aspects of English they find difficult. This is greatly appreciated by her multicultural group of students, some of whom have adopted her as a role model, saying they want 'to be like her'.

These brief sketches—which, although diverse, in no way represent all ESOL teachers—suggest the difficulty of regarding ESOL as one profession or one set of professional practices, or of thinking of 'the ESOL teacher' as having but one professional identity. Neither do ESOL teachers hold one unified set of knowledge. Indeed, the stories of individual teachers show their professional identities to be unsettled, perhaps unsurprisingly given that the ESOL field itself is unstable and subject to frequent revisions of curricula, funding crises, and repeated drives for quality improvement.

ACTIVITY 1   Your ESOL trajectory

Trace your own professional trajectory. Include the different settings you have taught in and the different students you have met. How different is your context today from when you first started?

The challenges of ESOL practice

Student diversity and student needs

Chapters 1 and 2 established that ESOL students are a very diverse group and discussed some of the reasons for this diversity. ESOL classes are themselves super-diverse and dynamic spaces, and their composition is constantly changing. This demands a high degree of flexibility and adaptability from teachers. It is not unusual for an ESOL class to contain students from a dozen different countries, as in the class we described in Chapter 2. In a globalized era, ESOL teachers have to cater for the reality of a range of abilities and needs in their classes because of the disparate backgrounds of their students. Some students' lives have been disrupted by poverty, war, and unrest at home. Consequently they arrive in their class with little experience of formal learning or with considerable barriers to learning due to trauma and stress. On the other hand, some students have had years of good quality formal education as children and young adults, and come equipped with highly developed study skills that they are able to bring to their English language education. Some students in the class may not have had the opportunity to develop foundational literacy skills as children, and are therefore learning literacy for the first time as adults. Conversely, other students have strong literacy skills in a first or expert language, and find that they can transfer those skills to their study of English literacy. The diversity of ESOL classrooms offers many opportunities, but can also be challenging for teachers. An institutional response to the extreme heterogeneity of ESOL classes can require that the teacher assumes the responsibility for 'differentiating' his or her teaching to meet the needs of each student. However, this is not always realistic or desirable. As Baynham and Roberts, *et al.* (2007: 10) point out, 'the super-diversity of ESOL students cannot be fully catered for by differentiation in the classroom alone', especially when it involves many hours of extra preparation on the part of the teacher, and when the diversity between students is so extreme that many of their needs cannot be met in a mixed group.

The managerial mechanisms in place to cater for students' needs can present a further challenge to ESOL teachers. In the UK, for instance, contemporary ESOL practice, as with other areas of adult education, is characterized by a strong orientation to 'individualized' or 'personalized' learning, in which each student must work towards their particular learning goals and targets with their own individual learning plan (ILP). With some justification, many ESOL teachers feel that formally personalizing learning in this way is unrealistic and counter-productive, especially when classes are large and many students are still at the early stages of English language development. Given that individualized learning has become a statutory requirement for which evidence must be provided and by which teaching is judged, teachers feel that the sound educational principle of addressing students' needs has been turned into a bureaucratic task. Efficient administration is important in teaching, and there are few teaching contexts where practitioners do not have to engage with bureaucracy at all. But the bureaucracy associated with individualization faced by some teachers leads them to regard it as a hindrance to authentic personalization because it detracts from the time needed to listen to students and the stories they tell of their daily lives outside the classroom.

Students' changing needs and attitudes

Students' needs also change over time, and this is another dimension of difference that ESOL teachers have to be aware of. The major concern for most ESOL students when they first arrive in a country is oral communication, the subject of Chapter 5. Some beginner ESOL students have very basic literacy needs as well, explored in Chapter 6. Looking at what people say about their learning gives an insight into their changing needs. Here, a group of students in an intermediate ESOL class talk about their learning needs. The students in this class are mostly female, mostly from Eastern Europe, and mostly work as nurses and care home assistants. Even within such a homogenous group, as Monika, Anya, and Milena show, needs and attitudes can vary from student to student and also over time.

Monika from Poland explains how, when she came to the UK, she concentrated on speaking, but lately has found that she needs to work on writing and building her vocabulary:

> *I need writing and vocabulary. It was pretty difficult for the first few months. I didn't understand nothing. It was really hard. Very hard. I really wanted to go home. I was really upset. But I said, 'No, you can do it'. And so when I start to speak with English people I had a dictionary with me absolutely everywhere. So it was funny. And I didn't write. So I started to write when I came to this college, which is a year ago.*

Anya, also from Poland, talks about how she can now understand people when they speak with a local accent. Her attention now is on improving her grammar and writing skills, partly because she needs to be able to write accurately for her job as a care home assistant.

> *It's not hard for me now to understand English people, even if they are speaking with different accent, like Yorkshire, because they are using different words or they are saying words in different way, like, they not saying, 'Thank you', they are just saying, 'Ta'. They are not saying, 'Because', they are just saying, ''Cos'. So, now it's easy but before I couldn't understand them. But now it's alright. And I still want improve my grammar. I want it strong. Because in my work I have to write a lot, like, write report and accident forms and everything. So I need to be better.*

Milena, from Slovakia, explains how she can speak in day-to-day conversation, but has more difficulty when speaking for a particular specific purpose.

> *I don't have problem to talk with people, especially old people. But make phone call a doctor because something happened. So you have to know what you have to say. You can't use slang, for example, which you use sometimes during the day or during conversation with residents. You have to tell exactly what is going on. It's not like children speaking. But it depends, of course, on some situation, on some events.*

Monika and Anya talk about how their needs have shifted from being primarily concerned with speaking, to a more recent attention on writing. Anya associates this shift with a growing competence in speaking gained through communicating with people from the local area, coupled with the writing demands of her job in a hospital. Milena, however, retains the focus on speaking. She notes that speaking informally to residents in the care home where she works is undemanding. But when the situation is more formal or specialized, for example when talking to the doctor, she has difficulty finding the words for the specific situation.

ACTIVITY 2   Students' needs

What are your students' language learning needs? How do you find out about them? Evaluate the 'learner-centred' approaches taken in your institutions. Can you think of other ways of finding out about students and their needs?

Diversity and group learning

Although there may be an institutional requirement to focus on individualization, most ESOL teaching takes place in groups. Time and again interviews with ESOL students reveal their preference for whole class and small group work because of the opportunities these afford for interaction and because of the social and cognitive benefits they offer. This quote from a student in London is typical:

> *I like this college because it's different. They make you talk more. We have small groups and you can speak, not like the other college. Here we get into small groups to talk and I like that a lot.*

An essential part of ESOL teachers' work is to generate the right conditions for effective group work, the most important of which is group cohesion. This can be a challenging task given the sometimes mixed nature of ESOL classes, but one at which teachers become extremely skilled.

Most of the importance teachers give to group work is concerned with what they often call 'group dynamics' or 'gelling'; a harmonious group is essential to the smooth running of the day-to-day activities of a class. However, it is also well established that being part of a group is important for learning in general. Interaction with a focus on learning with other students as well as with a teacher is termed 'collaboration'. The social theory of the Russian psychologist Lev Vygotsky is often cited in relation to collaboration in learning. Vygotsky was writing in the 1920s and 1930s, but his ideas came to prominence in the West only after his works were translated into English. In particular, the volume of papers *Mind in Society* (1978) provides a grounding in Vygotskyian thought on collaboration, mediation through language, and language play. Central to Vygotsky's theory is the view that learning depends to a large extent on social interaction between the learner and others, parents and teachers, fellow students and peers. Vygotsky proposed that a psychological space exists, which he described as being ' … the distance between the actual development level as determined by independent problem solving and the level of potential development as determined through problem solving under adult guidance or in collaboration with more capable peers' (1978: 86). He called this space the zone of proximal development (ZPD). The implication for language learning is that collaboration, either among learners or between learners and their teacher, is vital for learners' development and movement through the ZPD, the space where learning happens.

Vygotsky was concerned with children's learning, and it is not clear whether mental processes occur in the same way in adults' minds. It is sensible, however, to present students with linguistic demands which are slightly, but not greatly, beyond those which they are able to meet on their own, but which they can manage in co-operation with others. What is not in question is that students can be stretched beyond their current competence and concerns with topics that are intellectually challenging. Learning and teaching activities need to engage students adequately as adult, reflective learners with a range of interests.

Affective benefits of group work

A student in a class in Huddersfield, Yorkshire, said: 'When I arrived to start to English classes it was like being in a big family. They help each other and try to understand.' Within this short statement the student manages to summarize many of the reasons why the group is of such key importance in ESOL. He articulates the value of group processes for learning on a cognitive level ('They help each other and try to understand') and he also gives voice to other reasons why the group is important ('... it was like being in a big family'). The group can provide a sense of security and stability that is often missing in ESOL students' histories or daily lives. It can also promote people taking control of learning themselves, when they are encouraged to plan in groups, given opportunities to reflect on their own learning, choose activities, and decide what they want to concentrate on in future lessons.

Psychologists have suggested that certain needs have to be satisfied before learning can take place. Most famously, the psychologist A. H. Maslow (1943) proposed a hierarchy of needs, whereby fundamental needs have to be met before those higher up the hierarchy can be addressed. In Maslow's model, physiological needs (for food, sleep, etc.) have to be satisfied before safety needs (for example, security of employment and health) can be tackled. In Maslow's hierarchy, the needs that are concerned with love and belonging, for example, friendship, family, and sexual intimacy, come lower in the hierarchy than those concerned with learning (esteem and self-actualization). Maslow has his detractors, and it is unlikely that a strict hierarchy actually exists. Yet the idea that students have to feel secure before they can usefully learn is one which will strike a chord with ESOL teachers. Such security can be generated within a group or a class, as the student in Huddersfield says.

Each ESOL class has a unique atmosphere, which we can talk of as its 'ecology'. ESOL teachers face the challenge of generating, maintaining, and supporting a classroom ecology that is productive for collaborative learning. This can be very difficult when the students and their needs are highly diverse. While preserving an overriding orientation towards the group, ESOL teachers can support and strengthen the potentially fragile classroom ecology by using a number of possibly contrasting, but equally appropriate approaches. In some classes it might be fitting to focus very explicitly on students' needs, problems, and concerns as a way of promoting solidarity and helping students to learn from each other. This has echoes of the critical pedagogy of Paolo Freire (1970), which we discuss in Chapter 6, and of the stance whereby control of topics and texts rests with the students themselves, covered in Chapter 4. A different approach is to seal off the classroom from the harsh and uncertain reality outside by providing a predictable and structured environment. In her case study of an ESOL class for asylum seekers in Blackburn, Rachel Hodge talks of how one teacher has created a safe and supportive space for students. Here is an extract from her study (Hodge 2004: 31).

CASE STUDY 'This is not enough for one's life'

In order to support these vulnerable students and to aid their learning, Wendy has developed the practice of attending to their requests for help, such as phoning lawyers, outside class time, and of not making their past or present lives a part of any of the classroom learning activities. Her reason for this practice is to create a separate space inside the classroom as she explained in her interview:

> So if they've got problems we try and deal with them at other times; the classroom time is lesson time, and that is the time when they can be just a student and switch off.

Within this space she helps the students focus on their drive to learn the dominant language within a secure atmosphere of mutual support, where both she and they can put the complex and often negative demands on them to one side, as she explains:

> Within the classroom we've got a very definite focus, and, in that time they can forget everything else, but also I can as well be just a teacher for a little while.

In this way the teacher too finds a way to deal with the inevitable pressures and emotional stresses of supporting the learning and social needs of these students. So, for the first months of this class the students engage in tasks that have little reference to the rest of their lives, and Wendy approaches themes such as 'family' with extreme caution, knowing that this is a very painful subject for those students who have lost contact with theirs, or who fear for their safety. This approach has obviously been a successful one as the students get to know and trust each other and become familiar with the daily routines of the class. In addition, she has drawn on students' willingness and initiatives to support each other both outside and inside the class. Wendy actively encourages the students to look to their peers for learning support rather than setting herself up as the sole language expert in the class:

> Right, you can help each other, you don't have to work on your own, you can help each other with your meanings.

Wendy's experience encapsulates the classroom-oriented challenge of creating and maintaining group cohesion in the face of enormous variety and diversity. The trend for governments to adopt policies that focus on individualization and personalization, which are often imposed on ESOL teachers 'top-down' can, if they are allowed, run counter to the social solidarity and group cohesion which are so crucial in ESOL classes. How this plays out in practice is discussed in more detail below.

The challenges of audit culture: centralization and accountability

As well as the challenge of diverse student populations and their needs, the other challenge facing ESOL teachers is the bureaucratic and administrative demands made of them by their institutions. Publicly funded adult education programmes in colleges and other institutions are carefully audited and held accountable to their funders. They are also inspected for standards of teaching and learning; a failure to keep up standards means, in the long run, a removal of public funds. This is part of the larger phenomenon of the spread of audit culture from the business sector to all spheres of public life. The migration of methods of audit and accountability from the financial world to areas such as education and health have, since the 1980s, wrought deep changes in the nature of work, in institutions, and in what it means to be a professional. In education, the term 'audit' has become associated with a cluster of terms and practices such as 'performance', 'quality assurance', 'quality control', 'accountability', 'efficiency', 'effectiveness', 'benchmarking', and so on. For teachers this has meant their work has become more performance oriented and audit driven, and more directly accountable to a range of 'stakeholders', especially funding bodies. The need to provide evidence of learning is part of a trend towards the textualization of work, in which people are increasingly expected to write and talk about their jobs as well as carry them out.

These changes in education have created changes in professional identity and increasing job dissatisfaction, leading to high rates of teacher attrition in some areas. While the majority of ESOL teachers are ambivalent about audit culture, they expend a great deal of energy responding to the demands made upon them by funders and quality controllers. This is partly because teachers know their jobs are at stake in an increasingly unstable profession, but also because the individualization agenda draws on a distorted version of a powerful discourse of social justice which forms part of the belief system of many teachers in the field. This can be confusing to committed ESOL teachers who are convinced of the 'rights' aspects of individualization, but then find themselves struggling to cope with huge amounts of bureaucracy and having to find ever more creative solutions in their attempts to meet the challenges we describe in this chapter.

While certain levels of administrative tasks and record keeping are to be expected in any teaching job, some teachers face extremes of bureaucratic load, as this edited extract from an interview with a teacher describes:

> *We have the scheme of work for the year and a lesson plan for every lesson. They've got their ILPs [individual learning plans], that has to be filled in with all their personal information, their assessment results and diagnostic results from the initial assessments, their learning goals, what they're working towards. There's some information, such as asking asylum seekers how long they've been here, all that kind of personal information. Then they have a sheet that has the course objectives, the group goals with curriculum references, and then their individual targets for half term. We have a review form to do at the end of every lesson and then for every student we have to say what stage they are at. That comes from the inspection when they said we weren't keeping formal records enough. There's also a bit to put any test results on, for each student and whether you're taking any action on their ILP. There's an evaluation on the end of the lesson plan and for every student, an evaluation of every student's progress during that lesson. At the end of term there's all sorts of other forms …*

The teacher continues in this vein for a much lengthier description of the bureaucratic tasks she undertakes every academic term; in total she describes seventeen separate pieces of paperwork that have to be completed.

ACTIVITY 3   Reflecting on administration and bureaucracy

Reflect on the paperwork you are asked to do as part of your teaching. Can you describe the purpose of every administrative and bureaucratic task? Which, if any, do you find overly bureaucratic? What strategies do you adopt to manage them?

Meeting the challenges

Professional identity

Teachers struggle in many ways to meet the challenges described in this chapter, through skilful management of diversity and classroom ecologies and through different ways of being 'professional'. There are many different constructs of 'professionalism' in teaching. In their paper 'Unbecoming teachers: Towards a more dynamic notion of professional participation' (2007), Helen Colley and her colleagues identify two broad ways that academics have looked at professionalism. One is by invoking a set of externally judged features which are akin to a 'job description'. These features might be the adaptability and flexibility we describe above, specialist subject knowledge, reflective practice, tacit knowledge, and so on. The other way is a more internal model of the individual character of the professional person, that is, what she *is* rather than what she *does*. The latter way appeals to categories such as 'vocation' and commitment to students. In ESOL these two are very much in evidence at the same time.

Although not incompatible, there is a tension between the external view of ESOL 'professionalism' in which teachers have been expected to gain standardized qualifications and expert subject knowledge, and the traditional vocational nature of ESOL teaching. Many ESOL teachers display a strong sense of vocation in their practice and in the way they talk about their work. For many, their vocation and commitment are the reasons they stay in the field, despite unhappiness with other trends in their sector. Teachers' commitment to students and their strong sense of vocation are essential to the survival of ESOL. These are characteristics common to many long-term members of the profession, but do not always sit easily with the managerial demands and definitions of professionalism which have crept into the field in recent years.

ESOL shares similarities with the 'caring professions' of nursing and social work: the majority of ESOL teachers are female, and most are highly committed to their work. Teachers often work extra hours and many are employed on part-time or hourly-paid contracts. Many teachers have a well-developed political analysis of ESOL issues and express solidarity with their students, acting as advocates for them in their struggles outside the classroom. For many in the field, the political side of ESOL—its

The 2007 'Save ESOL' campaign

relationship with matters of social justice—is part of their identity as teachers. This commitment may come from teachers' own (or their parents') experience of migration, from a deep knowledge of minority or refugee communities, or from their own particular political or moral beliefs and allegiances. ESOL teaching has long been regarded as political work, as it has often been responsive to the needs of migrants seeking refuge from war and oppression, and suffering extremes of hardship and destitution. ESOL has a vociferous lobby in the UK; indeed, given that the field has often been marginalized even within adult education, and given the precarious nature of public funding it receives, this is probably one of its greatest assets.

ACTIVITY 4   Reflecting on professionalism

What is your definition of a 'professional' ESOL teacher? How far is this defin-ition shared by your colleagues and managers in your own organization? Do you consider yourself to be a 'professional'?

Approaches to language teaching in ESOL

ESOL teachers face the challenges of centralization, accountability, managerialism, and audit culture, along with the demands of a diverse and ever-changing student population. At the same time they are required to have knowledge about the linguistic and discourse features of English, as well as knowledge of how languages are taught and learnt. Teachers struggle with their professional identities when the demands made of them by their institutions conflict with their own beliefs about teaching and their own knowledge of their subject and their students. Many teachers complain that their knowledge of their subject is being undermined or overlooked in deference to institutional requirements such as high rates of exam passes. A common complaint amongst teachers is that they rarely get the opportunity to explore ideas about teaching and learning with their colleagues, or a chance to keep up with developments in the field. The final part of this chapter, therefore, turns to the core business of language learning and teaching, looking at approaches and methods in language pedagogy, and at how ESOL teachers can set about their classroom practice in the light of the challenges they face.

Teaching methods

Language teaching methods are coherent sets of techniques used by teachers in language classes. All teachers who undergo training to teach languages will be exposed to one or more teaching methods, whether this is made explicit or not. In many cases, methods are consistent with an overall approach or philosophy of language teaching. Teaching methods, and their correspondence with theoretical approaches, have provoked much description, discussion, and debate in the history of language teaching over the years, and any study of approaches and methods in language teaching will reveal the shifting fashions of the field (Richards and Rodgers 2001). The current dominant approach in language teaching literature and on teacher training courses in the West—and therefore the one we concentrate on in this chapter—is Communicative Language Teaching (CLT), a broad and general approach which has developed since the mid-1970s. Although teachers of ESOL draw on other approaches, most have been influenced by CLT to a greater or lesser degree, either directly through their professional training, or indirectly through materials and textbooks written according to CLT principles. Understanding what happens in ESOL classrooms therefore also requires an understanding of this influential approach to teaching.

CLT arose partly as a reaction against the perceived shortcomings of established earlier approaches to the teaching of languages. It is also based on a particular understanding of language in use, communicative competence. The term 'communicative competence' was coined by the sociolinguist Dell Hymes, in response to his concern that linguistics was overly focused on formal aspects of language. Hymes took particular issue with Noam Chomsky's (1965) distinction between linguistic competence and performance. Chomsky's work studied language as an abstract formal system (linguistic competence), rather than how it is actually used (performance). Hymes argued that it is a mistake to neglect the social and cultural dimensions of what it means both to know a language, and to have an ability to use linguistic forms appropriately according to the context at hand (Hymes 1972). For CLT, the attention is therefore not so much on teaching students how to produce language that is formally, grammatically accurate. Rather, there is an emphasis on effective communication in language that is appropriate to its contexts of use.

There is no rigid set of methods associated with CLT, and more or less any activity with a focus on using English for effective communication is seen as acceptable. Techniques such as role play, discussions, and jigsaw and information gap activities (involving the transfer of information from one person to another) prevail in communicative classrooms, where teachers manage activities which are designed to place students in positions where they are obliged to communicate. Recent years have seen the development of what many regard as the natural descendent of CLT, task-based language teaching (TBLT). In TBLT, the lesson is based around the completion of a central task related to a real-world activity, a task which might not begin with a specific language focus. The language studied in the lesson is decided as the students complete the task.

CLT is not without its critics and there are drawbacks to adopting the approach unquestioningly in ESOL classrooms. Pennycook (1994) regards

CLT as overly 'phonocentric', that is as subordinating the written word to the spoken, especially at lower levels. Other writers question the cultural appropriacy of exporting an approach developed in the English-dominant West to other parts of the world with different traditions of teaching and learning. In his book *The Struggle to Teach English as an International Language* (2005) Adrian Holliday describes how a communicative classroom can actually inhibit students rather than encourage them to speak and practice. Holliday taught the same group of Hong Kong students in England and then again a short while later in Hong Kong. In the first context he used a methodology commensurate with a communicative approach, carefully if subtly controlling students' language practice and production. Later, back in Hong Kong, Holliday found that the approach he had used in England had to be abandoned: 'I did away with the "communicative" classroom altogether because it simply did not work—the students simply did not like the corrective, controlling culture ...' (2005: 95). The lesson here for ESOL is that while some students will react well to a broadly communicative approach to teaching, others will be comfortable with what are more culturally appropriate approaches. A further criticism of CLT is that although it privileges spoken communication, talk can sometimes be promoted for the sake of it, with scant attention being paid to the *quality* of that talk. There is little focus on 'talk for learning ... or as a means for exploring ideas, and more specifically of argumentative or constative speech', says the language educator Catherine Wallace (2003: 68). By 'constative', Wallace refers to the kind of speech which is more debate-like, which elaborates and defends an argument and provides a bridge into expository written language, in other words the kind of talk students will need if they are to develop critical literacy or if they wish to pursue academic study later on. A further limitation of CLT is that it does not provide many good models for dealing with interaction when there are imbalances of power between speakers, a problem for many ESOL students and one to which we return in Chapter 5.

Despite the drawbacks of CLT, however, various methods associated with the approach are useful for ESOL, especially at beginner levels and especially in institutions where there is an over-emphasis on exam success, individualized learning, and functional literacy. For example, a communicative approach to language teaching stresses the importance of the group in learning; as such, it corresponds well with the points made earlier in this chapter about the group processes in ESOL classrooms. The focus on successful completion of tasks and activities ensures students are concentrating on meaning, and on the negotiation of meaning with other students, rather than primarily on linguistic form. Moreover, there is an emphasis in communicative classrooms on talk in small groups in order to maximize opportunities for practice. This is particularly important for students who have few opportunities to interact in English outside the classroom.

It almost goes without saying that ESOL teachers have to be flexible in their approach to teaching, and that each teacher will develop, adopt, and adapt teaching methods and techniques which are appropriate and responsive to the situation they are faced with. Taking such a pragmatic and eclectic stance might set teachers against some of the more rigid systemic structures which are characteristic of contemporary ESOL contexts. As we discuss in the final section of this chapter, the point is not to slavishly adhere to one method of teaching, but to take the aspects of that method which are most useful for a particular context and a particular set of students, mixing and matching it with other methods and techniques which may also be effective or beneficial.

Methods and principled pragmatism

Given the range and complexity of contexts of ESOL teaching and learning, there is no one best or right way to teach the language. Furthermore, the methods used in every ESOL class are not always the cutting edge ones promoted in the literature on methodology. Older and more traditional approaches and methods, including ones which some consider to be discredited, are frequently employed by ESOL teachers.

Many teachers use an array of methods in their teaching but do not necessarily feel bound by them. In a study of English language teachers who were also MA students at Ohio University, David Bell (2007) concluded that teachers have an outlook on the range of methods that is highly pragmatic. Teachers' interest is promoted largely by how far various methods provide options in dealing with particular teaching contexts. When discussing the methods they use, most of the teachers in Bell's study describe their teaching as 'eclectic'. Moreover, when asked to define 'method', none of the teachers in the study adopt a definition which views it as primarily theory driven. 'Teachers ... were far more ready to see method as emerging from practice and sensitive to context', says Bell (2007: 137). He goes on: 'Most teachers think of methods in terms of techniques which realise a set of principles or goals and they are open to any method that offers practical solutions to problems in their particular teaching context'. It seems that when teachers reflect on their methods, they see them as useful entities that can be employed with close reference to their particular teaching and learning situation.

So teachers view methods as a range of choices, to be drawn on and implemented according to the contingencies of the context. Some theorists have suggested that such an eclectic approach, in what has become known as the 'post-method condition' (a phrase coined by Kumaravadivelu 1994), can still be underpinned by a set of principles. Kumaravadivelu (1994, 2002) argues that methods themselves cannot take account of classroom realities. Instead, practitioners construct classroom-oriented theories of practice when empowered with knowledge, skills, and autonomy, through training, reflective practice, and the avoidance of impositions of methods. In an approach based on principled pragmatism, methods still play a role through selective borrowing, but theory, in the form of coherent and relevant pedagogy, is developed by teachers in relation to their daily work. Kumaravadivelu proposes ten 'macro-strategies' which can be used as 'a broad guideline, based on which teachers can generate their own situation-specific, needs-based micro-strategies or classroom techniques' (1994: 32).

These ten strategies are:

- maximize learning opportunities
- facilitate negotiated interaction
- minimize perceptual mismatches between teacher intention and learner interpretation
- activate intuitive heuristics (for example, by providing enough textual data for learners to infer underlying grammatical rules)
- foster language awareness
- contextualize linguistic input
- integrate language skills
- promote learner autonomy
- raise cultural consciousness
- ensure social relevance.

Of course, many teachers would say that some, if not all, of these macro-strategies are the implicit tenets with which they work as a matter of course. Moreover, the set of macro-strategies might themselves be said to constitute a method. Some of the macro-strategies are no doubt redolent of the prevailing theoretical positions at a particular point in time. Yet so long as teachers' orientation is towards their students and their learning context, argues another post-method theorist, Suresh Canagarajah, such a set of strategies can be fostered according to the learning styles of students and their lived experiences outside the classroom 'in a way that is less intrusive than the implementation of traditional methods' (2002: 144). It is important therefore to adopt such an orientation if the proposed macro-strategies do not themselves become translated into a prescriptive method. The hallmark of principled pragmatism is that theorizing should be done by teachers from the classroom itself. In the final chapter of this book we explore ways in which teachers do this, through engaging critically with theory, observation, and collaborative action research.

ACTIVITY 5   Your teaching theories

Try to identify your own personal teaching theories. Where do they come from? Think back over your teaching career. How have your own ideas about teaching and learning changed? Why did they change?

Conclusion

Rather than subscribing rigidly to particular methods or top-down curricula, ESOL practice can be based on strategies which teachers can relate to particular circumstances. Teachers themselves probably need a measure of confidence and autonomy to employ these strategies as the foundation for their teaching. This is because positioning themselves as people who are not bound by a particular way of doing things can lead teachers to certain tensions. These might be with what the applied linguist Bob Adamson (2004) calls 'systemic forces', such as a syllabus based on a prescribed curriculum, or a focus on examinations. Furthermore, many teachers have limited access to the knowledge on which to base their practice. This is true, but it is also the point, and these factors need to be challenged. Firstly, systemic forces are all too evident in ESOL, so it is important for teachers to adopt a critical stance towards their teaching. Such an outlook involves the effort of drawing on the study of individual classroom practice to develop methodology, rather than having it imposed from above. It also involves broadening a view of practice to encompass more than the classroom, to examine where it is situated in relation to the bigger picture of ESOL, engaging with the challenges outlined in this chapter. The second point, that many teachers lack access to the relevant knowledge about pedagogy, methods and language in general, can and should be addressed in initial teacher education and continuing teacher development. At the heart of teacher education policy should, of course, lie teaching and learning processes. Together with the depth of knowledge drawn from experience, teachers can become equipped to tackle the challenges of ESOL. As Canagarajah (2002: 140) says: 'This is perhaps the right moment to empower the local knowledge of teachers, deriving from their years of accumulated experience, wisdom, and intuitions about what works best for their students.'

Further reading

Teachers' knowledge and beliefs

These two books look at how teachers understand their teaching. Tsui's book is a collection of case studies on teachers' understanding of expertise and what it means to be an expert teacher. Borg's is a 'state of the art' study on teacher cognition.

Borg, S. 2003. *Teacher Cognition in Language Teaching: A Review of Research on What Language Teachers Think, Know, Believe, and Do*. Cambridge: Cambridge University Press.

Tsui, A. B. M. 2003. *Understanding Expertise in Teaching: Case Studies of ESL Teachers*. Cambridge: Cambridge University Press.

Collaboration in learning

Lantolf's book is a collection of papers exploring the application of Vygotskyian sociocultural theory to language learning and teaching. Vygotsky's papers themselves were first published in the 1920s and 1930s, and encapsulate his theories of learning through collaboration with others.

Lantolf, J. P. (ed.). 2000. *Sociocultural Theory and Second Language Learning*. Oxford: Oxford University Press.

Vygotsky, L. S. 1978. *Mind in Society: Development of Higher Psychological Processes*. Cambridge, MA: Harvard University Press.

Communicative competence

Canale and Swain's influential article reformulates Hymes' original model of communicative competence to make it relevant to language teaching and learning. Chapters 4 and 5 of Cook's book give an accessible overview of traditions in ELT and of communicative competence.

Canale, M. and **M. Swain.** 1980. 'Theoretical bases of communicative approaches to second language teaching and testing.' *Applied Linguistics* 1/1: 1–47.

Cook, G. 2003. *Applied Linguistics*. Oxford: Oxford University Press.

Approaches and methods in language teaching

Howatt's book gives an overview of the origins and history of the teaching of English, its methods and how they developed across time and in different contexts, from 1400 to the present day. Richards and Rodgers provide an overview and critique of approaches and methods in language teaching. Also included here is a selection of books on methodology. Harmer's book is the most widely read 'how to teach' book of its kind. Hedge's work is an excellent in-depth introduction to language teaching methodology based on a communicative approach. Chapter 2 gives an accessible introduction to the principles of communicative language teaching. Schellekens' is the first handbook devoted specifically to the practice of ESOL.

Harmer, J. 2001. *The Practice of English Language Teaching* (third edition). Harlow: Longman.

Hedge, T. 2000. *Teaching and Learning in the Language Classroom*. Oxford: Oxford University Press.

Howatt, A. P. R. with **H. G. Widdowson.** 2004. *A History of English Language Teaching* (second edition). Oxford: Oxford University Press.

Richards, J. C. and **T. S. Rodgers.** 2001. *Approaches and Methods in Language Teaching* (second edition). Cambridge: Cambridge University Press.

Schellekens, P. 2007. *The Oxford ESOL Handbook.* Oxford: Oxford University Press.

4 THE CONTENT OF ESOL LESSONS

I'm happy to take risks in a classroom; someone will have something to say, or something happens. There's always something. Today there was an accident and the road works and a crying student. Then it was a lost key. So there's a story behind everything, and that gives me a lesson.
ESOL teacher, London

Introduction

This chapter is about the topics, the activities, and the materials which make up the content of ESOL lessons. The teaching of language inevitably involves the teaching of culture, whether this is made explicit or is embedded in the approaches to pedagogy in institutions, and in specific classrooms (see Byram and Morgan 1994; Kramsch 1998). Materials designed for pedagogy reflect the culture within which they are produced; in ESOL this might include prevailing ideologies with respect to the role of migrants. The last chapter suggested that there is not one best or right approach to language teaching and that teachers should ground their practice in their particular contexts and knowledge of their students, as well as in their knowledge of theories of language learning. Similarly, just as there is no one single method that will be appropriate for all ESOL teaching, so there is no unified lesson content, no single set of topics, activities, and materials, that can cater for the needs of the diverse body of students who make up ESOL classes. The appropriate content for ESOL lessons is likely to be identified not in prescribed or generic material, but embedded in the contexts of practice.

The tensions of lesson content

This approach, however, is often difficult to reconcile with the political world in which ESOL is situated, particularly when working within the framework of a statutory national curriculum, and an audit culture which requires accountability in the form of exam success. As Chapters 1 and 2 showed, at a time of mass migration and globalization, ESOL has to respond to constantly shifting populations and increasing cultural and linguistic diversity in towns and cities. In recent times ESOL has become central to a range of social, political, and economic issues, all of which have had an impact on pedagogy and the content of ESOL classes. The realities of global capitalism are unlikely to be ESOL teachers' most immediate concerns as they prepare and teach their lessons, yet macro-economic factors impinge on ESOL in various ways. One of the main concerns of government, for example, is to ensure that the workforce has a level of skills high enough to match its competitors. Publicly funded language and literacy programmes are therefore more likely to be oriented towards business and workplace needs. Employers are increasingly expected to be willing to contribute to the cost of training their workforces and in turn expect, and are permitted, to have a greater say in the content of ESOL and other basic skills courses. A second socio-political factor affecting the content of ESOL is a concern for the integration of immigrants into mainstream society and the larger issue of 'social cohesion'. A perceived lack of English language competence in some minority communities in England has been connected by some politicians and the media with a failure on the part of some communities to integrate; the solution in the UK was to introduce citizenship testing and teaching as part of ESOL, thus adding a further expectation in terms of the content of lessons.

Inevitably, a top-down approach to language education positions ESOL students in certain ways, particularly in relation to their perceived language learning needs and the needs of the economy. This might well be at odds with the perspective of individual ESOL teachers and students 'at the chalk face'. However, if national curricula and their associated materials can be criticized for the assumptions they make about learners' needs, the generic English Language Teaching (ELT) coursebooks, which teachers frequently turn to, bring concerns of a different kind. Looking for range and variety, teachers find that authors and publishers of such materials tend to avoid many issues which are pertinent to ESOL students. Consequently they may be rejected by teachers (and students) as not fitting the needs of their groups. How then can teachers work with lesson content in ways which *are* appropriate for particular groups of students, which conform to what students both need and expect? What are ways in which teachers and their students can work together on lesson content appropriate to their respective needs? When content is negotiated with students, and in particular when content is learner-generated, it is likely that topics close to students' personal concerns will emerge. A challenging issue for ESOL teachers, then, is the extent to which sensitive matters of risk and taboo that arise in such lessons can and should be managed. These are among the questions we explore in this chapter.

From home-produced materials to the global textbook

ESOL teachers have several sources of materials to draw on when planning their lessons. Looking back, the material from the 1960s, 1970s, and early 1980s tended to reflect the political trends of the time. Early ESL attempted to respond to the needs of large numbers of non-English-speaking people who migrated from the 1950s onwards; in Britain these students came especially from the Indian sub-continent and East Africa. Students needed to be prepared for daily life; ESL materials were home-produced and heavily functional, dealing with basic survival and adjustment to life in the new country, and activities such as going shopping, going to the doctor's, and filling in forms for welfare benefits. 'Survival' ESL was later criticized by writers such as Elsa Auerbach (1986) and Jim Tollefson (1986) for its reliance on materials based on unreal situations in which problems are easily solved and people in positions of power are co-operative and helpful, and for its hidden curriculum 'which prepares students for subservient social roles and reinforces hierarchical relations both in and outside the classroom' (Auerbach and Burgess 1985: 475). Perhaps inevitably, echoes of 'survival English' can be seen in materials and methods used in ESOL classrooms even today.

By the late 1980s and 1990s, a lot of the earlier ESL material was either out of print or seemed irrelevant to new students coming from different countries from previous groups of students, so teachers turned to alternative options. These included commercially produced materials, such as the type of textbooks commonly used in the teaching of English as a Foreign Language around the world. Just as ELT in general has a strong ideological agenda, which Robert Phillipson, among others, has linked to the notion of linguistic imperialism (Phillipson 1992), so teaching materials are not without an ideological dimension. Materials inevitably present a particular view of the world to their users, reflecting the wishful thinking and ideological positioning of publishers more than the local realities of students or teachers. EFL coursebooks in the 1970s and 1980s, such as the *Kernel* series (O'Neill 1972), *The New Cambridge English Course* (Walter and Swan 1984–1987), and *Streamline English* series (Hartley and Viney), tended to reflect the culture—invariably the dominant, usually conservative version—of English majority countries such as the United States or Britain. These materials were not without their critics; overseas teachers often had difficulty 'translating' the very British or American content for their local settings and feminists in particular condemned the way men and women were represented in traditional gender roles (see Clarke and Clarke 1990 and Sunderland 1994).

ACTIVITY 1 Global coursebooks

Take an EFL coursebook you are familiar with. How does the book represent:
• women
• men
• social class
• ethnicity
• native and non-native speakers of English
• cultural norms?

What are the issues arising for ESOL classrooms?

Do teaching materials necessarily work better if they reflect their 'users'?

Of course, ELT is above all a commercial endeavour so coursebooks with a very particular British or American flavour soon had to accommodate the globalizing trends of English language learning and publishing. It is now in publishers' interests to make coursebooks appeal to as wide a market as possible, hence the emergence of generic English Language, or 'global' coursebooks—such as the best-selling six-level *New Headway English Course* (Soars and Soars)—that can be marketed and sold anywhere ELT is practised. However, the extent to which global textbooks are appropriate in ESOL classrooms is questionable; in particular, the sort of apolitical, carefree, and overwhelmingly middle class culture that such coursebooks present opens them up to criticism.

These concerns regarding global ELT coursebooks are the subject of research by John Gray (2002). Gray describes how publishers of modern ELT coursebooks written for the global market have adopted particular guidelines for their authors. These cover two areas: inclusivity and inappropriacy. The guidelines for inclusivity put pressure on coursebook authors to avoid the bias and stereotyping they were criticized for in the past, and to ensure fairness and balance in representations of gender in particular, and also of age, class, ethnic origin, and disability. Gray describes how the authors of one popular coursebook have adhered to these guidelines:

> *Women are highly visible and are shown in a variety of roles—as journalist, high-earning graphic designer, artist, writer, intrepid nun and TV presenter, happy unmarried and middle-aged aunt, businesswoman, judge, and film director. Men too are shown in a variety of jobs and in situations where they wear aprons, prepare meals for their female partners, and talk knowledgeably about housework.*
> Gray 2002: 159

Ironically, of course, inverting stereotypes often serves only to reinforce them. Changing the way a group is represented only goes part way to challenging the way that group is positioned in a particular society—students also need the chance to critically engage with stereotyping and discrimination.

Many publishers also have guidelines for inappropriacy, including lists of proscribed topics, risky or taboo areas which authors should either handle with great care or avoid altogether. One publisher's list cited by Gray contained 30 items to avoid, including: alcohol, anarchy, AIDS, Israel, politics, religion, racism, sex, science when it involves altering nature, terrorism, and violence. The result, says Gray, is that coursebooks begin to resemble one another, and there is a danger that they will misrepresent the 'target culture' because its distinctive characteristics have been bleached out and content becomes bland and dull.

ACTIVITY 2   Global coursebooks and taboo topics

Examine a widely used coursebook you are familiar with. Which topics does it cover? Which topics does it seem to avoid?

A commercially driven policy prevents 'dangerous' or taboo topics from being included in coursebooks, which sanitizes them for consumption in certain countries. Reliance on such materials in ESOL classes means that opportunities for students to engage critically with unsafe topics will be missed. Yet such topics are frequently the stuff of interesting communication and many practitioners believe that the risk of offence is overstated. In fact, in her book on reading in English language classrooms (1992), Catherine Wallace suggests that students are more likely to be offended by being patronized or having texts censored for them.

The tendency of global coursebooks to avoid unsafe topics may also represent missed opportunities for learning on a cognitive level. In his book *Language Play, Language Learning* (2000) Guy Cook brings to our attention the importance of language play for second or foreign language development. Language play can be observed on a formal level, as linguistic patterning (repetition, alliteration); on a semantic level, for example as fiction; and on a pragmatic level, as humour, display, and contest. Language play is central to human thought, and is found in the language of religion, ritual and aggression, verbal competition and duelling, and sex. As Cook notes, the topics proscribed by textbook publishers are often the very ones which are associated with language play. Thus the avoidance of these topics will lead to a reduction of a focus on language play, at the expense of opportunities for play-related language development such as attention to language form.

The attitudes of ESOL teachers and students towards global coursebooks is ambivalent. A study carried out in a London college shortly before the introduction of the national curriculum (Cooke 2000) found that ESOL teachers were using global EFL textbooks for a number of reasons. Some of those cited were:

- teachers are familiar with these coursebooks
- there is a lack of availability of appropriate ESOL materials
- ESOL materials are not relevant to today's students
- few new ESOL-type materials find a publisher
- teachers have too high a workload to develop their own materials
- no paid time is allotted for development of materials.

Some teachers in the study said they spent considerable time 'cutting and pasting' EFL textbooks in an often hit-and-miss attempt to present the asylum seekers and refugees in their ESOL classes with materials they might relate to culturally and linguistically.

In the same study, the attitudes amongst students to global coursebooks also varied, but many felt the materials were boring and had considerable shortcomings. Some of the comments made by students regarding materials, and the way they are used in ESOL classes, suggest that in many cases they fall short of meeting students' needs as they themselves perceive them:

> *We use the same materials as in my country, I expected something better here in the UK, something more.*
> Ecuadorian man, London

> *There is one style in the book and you can feel it, and there are many things more that we need, but we go from one page to another every day. There are things that are difficult for us but we don't learn them. In this book it's just like a short reminder as if we already knew it.*
> Russian woman, London

Some teachers in Cooke's study doubted how appropriate global EFL materials were for all their students, echoing the concerns outlined by John Gray in his research. Representations in global coursebooks written for the EFL market are generally of young people living fairly affluent lifestyles, the content presupposes a general knowledge base and linguistic background that is eurocentric, and the books contain little specific local subject matter. However, because of lack of time and support these teachers were unable to produce anything more relevant for the asylum seekers and refugees in their ESOL classes. Other teachers however, found this less of a problem—they found that they were able to use materials which seemed inappropriate as long as students were encouraged to engage critically with the images, ideas, and texts they contained (see Wallace 2003).

Adult ESOL in England, Wales, and Northern Ireland: curriculum and materials

The attempts by teachers to adapt global coursebooks for their ESOL students led to a great deal of photocopying and cutting and pasting, as well as much confusion as to exactly what ESOL students *should* be taught in their lessons and what materials were appropriate for them. There was a general feeling that there was a dearth of resources and that ESOL was a sector which lacked professionalism and public funds. This changed with the introduction of the national adult ESOL curriculum in 2001 and the subsequent publication of materials to accompany it.

The materials were professionally produced and distributed free to all colleges and adult learning centres who requested them. Just as the materials of earlier times were influenced by prevailing attitudes to immigrants and how they should ideally be behaving in their 'host country', the new materials reflected current concerns with multiculturalism, integration, and social cohesion. They therefore show thriving and dynamic multicultural communities in which migrants are welcome to maintain their traditions and identities, but within a firm framework of integration and social responsibility. Thus there are activities which draw on festivities such as weddings (an inexhaustible subject for coursebook writers!) and traditions from various cultures and religions, alongside examples of harmonious interactions between neighbours from different ethnic backgrounds using English as a lingua franca. Ethnic minority people invite their English neighbours and colleagues home for a cup of tea, help out the old people in the neighbourhood, ask for directions when they are lost, and chat to each other when they meet in the street. The 'survival' English of the 1960s and 1970s is evident in the extensive coverage of subjects such as local transport, local neighbourhoods, finding a doctor, phoning the emergency services, and housing. The radical anti-racism of the 1980s has given way to a milder 'rights in the workplace' representation in which workers ask their employers for time off to go to appointments.

The current orientation towards work and creating an economically productive workforce is evident in the materials, several chapters of which cover job seeking, interviews, and work relations. There is also an emphasis on adult education and training, volunteering, community resources and, inevitably, people exercising their rights as good consumers in shops, markets, and with suppliers of goods and services. Occasionally there is a foray into the geography and history of the British Isles in which students might be encouraged to plan a day out or learn about social changes such as the decline of the mining industry, but this is kept to a minimum.

The response of the ESOL teaching community to the ESOL learning materials was mixed. In some institutions the materials were implemented as part of the statutory curriculum and were used from the start as the syllabus for ESOL courses; this policy tended to lead either to slavish adherence to the materials or to their outright rejection. Confusion reigned over whether these materials should form the syllabus for courses, and whether inspectors would demand they be used to the exclusion of other materials. One teacher explains further:

> When it was inspection earlier this year we were discouraged to use EFL-type books when the inspector was around because they had to be ESOL materials for ESOL students. So I go and use the ESOL books, the Skills for Life stuff and I got inspected in one of the classes, in the community, and it was fine. But one question she did ask was, 'Do we just use Skills for Life material?' and I said, 'No', because we use other books as well. So, I was able to give

examples. I didn't like to say, 'Oh, this is one of the very few lessons I've used this, and that's only because you're here, otherwise I wouldn't have used it.'

More typically though, teachers were given the materials as a new resource which they could use as they deemed fit. Some were pleased that their field was at last being treated seriously and that money was being spent on it after many years of underinvestment. Others praised the fact that the characters peopling the pages of the new materials at least resembled the students in their ESOL classes. There was, however, more criticism than praise amongst teachers for the materials, especially in their scant coverage of grammar and very functional approach to literacy, an issue revisited in Chapter 6. Once again, teachers were spending time supplementing and adapting the very materials that were supposed to be an answer to their problems.

ACTIVITY 3   ESOL materials

Examine a copy of materials based on a national curriculum. Evaluate it in the same way as for EFL coursebooks (Activity 1). How do the materials represent:

• women
• men
• social class
• ethnicity
• native and non-native speakers of English
• cultural norms?

What are the issues arising for ESOL classrooms?

Do teaching materials necessarily work better if they reflect their 'users'?

A problem which is perhaps inherent in all published generic materials is that of relevance to specific contexts and the feeling of the activities becoming 'dead' on the page, no matter how contemporary or high quality they might be. The very fact that the characters peopling the materials were everyday folk going about their everyday business made the ESOL learning materials seem curiously *less* relevant to ESOL students than even some global textbook materials; if students in east London need to learn how to shop in the market for cloth, for example, will they be best served by listening to a tape of people going to a market in Liverpool? Carol, a teacher in London, put it like this:

I thought well why do something that's made up if it's not relevant? I don't have anyone in my class called that. So I would rather use my real students' news in the class for us to be listening to. More and more when I try to use the units I suddenly feel that it's not relevant to my class and I keep coming back to what my students bring to the class. So my first reaction to the new materials was 'hah brilliant' thinking that that was my lesson; it's not my lesson, it makes me switch off.

Despite the best intentions of the writers of the curriculum and its associated materials, teachers return to the dilemmas of relevance and local context. It seems that ESOL teachers are still in a neither/nor position when it comes to their choice between global coursebooks and the curriculum materials. Teachers need to explore other ways to address the curriculum, one of which we turn to now—lesson content generated by students themselves.

Student-generated content

Opening up spaces for students to generate the content of their lessons is one way to avoid the shortcomings of generic curriculum materials and global coursebooks. Classrooms where this happens are characterized by a high degree of student participation and can sometimes bring surprising results. One teacher, James, wished to explore ways of handing the content of lessons over to his students (an example from one of his classes appears below). He noticed that his upper-intermediate students were struggling with idiomatic English and expressed a wish to use idioms more accurately. He encouraged them to spend a week compiling an idiom diary, recording when they heard idioms which intrigued, attracted, or baffled them. They then held a workshop in which they discussed with each other the idioms they had learnt. In this extract, Ursula, an au pair, is explaining to other students what she had observed:

> **J=James, U=Ursula, B=Bettina, N=Nadia**
> U So I went down to check what's going on in my child's room, I mean my host child's room and then it was nothing and I didn't know how to say that I did think that I heard something. So I asked him, 'how do you say it in English?'
> J yeah
> U and I learnt an expression
> B phrase
> U my ears
> B my eyes are playing tricks on me
> U my ears were playing tricks on me
> J yeah. So, my eyes or my ears are playing tricks on me. And it means?
> U that you think that you heard or saw something but you
> B or you
> U but you didn't because it was only
> N oh, OK
> B so you think
> U but you think that you hear or see something but it's not true—there is nothing.

Reflecting on this and other lessons in which he handed over the content to his students, James wrote that there was a noticeable difference in the level of interest and involvement when his students had control of the topic. After one unplanned heated discussion about the problems facing foreigners of opening a bank account, he wrote: 'I had previously put a lot of effort into thinking of tasks which would encourage learners to have these kinds of discussions, which often ended up feeling false and contrived.'

ACTIVITY 4   Learner control of lesson topics

What is your attitude to handing the topic of lessons over to students?

What are the drawbacks of the kind of lesson in which learners themselves generate the content?

There now follows the first of two case studies presented in this chapter, both of which look in some detail at extracts of lessons. The first is an ESOL lesson taught by Catrin, a teacher who routinely draws on students' own lives to generate lesson content. The study shows how adopting this stance can produce longer and more complex utterances when even low-level learners speak 'from within'.

CASE STUDY 1   Catrin

Catrin teaches a beginners' ESOL class in a community centre in a working class neighbourhood in London. The nine students, all women, come from diverse language and ethnic backgrounds, from Poland, China, Congo, Iraq, India, and Somalia. Most of the women are refugees and asylum seekers, and past experiences as well as childcare responsibilities sometimes interfere with their learning. Catrin is a very experienced teacher and has taught English for over 20 years, in a wide variety of settings. Because there is no common *subject* knowledge to draw on in the group the teacher relies on everyday knowledge and experiences. On the other hand the students are able to maximize their communicative resources and the student-generated material achieves high authenticity for the students.

In this activity Catrin is encouraging students to develop spoken narratives using past tenses. To do this she will tell a story about her own childhood and then students will tell their own 'scary story', first in small groups, and then to the whole class. In this way, the topic of the lesson—its content—is handed over to the students.

First Catrin introduces the activity with her own personal example:

> I'm going to give you one word and my word is 'photograph'. Do you understand what a photograph is? Are there any photographs in this room? Yes these are photographs, with a camera. I'm going to tell you a story when I was a child. This is the important word in my story. When I was a small child, when I was three years old my mother was with a friend and they talked and talked and I listened

*and I heard my mother say we want to take a photograph of Catrin and put
it on the wall we want to take a photo and put it on the wall and I was really
terrified because I thought that when you had photographs you killed someone
and took them and put them in the photograph I thought it was really them in the
photograph. Do you understand? My mother wanted to take my photograph. I was
three, I didn't understand photographs. I thought when you had a photograph that
these were people you killed, dead people—that you took the dead people and
you put them in the picture. So I thought my mother and father wanted me dead
and in the picture and I was really terrified. I cried and cried and cried.*

Catrin goes on to introduce the activity for the students. Again she is very
explicit about what she wants the students to do:

*First of all think about a story about when you were a child when you were really
terrified. OK. When you were really scared, really terrified. Then I want you to
write one word, the important word from that story. Just like my important word
was 'photograph'—think of a story and write one word.*

The student Belinda starts to tell her story to her group. From the extract
we can see that Belinda's story is very personal and painful rather than scary.
Nonetheless it seems that she is anxious to pursue it; at one point she says, 'no
wait', and her fellow students allow her to continue telling the story:

B=Belinda, S=other students

B ah yes no wait. After, my mum called the pastor pray for me the pastor
pray God for me is leave the oh my god [laughs]. No sleep the problem
my grandmother she's give me what's the name the the hex? The devil?
You understand devil? In the end somebody sleep she's got [students
laugh] I'm finish, yes the pastor come pray for me every time pray pray for
me if I'm sit here I'm looking the problem past.

S Belinda today good?

B is good my God is give me I'm no sick now is good for me I believe God I
pray God

S no brother no sister?

B no I'm no brother no sister I'm one I'm sad my mum she is going I am
sad

S your mum in London?

B no she died long time in my country

S your father?

B my father he's died

In this class, Catrin relies on everyday knowledge and experiences of the
students to provide the content. In other words she brings the outside in.
This has the advantage of allowing students to maximize their communicative
resources, for instance when they ask each other questions spontaneously.
What is more, the student-generated material achieves high authenticity for the
students, who are very supportive of each other. Although Belinda's story shows

how drawing on funds of knowledge and previous experience can be potentially problematic when people produce stories which raise painful memories, there is a strong sense of a shared experiential world as Catrin too has disclosed quite a personal story.

Taboo subjects

Enabling content to be generated from students themselves brings with it all the virtues of a participatory curriculum: agency and control rests with students as well as teachers, and topics are relevant to students' interests and perceived needs. Some teachers nonetheless have concerns with this approach to content. Although the issues brought up by ESOL students are often everyday and routine, there is sometimes an echo of the dilemma faced by writers and publishers of global coursebooks: the possibility for topics to arise which are somehow dangerous or taboo. The circumstances in individual classes will dictate the extent to which taboo topics are encouraged in ESOL classes, whether they are opened up or closed down. It might be thought best to steer clear of issues that are sensitive or difficult to engage with. Yet what if students clearly want to pursue a theme? Is it really up to the teacher to cut them off? The students, the people actually doing the learning are, after all, independent thinkers with adult sensibilities.

The decision on how to deal with taboo and risk lies ultimately with the teacher, and how they choose to deal with the themes which arise. Some teachers insist on convergence and harmony in their classrooms while others encourage debate and discussion, while making sure that certain boundaries are respected. Here Sarah, a teacher in east London describes her approach to potentially risky subject matter:

> When they're having these heated discussions I do make sure that people don't overstep the mark; to be honest, even though they're very heated and they do have their opinions, I think they're intelligent enough to gauge for themselves when they're about to annoy someone or whether they're about to say something that's a bit too much, and they know that there are certain opinions that are not going to be tolerated in the classroom. You know that you can't say something that's racist or whatever or sexist. They know that if they say something and I don't like it then I'll say you know what, I don't think that that's appropriate or you know I don't agree with that.

This is not to say, though, that even teachers who encourage students to discuss controversial topics do not sometimes find themselves at odds with or embarrassed by students' opinions. In these situations teachers often fall back on their pedagogic role either to divert attention from potentially embarrassing or difficult issues or to diffuse argument. In this extract, taken from a research report by Melanie Cooke and Catherine Wallace (2004), Alice's students are learning some terms and words they need to read a newspaper text on the plight of women worldwide. The topic of bride burning has come up, much to the consternation of a female student, Raquel from Lebanon. Alice focuses on the word 'bride' rather than 'bride burning' and on two occasions postpones the discussion of this issue till later in the lesson. In this way she uses her authority to control the proceedings to avoid confronting a potentially distressing topic:

R=Raquel, T=teacher, S=other students

R   [quietly] could you believe this in India still until now? They still do it until now? I can't believe it.

S   bride. Bride.

T   [indistinct] every year

R   [louder] Still exist uh? This, about India?

T   yes, happens here sometimes. What's the meaning of 'bride'?

S   bride is the

S   to marriage

T   a woman when she gets married, a woman when she but when they say 'brides', for the Indian bride burnings, it doesn't mean the day she gets married, it means maybe the first year after she got married.

R   when they reach the age, maybe.

T   more of that later.

S   when the people die

T   petrol

S   petrol, yes I know

R   fire, oh my God

T   why, why? We're going to do it afterwards.

As this lesson unfolds there are many examples of students bringing the topic back to difficult issues which have been brought up by the text but which the teacher deflects, not always successfully, by appealing to her pedagogic aims for the lesson. The problem of sensitive topics is one which does not seem to have a clear answer, but is one which ESOL teachers need to work with consciously in their heterogeneous classrooms.

The playful side of language learning

A fear amongst teachers is that if content is always learner-initiated, topics will descend to the grim and gloomy, or will be solely associated with the immediate daily life and employment-related needs of students. The second case study in this chapter is a teacher who employs a very different approach from Catrin, one which recognizes the importance of the playful side of language learning, both from a cognitive as well as a social point of view.

CASE STUDY 2   Carl

Carl's beginners' ESOL class takes place in a large community centre in Leeds.
It has a mix of students from very different backgrounds from across the city.
All but one of the students are asylum seekers and refugees and Carl views
the classroom as a sanctuary. Of the classroom he says: 'This is our living
environment, here in the classroom'. And of students: 'They've got to know
they're safe. They've got to know that when they come to class they're going to
have fun. They're going to enjoy what they're doing.'

In this lesson, Carl brings in a mime activity as a way of getting students to
practise using the present continuous form of verbs. This extract of interaction
comes as he introduces the mime activity.

T=teacher, S=student(s)

T I've got lots of little cards OK and they have a sentence written on them so
here's this one says you are standing in a crowded bus you know crowded

S yeah

T what's crowded?

S all people

T lots of people too many people busy very busy you are standing in a crowded
bus

S yeah

T OK so you have to mime this so you could be phew [teacher mimes standing in
a crowded bus]

S tired

S oh what are you doing? [students laugh]

T because people are pushing into me and the bus driver starts

S like when you have a baby you go

T oh if you have a baby on a bus it must be very difficult

The students take turns to act out situations. Some of the situations which
students mime are copied from a teachers' resource book (*you are watching
a funny film; you are eating something you don't like*) and some are invented by
students (*you are bringing a baby to the crèche; you are dreaming in the night*). As
the activity progresses, the teacher models and elicits full, accurate sentences.

[student acts an elaborate mime of buying flowers]

S she want to buy

S she is buy

T she is buying

S she is buying flowers [students laugh]

T yes fantastic flowers she is buying some flowers

S she is buying some flowers

Carl's lessons include many 'fun' whole-class activities such as this one which
have a focus on form or skills development. These are popular with the students

for whom, in the great majority of cases, this ESOL class is their first experience of formal learning in England. The mime game has no immediate bearing on students' everyday lives, and does not seem to be preparing them specifically for the difficulties they encounter outside. Nor does it particularly demand that students draw on their own personal resources, their memories, or opinions. And yet the pace, fun, and predictability of the activity are much appreciated by the students.

The content of language learning does not, indeed should not, always have to relate to the immediate concerns of ESOL students' lives. As Guy Cook (2000) among others notes, the playful function of language has an important role in learning as well as in daily life. A lack of understanding of this vital aspect of learning can make learner-initiated content of ESOL overly needs-driven. The philosophy of language teaching where content is dictated by a perceived end need, even if the need is that perceived by the students themselves, can lead to a situation where only content which has been identified as practically useful to students' lives must be admitted to ESOL classrooms. This excludes a play element in learning which might usefully be encouraged in ESOL lessons and materials. It may also restrict the range of texts that students can read and critically engage with. It is perhaps the teacher's role within a participatory framework to integrate the range of texts, as well as games, song, jokes, poetry, fiction and literature, and purely form-focused activity into ESOL lessons, thus satisfying needs in learners that are other than the routine and everyday.

ACTIVITY 5 Comparing approaches

Compare and contrast the approaches of Catrin and Carl. Which is more similar to your approach? Comment on the way in which the students control the content of Catrin's lesson. What difficulties might she face as control of a topic shifts from her to her students? What might be the drawbacks of a very 'safe' approach such as Carl's?

Conclusion: principled pragmatism in lesson content

ESOL is located at a place where the social, political, and economic effects of globalization play out 'on the ground'. By its nature it is a shifting field: it exists as an area of ELT which must be responsive to the changes in the student population, as well as the constant realignments of policy at global, national, and local levels. Pedagogic materials themselves are only one dimension of lesson content; what matters is how materials are approached and used by students and teachers. In Chapter 3 we suggested that teachers approach their classrooms from a position of 'principled pragmatism', drawing on both their knowledge of language learning theory and their particular knowledge of their own classrooms and students. The same principled pragmatic approach to lesson content is one in which teachers use and adapt a range of materials in ways which suit a particular group of students and their learning needs. Prescribed and generic materials can be supplemented, adapted, or subverted in creative and critical ways. Published materials can be used strategically to focus on linguistic form through activities and games and to provide more structured progress in a safe and predictable classroom. At the same time, teachers might try to develop the skill, confidence, and ability to use the shared experiences of individuals and students as a group to generate lesson content. As well as media texts such as newspapers and material from the internet, brochures, recordings from the radio and television, teachers can encourage their students to bring along texts and language puzzles of their own and try out different approaches using innovative and 'riskier' materials and activities which raise difficult topics to stretch learners in unexpected ways.

Further reading

Critiquing 'survival English'

The ideological aspects of lesson content are explored in Auerbach's work.

Auerbach, E. R. 1995. 'The Politics of the ESL classroom: Issues of power in pedagogical choices' in J. W. Tollefson (ed.). *Power and Inequality in Language Education.* Cambridge: Cambridge University Press.

Auerbach, E. R. and **D. Burgess.** 1985. 'The hidden curriculum of survival ESL.' *TESOL Quarterly* 19/3: 475–95.

Language lesson content

Cook's book is on both the extent and the importance of language play in everyday life and its crucial and neglected role in language learning. Gray's paper presents a clear critique of the 'global coursebook' through an analysis informed by interviews with EFL teachers.

Cook, G. 2000. *Language Play, Language Learning.* Oxford: Oxford University Press.

Gray, J. 2002. 'The global coursebook in ELT' in D. Block and D. Cameron (eds.). *Globalization and Language Teaching.* London: Routledge.

Teaching language and culture

Byram and Morgan's book stresses the importance of the cultural dimension of language learning through a discussion of the theories underlying the teaching of culture and several case studies. Kramsch's work is a brief, readable introduction to the complex relationship between language and culture.

Byram, M. and **C. Morgan.** 1994. *Teaching-and-Learning Language-and-Culture*. Clevedon: Multilingual Matters.

Kramsch, C. 1998. *Language and Culture*. Oxford: Oxford University Press.

5 | ORAL COMMUNICATION

Before, our tongues were heavy and we didn't know what to say. Now they are light and I feel my tongue can fly.
ESOL student, London

Introduction

This chapter looks at oral communication in English and its fundamental importance for migrants to countries where English is the dominant language in the public domain. Most researchers in second language acquisition (SLA) agree that in order to achieve a good level of speaking and understanding in a language, learners must have opportunities to practise and interact in varied settings with expert users of the language they are trying to learn. This has been theorized in different ways: Stephen Krashen (1985), for example, proposed that language learners need to be exposed to 'comprehensible input', which he calls i+1. This input is available to learners from their surroundings, from speakers who can provide language which is just above learners' current level, and which will therefore stretch them to first understand and then to acquire new forms.

Other researchers, for example Merrill Swain (1995, 2005), say input alone is not enough without *output* and conversational interaction. As well as exposure to a new language, learners also need plenty of opportunities to practise that language with other, more advanced speakers. Researchers who study learning in the sociocultural tradition stress the importance of interaction between learners and others who are more knowledgeable than they are: the support and scaffolding received in this type of interaction takes place in the zone of proximal development (Vygotsky 1978), as discussed in Chapter 3. Some researchers (for example, Roberts 2001, Zuengler and Cole 2005) prefer the term second language 'socialization' rather than acquisition, in order to stress the fact that people coming from abroad to settle in countries such as the UK are learning about the social and cultural contexts of language use as well as its linguistic forms; this socialization also usually takes place in interaction with more experienced members of local language communities.

SLA has its share of arguments and disagreements about the nature of language learning; for example, traditional SLA researchers have been criticized for focusing on the cognitive side of language learning and failing to take the social aspects fully into account. However, most theorists are in agreement that without opportunities to practise the language, to actually speak it in varying settings and with an assortment of speakers, acquisition can be a long, slow, and difficult process. It is to this that we turn in this chapter. We look first at speaking and listening outside ESOL classrooms and see to what extent the networks which ESOL students belong to provide opportunities for interaction. Secondly, we consider the barriers to English language use that ESOL students face. For many, the ESOL classroom is one of the few places they use spoken English, so students' needs are great and their expectations are high. The first concern for teachers is how to set up opportunities for practice in the classroom. What do students wish to discuss? What concerns do they bring with them from the world outside the classroom? Which activities produce longer stretches of talk? Teachers must then decide how they can best respond to the talk that is produced by students in the classroom setting. What kind of talk is it? What are they trying to express and how can the teacher help them to express it more effectively? Thirdly, we look at the problems for students when facing tests of their speaking and listening abilities. And perhaps most difficult of all: how far does—and can—the classroom address the challenges of the outside world?

Oral communication outside classrooms

Many members of language minority communities lead fulfilling lives and participate in their local communities in the same way as those who have been born in English-dominant countries. People differ of course in terms of the degrees of integration they feel. At one end of the scale, some suffer extremes of isolation and speak very little to anyone, even in their expert languages; their experience is one of eavesdropping on other people's lives. Others move in large multilingual networks of other migrants, refugees, and minority workers, while some have busy lives in large ethnic minority communities. Most people attending ESOL classes, however, express a certain sense of frustration at their progress and lack of opportunities to practise English with expert speakers of the language.

The advantages of speaking English in English-dominant countries (as well as in a globalized world), and speaking it well, are more than apparent to the majority of migrants. There are multiple reasons why those settling in a new country are motivated to learn English, ranging from the urgency of finding a job to the desire to socialize and integrate in a new community. For many people one of the most pressing motives to invest in learning English is that of employment. Statistics show that migrants, especially from non-white backgrounds, fare much worse in terms of unemployment and low pay than non-migrants (see Vertovec 2006). Lack of English language skills is cited by most job seekers as a major reason for their unemployment or lack of progress, and is therefore their main priority. As shown in Chapter 2, ESOL learners often have a wide range of qualifications, skills, knowledge, and prior experience, but many are employed *below* their professional level and may remain in this position for years.

Another reason for many to invest in learning is the day-to-day difficulty of being a low-level speaker of English. Some ESOL learners experience fear, isolation, and a feeling of disadvantage or incompleteness. Institutions such as government employment offices, welfare offices, and banks loom large in the lives of linguistic minority people and some of the stories told by students about their interactions in English are of miscommunication, hostility, and sometimes racism. A common feeling reported by some students is discomfort at their dependence on interpreters, friends, or even their own children to help with bureaucratic and medical encounters; many talk of their language learning achievements in terms of breaking this dependency.

The experiences of ESOL students in their day-to-day interactions have a serious effect on the development of their understanding of English and their listening skills. Outside class, it is often assumed that people will acquire language through listening, simply by dint of living in English-dominant countries. However, ESOL students do not necessarily have much day-to-day interaction with English-speaking people, and even when they do, the power imbalances inherent in many of their everyday lives have implications for the development of their understanding. In their book *Achieving Understanding* (1996), Bremer and Roberts and their colleagues show that for many minority language speakers their main interactions in the target language (in this case in English, French, German, Dutch, and Swedish) are in encounters with service providers or bureaucrats. These encounters are by their nature unequal and do not provide environments conducive to developing either spoken skills or listening skills. In a paper which approaches listening from a sociolinguistic perspective, Karen Carrier (1999) discusses a number of factors which hinder listening ability for people who perceive themselves to be of a lower social status than those who they are speaking to. She points out that in asymmetrical encounters with an imbalance of status between participants, low-status listeners are less likely to engage in negotiation of meaning (for example, by asking for repetition or clarification) and are thus less likely to understand what is being said or to acquire spoken language. ESOL students are at a disadvantage in listening encounters outside classrooms, encounters which are habitually asymmetrical.

ACTIVITY 1 Reflecting on day-to-day interaction

Think of all the times in the course of a day in which you need to speak. How does the context affect what you say and how you say it? How is your way of speaking affected when you are talking to someone with a higher social status than you, or someone who intimidates you for whatever reason? How does this affect the way you speak to them? How important are these questions in the ESOL classroom?

Students have aspirations regarding their English which are not only connected to work and survival, but are also social in nature. For example, people need to understand English to connect with outside events through the media or to understand what people are saying to them: as one Chinese student in Leeds explains, 'My wife and I used to joke with each other, saying that we might have said thanks in reply to someone else's curses.' Others expressed a strong desire to socialize with English speakers such as neighbours or others in the local community; here, a woman from Ecuador speaks of her wish to be as sociable in English as she is in Spanish:

> *I am very communicative in Spanish. For example if a woman comes along and we have to wait I'm 'Hello how are you, how's it going, what's your name?' and all that, and in English I would like to do the same. I like making conversation but I limit myself because I don't know English.*

Of course, learning a new language and culture can challenge established identity on a profound level. This is described movingly by Eva Hoffman in her book *Lost in Translation: A Life in a New Language* (1989), and echoed by many ESOL students. A Russian man from Leeds describes the anxiety of never being able to be 'fully himself' in a language other than his own:

> *If we were sitting on the bench like now and wished to talk about life, I don't think we would be able to do it in English. We would wish to talk about nature, flowers, art, pictures, images, impressions. I am sure we would not manage to talk about them. But it is a very important part of my life, and all that is in Russian. How can I translate it into a different language? What about my feelings and the like?*

ACTIVITY 2   Student interaction outside class

Think of the students in a class you are teaching or have taught recently. What do you know about their interactions outside of class? Who do they interact with? In which languages? What do they feel they cannot talk about in English? Is it important to know this information? How might it affect the way you plan your courses?

Research on people in ESOL classrooms shows that they are highly motivated to learn English. However, some have been in the UK for many years without reaching a level of English language and literacy they find acceptable, not because of unwillingness to learn or reluctance to integrate, but because of structural and institutional factors such as employment patterns, housing, and the legislation governing the rights of asylum seekers. Almost all the students populating the studies we have drawn on for this book talked of lack of access to English and to English-speaking communities. There are many possible reasons for this, some of which we explore below.

Some migrants to the UK in the 1970s found work in industries and services in local economies. Often this meant working with people with the same first or expert language, or in so-called ethnic work units, sometimes for many years. This is still a typical pattern of work for people arriving today: 'I worked in a take-away which is owned by our people. There I could not speak English, which I think was a great disadvantage to me because I could not learn any English there' (Pakistani man, Leeds). Others find work in jobs where interaction is required with no one at all. This is particularly common in jobs such as cleaning and hotels: 'In housekeeping it's quite boring: you come to work, take your mops, and go up to clean without seeing almost anyone' (Lithuanian hotel worker, London). Unemployment is also a source of isolation. This is exacerbated by laws which prohibit asylum seekers from employment, as Haxhi's story in Chapter 2 illustrates.

Feminist writers in the US, Canada, and Australia have researched and written about the differences for men and women in terms of access to English classes and opportunities to practise English. The picture is of course far from straightforward. For some women, moving from one place to another can mean changes in the family structure which result in changes in gender relations and access to work and education. Where previously local economies may have disallowed female employment, some women find themselves in their new countries as the family's sole breadwinner, and with considerably more freedom than they would have had in their countries of origin. On the other hand, for many women a major reason for a delay in progress in acquisition of English is that of child raising, made worse by a chronic lack of crèche facilities in many colleges and community venues. People, usually women, who are responsible for looking after children sometimes learn in fits and starts and at a much slower rate than they otherwise might: 'I must look after my daughter and sometimes I must work. The timetable of these classes sometimes is suitable for me and sometimes is not, therefore I learn in a piecemeal way' (Chinese woman, Leeds). Kathleen Rockhill (1987), writing about Latina women in the USA, describes how for some women gaining access to literacy and language classes amounts to an act of resistance against the particular patriarchal constraints under which they live. The acquisition of literacy is also a matter which affects women differently to men, and one which we return to in Chapter 6. Many classes dedicated to ESOL literacy are dominated almost entirely by women; one of the reasons for lack of literacy is the fact that some did not get access to education in their countries of origin when they were of school age.

Some migrants live in communities or work in settings where their own expert language or even a different language altogether is more necessary than English (see Goldstein 1996).

As we described in Chapter 1, people living in these communities often come under attack from the media because of their supposed reluctance to learn English and therefore to integrate. Again, the story is far from straightforward. There are many reasons why people (including those in homogeneous white areas) live in communities where their ethnic group is dominant. Migrants have traditionally tended to live in communities with others from the same ethnic background, partly for mutual support in the face of hostility from the majority ethnic population, and partly because of reasons of affordability. However, where people live is far from a matter of individual choice, and there is a long history of discrimination in the policies and practices of public and private housing agencies. In some cities there are both settled minority ethnic communities and areas marked by a high degree of super-diversity. Some migrants live in communities together with locally-born people, and wish to mix with them, but are unsure exactly how to socialize: 'I don't avoid it or do it on purpose; it is just that there are no ways to mingle with people, you have to know them, most people in this country are normally conservative' (Somali woman, London).

Added to all of this, of course, are those individual factors more commonly discussed in the SLA literature, such as age, personality, motivation, attitude, and aptitude (see Skehan 1989). One ESOL student from Spain describes her shyness as the main obstacle to her learning:

> *I remember someone saying to me 'you, what you have to do is go to the street and ask questions [laughing], anything, where is this street, where is the other' and I say that I can't even do that in Spanish. I understand that it is my own problem as well, and the way I am, but if I can't do something in Spanish it's even more difficult in English.*

Factors such as shyness can affect all learners of other languages; this might, of course, be exacerbated if an already shy speaker is attempting to interact in a situation in which they also have to confront hostility, impatience, and prejudice, as is the case for so many ESOL students. Many of the traditional notions about what constitutes a good language learner may apply to all learners to a certain degree but they are most certainly complicated and compounded by the social inequalities and stresses we have described in this chapter so far.

Speaking in ESOL classrooms

As well as promoting social inclusion, particularly amongst vulnerable groups such as refugees and low-paid migrant workers, access to the majority language of a country is a right. ESOL students often express regret that it is not easier to communicate even in everyday run-of-the-mill situations, for instance, when they want to chat to their neighbours:

> *Our other neighbours are a younger husband and wife. I would really like to go and talk to them to get to know them. If they ever have time then it would be nice to just sit with them for half an hour and have a chat*
> Iranian woman, London.

What is more, people meet huge difficulties in trying to communicate meaningfully at times when there is an unequal balance of power between speakers. This rarity of routine daily communication means that the classroom is often the only place where people have an opportunity not only to learn English, but to use it regularly. Yet, however important the classroom is, it is limited in the extent to which it can be effective in addressing the challenges and inequalities of what happens in the outside world. In Chapter 4 we discussed materials and activities in ESOL lessons, including how learners themselves can be a learning resource, and how they can generate their own topics and texts. Here we take a closer look at talk in ESOL classrooms and at how skilled teachers manage classroom discourse to encourage meaningful spoken interaction, which in turn creates opportunities for learning.

Opening up and closing down

Many teachers are responsive to their students' talk and have a genuine interest in what they are saying; after all many ESOL students lead interesting lives. But when students take control of classroom discourse, a lesson can move away from its planned route. This might seem to be a problem if a teacher wishes to get through her lesson plan, or if the lesson is being observed, or students have to prepare for an exam. However, when carried out in a systematic and principled way, the opening up of classroom discourse can lead to opportunities for learning that would never exist if the teacher was overly attached to a predetermined plan. For example, in this extract from a lesson in London, Melinda, a shy student, has just finished speaking to her teacher, Carol, about her homework. Carol says:

> *Well done Melinda, very brave, but just remember when you feel a bit worried slow down don't panic, there's no bus no tram, we've finished the rush.*

The mention of the tram prompts Melinda (M) to tell the class about a recent incident which surprises Carol (C):

Ss [laughter]
M yesterday I left my children in the tram they didn't
C tram
M the tram closed the door I leave my children inside
C [intake of breath]

At that point, Carol could have diverted the lesson back to its course, perhaps by asking the next student to talk about her homework. Instead she makes the choice to open up the classroom talk to allow contributions from other students. The extract continues:

D=Dalia, M=Melinda, C=Carol, the teacher
D yesterday I saw you get down
C what, Dalia was getting off?
D yeah getting off out
M I am inside, my children both out
C so you were left on the tram and your children
M out
C were on the pavement?

The episode goes on for some time in this vein, with Melinda telling her story of being left on the tram without her children, a story helped along by supportive and collaborative interjections from both Carol and Melinda's fellow students. Both teacher and students seem to be interested in what happened next. Carol also wants to encourage Melinda to speak, because previously in lessons she has been quite reticent.

We can describe this behaviour by teachers and learners using the terms 'agency' and 'contingency'. Agency refers to how an individual takes control

over some aspect of his or her life; in this case it refers to how students claim a space to talk in the ongoing classroom discourse. Contingency refers to a way of responding to events as they arise, in this case how the teacher allows students to claim the discursive space. In a paper on this topic, Mike Baynham writes of learner agency and teacher contingency in ESOL classrooms, how they are connected, and how they allow for relevant and meaningful talk:

> *We see … how agency and contingency are interrelated: realized both in the ways that students make their place and take their place in the classroom and the ways that teachers are challenged contingently and responsively to open up spaces where this becomes possible, responding interactively to demands for space. Momentarily the students are engaged in finding solutions to a real problem, not a manufactured hypothetical example: the outside has been brought in.*
> Baynham 2006: 31

Contingency on the part of teachers is a valuable reaction to attempts by students to take control of their classroom talk, and hence, their learning. It is a way of relating classroom content to students' lives while retaining the freshness and responsiveness of on-the-spot planning.

We can contrast the talk in Melinda's class with an example from a class of teenage migrants. Rather than opening up the classroom talk, the teacher, Marie, closes it down by not allowing opportunities for talk to develop. This is in part because Marie does not show a lot of interest in her students' lives outside her classroom and in part because she wishes to stick to her lesson plan. Here is an extract from field notes from a lesson observation in Marie's class.

> *Marie is using a reading text about a refugee and his journey from Afghanistan to England. The text is thoroughly exploited for comprehension, new words, and reading aloud. It is then used as a gap fill exercise. Marie does not invite the learners to reflect on what the text is about, or on the fact that they have had similar experiences. The attempts by the learners to discuss this theme further (some of them have seen a film on asylum on TV the night before and are keen to talk about it) are not encouraged by their teacher, who wants to get back to her lesson plan.*

Catherine Wallace has written about this class in more depth in her paper 'The text dead or alive: Expanding textual repertoires in the adult ESOL classroom' (2006). Wallace points out that the classroom treatment of this text closes down wider interpretive possibilities, in the same way as the tight curriculum planning and controlled approach to the students closes down opportunities for their input and contribution to their lessons. Real talk *can* take place in ESOL classrooms, and students *do* have things to say, and teachers often have a choice: they can either open up talk or close it down. If the teacher is prepared to respond contingently and let students take control, the talk that emerges can be both productive and beneficial for its immediacy and relevance.

ACTIVITY 3   Opening up interactional spaces

Reflect on your own teaching, and on the teaching of your colleagues. Think about occasions when you have opened up wider interpretive possibilities and interactional spaces for your students. What happened? Think also about occasions when you have closed them down, and why.

Encouraging learners to talk

In SLA terms it is not enough to provide *input* for language learning to take place; producing language *output* is also essential. This is one of the benefits of encouraging students to take control of classroom discourse as it gives them an opportunity to generate language themselves. A consequence of a teacher promoting learner agency is that room is made in the classroom discourse for students to speak. This is termed 'interactional space' by analysts of classroom discourse. By claiming interactional space, students are allowed the thinking time to rehearse what they plan to say, as well as the time to actually say it. This results in more extended learner turns in talk. Learners will also have control of the topic and of turn taking. Learner talk is particularly beneficial if students are talking about what they *want* to talk about, and if students are making most contributions to classroom talk, the teacher's turns will be short or minimal. They will be particularly useful when they are focused on prompting students to elaborate upon or continue a turn, to say what they mean as clearly as possible.

So rather than promoting talk for talk's sake, some particular types of oral classroom interaction can be seen as beneficial to learning. How can such talk be encouraged in the classroom? What are the circumstances under which it emerges? Here we look at an example of how one teacher, Patrick, worked with his class to promote high quality oral work. This is taken from an action research project, Turning Talk into Learning (published as Cooke and Roberts 2007a, 2007b), which we discuss further in Chapter 8.

Patrick is teaching an intermediate level class called 'Speak Clearly', for students who want or need extra lessons to develop their oral English. He has tried to find activities which will encourage them to produce longer turns, such as talking for one minute about a pre-set topic. He notices that for some reason these activities are not really working:

> *My students were often in a position when they needed to explain something that had happened, in other words tell a narrative, but were having some difficulty in getting the events in order and giving answers which were not vague and/or lacking in substance. Topics rich in potential, such as 'the worst job you ever had', were only being touched upon while other students seemed to be more interested in getting to the end of the time limit for the next turn to arrive. It was clear that the objectives for which the task was designed were not being met.*

Patrick decided to take a step back and do some work with his students on the typical structure of narratives. One of the first researchers to look closely at this matter was the sociolinguist William Labov (1972), who analysed what he called standard western narrative. Using the internet and other resources, Patrick found it relatively easy to read about what Labov and others had to say about narrative structure. As Patrick writes in the project report:

> *Labov argues that narratives have distinct stages which can be simplified to setting the scene, main events and evaluation. Setting the scene deals with where and when it took place and the background relevant to the story. In the main events the speaker develops what happened. In the final stage the speaker gives an opinion, or evaluation on the narrative and how it affected her/him and the present situation.*

Patrick then devised a series of lessons in which he taught his students about the structure of western narrative. He asked them to listen to a person recounting a narrative and analyse it, noticing the features of narrative they had previously discussed. They were given time to prepare their own narratives and to recount them several times in pairs and to the whole group.

This was repeated over several lessons, during which Patrick encouraged his class to produce narratives suitable for different settings, such as answering a question in a job interview along the lines of 'How did you cope with a difficult situation at work?'. The transcripts from those lessons show that the students do indeed begin to produce longer, more involved narratives with an identifiable structure. Here is an example from Patrick's students. Charmaine (C) is telling Aynur (A) about a difficult time in her life and how she overcame it. Charmaine's turn is a much longer utterance than usual for her and the three turns together constitute a well-structured narrative:

C   I want to speak with you about the first time I drove a car at Peckham Park in the summertime. I was with my husband and my husband was teaching me how to drive and it was so hard for me I was sweating. I was scared and depressed. I couldn't change the gear, I couldn't use the clutch, I couldn't go on the hill. I was scared I couldn't, I can't use the speed, the speed I can't. It was so hard for me and thank god I didn't crash my car. I didn't crash anybody car from that time and now I drive safely. I know how to drive I'm happy when I'm driving.

A   So did you get driving licence?

C   Ah I get. I took my driving licence everything and I am happy now because I'm driving safely. I can go wherever I want without depress, without scaring again like before so I'm so very glad [laughs].

One of the interesting things about working like this with students is the fact that basic structures such as narrative occur again and again in many situations, not just in storytelling or recounting anecdotes. This is one way of beginning to help students make the bridge from the language of the classroom to the challenges of out-of-classroom daily life.

Tackling real-world challenges in the ESOL classroom

The interactional challenges faced by ESOL students in the outside world range from everyday activities such as shopping to encounters with medical professionals, interactions with officials in settings such as banks, benefit offices, and employment bureaux, and interviews for employment. One of the traditional ways in which English language pedagogy has attempted to prepare people for real-life interaction has been through the use of dialogues such as this scene from a doctor's surgery:

   R=receptionist, F=Filiz
R   Hello. Ashlea Surgery.
F   Hello, can I make an appointment for my daughter to see Dr Green please?
R   Yes. What's the name?
F   Gulay Akpinar.

R Can you spell her first name please?
F Yes. It's G-U-L-A-Y. Gulay Akpinar.
R OK. Dr Green's next appointment is on Thursday morning.
F Thursday. OK.
R Right. Is 9.30 OK?
F Yes, that's fine. Thank you very much.

(From *Skills for Life ESOL Learning Materials* Entry 1, DfES 2003)

In class, students might go on to use the dialogue as a model, modify it with their own details, rehearse it, and perhaps learn it by heart to perform in front of the class. However, teachers often have a feeling that these dialogues do not exactly 'work' as learning activities and somehow fail to hit the mark in terms of what really goes on in encounters outside the classroom. Students themselves sometimes echo the same frustration: in this particular lesson they lamented that in their own doctor's surgery they would be unlikely to get an appointment so easily at a time to suit them or with the doctor of their choice.

ACTIVITY 4 The 'Skills for Life' job interview

Read the following transcripts of job interviews. The first is from the *Skills for Life ESOL learning materials*. The second is adapted from a real interview from *Talk on Trial* (Roberts and Campbell 2006). How does the first extract compare to the real interaction shown in the second? How do they both compare to job interviews you have had? If you wished to prepare your students for a real-life job interview, how would you decide what to teach them?

Extract I
I=interviewer, M=May
I Good morning, Mrs Lee. Did you have problems finding us?
M No, no problem at all.
I Good. Well then, please take a seat.
M Thank you.
I So, you want to work for ACE Stores? Have you worked in a supermarket before, Mrs Lee?
M No, but I worked in a shop. I was a stockroom assistant.
I So why are you applying for this job?
M Well, I enjoy my present job but it's a long way from home. It takes me an hour to get to work. This job looks interesting and it's near home.
I I see. Most staff here work early and late shifts. Can you do that?
M Sorry, I don't understand. Could you explain?
I Yes of course. It means that some staff work from 8 in the morning until 3 in the afternoon. That's the early shift. Others work from 3 until 10 at night. That's the late shift. So one week you work the early shift, the next week you work the late shift.

M I see. That's fine.
I   Is there anything you would like to ask me?
M Yes. Do staff have to wear a uniform?
I   There's a company T-shirt.
M And what about the pay? Do you pay weekly or monthly?
I   Weekly.
M That's fine.
I   Do you have any more questions?
M No, I think that's all.
I   Well, thank you for coming. We'll let you know in a couple of days.

(From *Skills for Life ESOL Learning Materials* Entry 2 Unit 8, DfES 2003)

Extract 2
C=candidate, I=interviewer
I   okay that's all right erm. What about in oth- other jobs er- were there changes, either because the nature of the job changed while you were there or you moved into something that was very different from what you've previously had experience of because your work in the opticians must have been a little bit different?
C mm well what p-between the two companies or
I   yeah
C or as in
I   eh-I mean that's quite an unusual you know actually making the spectacles
C mhm
I   ehm and the time pressure that- that you're under to achieve that
C mhm
I   that must have been quite different from just about anything else you've ever worked in?
C erm well it is I think the -m-majority of the jobs that I have worked in I have been erm customer focused and deadlines and under pressure, erm catering I've — you know my family own a business and I've worked in that since the age of nine, you know helping them out erm but that that's I suppose that's a different field altogether from
I   yeah
C customer focus but I've sort of gone off on a tangent now
I   no it's I mean the range of experience just shows you
C mmm
I   in many ways that you're used to
C yeah I'm quite
I   having new things thrown at you.

(Adapted from *Talk on Trial*, Roberts and Campbell 2006: 103)

Research in fields which deal with spoken language, such as conversation analysis and interactional sociolinguistics, shows that language in interaction is usually very different from that given as models to students. There is a wide gap between real spoken interaction on the one hand, with its pauses, hesitations, false starts, repair, and unequal power relations, and orderly classroom dialogues on the other, in which interactive tasks are accomplished with the minimum of misunderstanding and with the maximum co-operation between participants. An additional concern for teachers is the challenge of how they can know what the interactions that take place in institutional encounters such as job interviews are actually like. The classroom dialogues presented by teachers to students as preparation for employment interviews are likely to be based on either the teacher's own experience, which may be from a different sector or era, or from what the teacher or textbook writers *imagine* to be the procedures of modern day job interviews. The reality in the outside world, however, is often very far from the imagined interaction of classroom dialogues.

For the report *Talk on Trial* (2006) Celia Roberts and Sarah Campbell analysed over 60 videos of real interviews for jobs in factories, supermarkets, and delivery firms. They found that candidates born overseas who spoke a language other than English fared less well in the interviews than those who were British born, even though their skills more than met the requirements of the job itself. These candidates had greater difficulty in presenting themselves in expected ways and there were more interactional problems between interviewers and candidates. Roberts and Campbell call this a 'linguistic penalty', which they describe thus:

> *The linguistic penalty arises ... from the largely hidden demands on candidates to talk in institutionally credible ways and from a mismatch of implicit cultural expectations, evidenced by mutual misunderstandings, protracted attempts to resolve them and negative judgements by interviewers.*
> 2006: 1

The writers go on to describe the hidden meaning behind questions such as 'what attracted you to this job?' (i.e. what is it about *this company* which makes you want to work here?), the implicit expectations interviewers hold with regard to candidates' answers, and certain features of modern day interviews such as the 'competencies framework' and the taking of extensive notes during the interview itself. These practices are unlikely to be dealt with in an ESOL classroom, not least because the teacher is unlikely to have the detailed knowledge required to navigate interactional situations of this type.

The question remains, then, how can ESOL teachers best prepare their students for the challenges they face in the outside world, especially in high stakes encounters such as job interviews? One approach is to raise awareness with both interviewers and candidates of the practices of modern interviews and of the misunderstandings that can arise when interviewer and candidate do not share the same culture and/or language. This might be done through materials, such as DVDs or transcripts of authentic interaction, which raise awareness of real-life language issues. This approach is of course dependant on more data being made available from different interactive settings, which inevitably has implications for resources and funding, and therefore depends on the political will to pay for such research.

Testing oral communication in ESOL

ESOL students need to take English language tests for a variety of purposes, some of which—in testing terms—are very high stakes indeed. As well as the 'linguistic penalty' they face in job interviews described in the previous section, migrants who seek employment are sometimes obliged by employers to demonstrate their English competence formally through language qualifications. Also, as we discussed in Chapter 1, success in an English test is in some countries used to satisfy the language requirement for citizenship. Adult migrants with little or no English and enrolling on an ESOL course are likely to undergo a series of externally accredited language assessments from the very first level, and later progression and further funding can depend on success in such tests. At the same time, some ESOL students have low levels of educational attainment and little experience of school. It follows that they also have little previous experience of formal testing situations of the type which they may have to undergo in their current learning environments in the English-dominant West. This section concentrates on the experiences of speaking tests for students like these, and on some implications for testing speaking in ESOL. It draws on work by James Simpson (2006).

Because they have not experienced language testing before, many beginner and low-level ESOL students have a limited understanding of what they are supposed to do in a speaking test, which is generally to produce a large and extensive enough sample of language by which they can be assessed. This is partly due to the wider difficulty of being clear about what it is a speaking test is designed to test. Interviews with students themselves reveal a misunderstanding of the purpose of a test. A student in a beginners' ESOL class mentions the speaking test she has recently undergone:

> *When I did the interview with Mr John and Mr James they asked, 'Do you like English?' I said 'Yes'. They asked 'Why?' A strange question. You need it when you go out.*
> Yemeni woman, Leeds

The student uses the word 'interview' in preference to 'test', and reports that she takes the intention of the question 'Why?' at face value ('A strange question'). She is perhaps unused to being asked questions by near-strangers which have no purpose beyond eliciting language for assessment. She may also be completely unfamiliar with speaking assessments, her closest experience being an interview of one kind or another.

A fundamental question for language testers involves identifying exactly what a particular test is testing: as testers say, what is the *construct*? As it relates to speaking tests for low-level learners this question can be reformed in two ways: (1) if an assessment is testing conversation, how conversation-like is it? And (2) if it is not testing conversation, then what *is* it testing? It is often assumed that in a formal assessment of speaking, the construct being tested is conversation, viewed by many as the basic form of oral interaction. Yet an examination of conversation, and a comparison with speaking test discourse, suggests that they are quite different in nature. Spoken casual conversation is defined by the linguists Eggins and Slade (1997: 19) as talk which, in contrast to other events such as interviews and service encounters (in shops and so on), is not motivated by any clear pragmatic purpose, that is, there is no need to get something done. Within this definition, Eggins and Slade suggest certain differences between casual conversation and pragmatically oriented interaction, that is, interaction with a broader purpose: in terms of number of participants (often there are more than two people in a conversation); whether or not a pragmatic goal is achieved (this is not the aim of casual conversation); length (pragmatic interactions tend to be short); and level of politeness and formality (casual conversation often displays informality and humour).

By these criteria at least, formal speaking tests are clearly not conversations. But how conversation-like are they? This is a question which has exercised testers of spoken language since the publication of Leo van Lier's paper 'Reeling, writhing, drawling, stretching, and fainting in coils: Oral proficiency interviews as conversation' (1989), in which he questioned the extent to which an oral proficiency interview (OPI) was actually an example of conversational language use. Van Lier's analysis of language test data demonstrated that it was not conversation-like; instead it exhibited many of the features of formal interviews, for example asymmetry and interviewer control.

In response to concerns over the asymmetrical nature of participation in speaking tests, testing organizations have developed other test formats which attempt to elicit a range of responses beyond the question-and-answer format of older tests. These include, for example, the paired format test developed by Cambridge ESOL. Even so, in their review of research methods in language testing, Lumley and Brown summarize the general findings of discourse analysis approaches to the question of speaking assessment (2005: 842):

> *A general consensus has emerged … that although oral interaction shares some features with non-test conversation, it is essentially a distinct and institutional form of interaction, and that because of its non-symmetrical*

nature, it is limited in the extent to which it can provide an indication of non-test conversational performance.

But if the speaking assessment is not testing conversational performance, then what is it testing? In their asymmetry, power discrepancy, and inbuilt intention, many if not most formal speaking assessments correspond to a definition of 'interview', and can be viewed as interview-like events. Testing the ability to interact in an interview situation is not an unrealistic or irrelevant aim: in the course of their day-to-day lives, ESOL students face institutional interactions where similar power relations exist, and being able to interact appropriately in such interactions is a vital skill. Perhaps speaking assessments for low-level learners can, and indeed should, be thought of as interviews rather than conversations. This view is supported by Moder and Halleck, who state that the use of questions in speaking tests: 'clearly reflects one of the elements of the interview frame: it is the role of the interviewer to ask questions and the role of the interviewee to answer them adequately and appropriately' (1998: 121). Furthermore, in terms of procedure the speaking test may be more interview-like than conversation-like: one participant in the test knows what is going to happen in advance—what questions will be asked, and so on—the other does not. This corresponds with other types of interviews students may have experienced, for example with a prospective employer, a housing officer, or an immigration official. And like those interviews, speaking tests are increasingly important, or as testers put it, *high stakes* for ESOL students.

Here is an example of the way in which a speaking test is not conversational. It also raises questions about the ability of a speaking test to allow students to produce as wide and extensive a range of language as they are capable of. In most speaking tests, the tester asking the questions, who is known as the interlocutor, uses a script called an interlocutor frame to maintain reliability in the test. That is, the more all takers of a particular test are asked the same type of questions, in the same type of language, the more the reliability from test to test is assured. In this case the interlocutor behaves according to the requirements of the speaking assessment by deviating only minimally from his script, while the test-taker with limited experience of the assessment experience is addressing the questions she is being asked as if they are part of a conversational exchange. The student is Hanan, a Somali woman in her forties, who spent only two years at school when she was young. There is an instance here where the interlocutor stays with the script, generating turns which would be very out-of-place in a conversation. In these examples, the turns of the speakers are numbered, and pauses and other conventions are marked:

(.)   a short pause of less than one second
(3)   a longer pause (with length in seconds)
(xxx)   inaudible talk

H=Hanan, I=interlocutor
1 I   and what do you study?
2 H   learn English
3 I   yeah (.) and do you like it?
4 H   yes I like
5 I   Why?
6 H   because when I come here I don't understand English because difficult (xxx) appointment with your children or and you can't speak English and it's important you [should]
7 I   [hmm]
8 H   for me and I would when I my language perfect I want work
9 I   OK
10 H Yes
11 I   thank you (.) Hanan how long have you been here in London?

In turn 9 the interlocutor does not ask a question along the lines of 'what sort of work?' but instead cuts the topic short with 'OK'; in turn 11 the pause after 'thank you' signals a very abrupt end to that topic. The repetition of the student's name in turn 11 also indicates adherence to a script, and is thus very much more test-like than would be found in a conversation. Hanan on the other hand, responds to the interlocutor's elicitation (turns 5 and 6) with an elaboration which might be seen in either a test, a conversation, or another type of interview; she could be taking part in any event which in her view would require a full response to a question addressed to her. Because the interlocutor is constrained by the use of a script, Hanan is not allowed to expand her responses to the extent that she is potentially able.

In other cases candidates say very little in the test itself, but when it is over they become voluble and expansive, presenting the assessors with a long turn. This is the case with the examples below. They are from a speaking test undergone by Tam, a woman in her forties from Vietnam, who went to school for just one year as a child. It is possible that Tam brings to the test the background knowledge of a formal speaking experience where she is not expected to respond at length. So rather than producing a substantial sample of language which can form the basis of assessment, it is only when the test has finished that she feels able to engage in more conversation-like behaviour.

T=Tam, I=interlocutor (during the test)
1 I   Tam where do you come from?
2 T   um (2) Vietnam
3 I   And which town are you from in Vietnam (2) which city?
4 T   (.) (xxx)
5 I   Are are you from Saigon?
6 T   (xxx)
7 I   Ok thank you (.) Do you work in Leeds? (3) Do you have a job?

8 T   No.
9 I   Are you a student?
10 T   Yes (xxx)
11 I   What do you study? (4) What subject (1) Do you study English?
12 T   Yes I…
13 I   Do you like it?
14 T   Yes.
15 I   Why?
16 T   (2) I need er I need (.) I need company I (xxx)

Tam says very little in the test itself. In some cases, turns 7 and 11, the interlocutor even has to use back-up cues (part of the interlocutor script) to elicit a response from Tam. This reticence on her part is in sharp contrast to the episode immediately following the test:

T=Tam, I=interlocutor, A=assessor (after the test)
1 A   Thank you very much indeed
2 I   Relax now
3 T   Because I have problem stomach yes yeah illness long years ago begin I am in Vietnam. I'm er come to UK twenty second May 1999. I can see doctor, tablets now and when and when mmm usually I am very tired yeah er I need tablets. Yeah I am sleeps er less sleep late yeah sleeps very late one or two in the morning yeah very tired before I am um learning English because student in the last. Yeah I am teacher change class in there yeah um before my learning English Tuesday and Thursday er ten in the morning come here finish and afternoon three o'clock begin yeah I go back full time very tired
4 A   Yeah.
5 T   Yeah really yeah
6 A   And you're tired now?
7 T   Tired yeah before I am problem, go to hospital yeah er check in inside. Yeah problem with stomach, is about er two year er three year. Yeah about 2000 and 2001 go to hospital check in stomachs, yeah take tablets I can see doctor take tablets eat now.
8 A   Which make you tired?
9 T   Yeah.

It is clear that Tam is quite able to embark on a long turn, trying to get across a complex message, but did not do so in the test itself. The background knowledge which she brings to the interaction leads her to produce minimal responses until the formal aspect of the test is complete (signalled in the second extract, turns 1 and 2). At that point, outside the bounds of the test, and when all participants are engaged in an informal chat, she is able to produce the long turns (turns 3 and 7).

ACTIVITY 5   Assessing speaking

Before you read the section below, think about how you might answer this
question: Why do students like Tam fail to perform in a test to the extent of
their ability?

There are a number of possible answers to this question, some of which are
listed here. The first two are suggested by Steven Ross in his paper 'Divergent
frame interpretations in language proficiency interview interaction' (1998).

- Learners might not possess the pragmatic competence to tackle or answer
  the question. That is, they do not possess the knowledge and ability to use
  communicative language (in this case, test-taking language) appropriately
  in its sociocultural context (in this case, a speaking test).
- The phenomenon of saying little in a test is called by Ross 'under-
  elaboration'. Under-elaborate answers might 'mark the boundaries of
  what are considered by the candidate as private matters' (Ross 1998: 345).
- A student's idea of how to perform in a speaking test may not match that
  of the test designers' expectation. Nonetheless they possess a notion of
  correctness. Even if they have little experience of formal schooling, they
  come to the test with some knowledge, possibly based on knowledge of
  the overall dominant educational culture in their home countries or of
  their prior learning experience in their new countries, that encourages
  them to focus on getting the answer right rather than demonstrating their
  range of ability at the risk of making mistakes. This, coupled with lack of
  experience of the formal testing situation, may prompt 'new' test takers to
  feel that it is better to say little in the test itself than to produce incorrect
  utterances.
- Speaking test candidates in general are undoubtedly under an amount of
  what Brown and Yule, in their book *Teaching the Spoken Language* (1983),
  term 'communicative stress', where they are in the presence of unfamiliar
  listeners, where it is not entirely clear what they are expected to produce in
  terms of length and complexity of utterance. Like actors with stage fright,
  an effect of communicative stress is for people to 'dry up'.
- During a test, there is a clear inequality between the less powerful test taker
  and the more powerful tester. When a test ends, there is a corresponding
  shift in power relations. When students no longer feel that they are the
  subordinate partner in an unequal interaction, they are able to expand
  their responses, just as Tam does in the example above.
- Different cultures have different expectations of conversational style.
  The insight from Dell Hymes' work on the ethnography of speaking
  (1974) is that descriptors in a speaking test may well describe aspects of
  conversational style valued by a particular speech community and not by
  others. That is, the descriptions of language in a speaking test taken by
  ESOL students might well correspond with what is deemed desirable by

test designers in western, English-dominant countries. There is a norm in such tests based on a 'western' model of communication to which all learners are obliged to aspire.

What emerges from this complex range of possibilities is that conclusions drawn from any hesitations and minimal responses on the part of the candidates in a speaking test risk conflating lack of ability with a number of other potential accounts.

The obvious implication for testing oral communication in ESOL is that test takers should be made thoroughly aware of the test format and properly trained before embarking on the test. Given the high stakes nature of tests which are designed to satisfy a language requirement for naturalization or employment, as well as the widespread introduction of national tests for ESOL students, test-taking training is becoming an integral part of ESOL lessons even at the very lowest levels. This will perhaps combat, if not solve, the problem of inexperienced test takers having to be taught how to undergo complex assessments of which they have little previous experience. Some students in low-level ESOL classes had little or no experience of school as children, which means that they also lack experience of what is expected in formal teaching and learning situations, rendering the training of test-taking techniques difficult. Ultimately, it is questionable whether it is fair to expect migrant learners with little or no previous educational experience to possess appropriate and adequate interpretations for a speaking test. If not, other alternative assessment approaches may have to be explored.

Conclusion

As we have seen in this and earlier chapters, learning to speak English to a level students find acceptable for their needs is not always a straightforward matter. Learning any language to a high level is, for most adults, challenging and time-consuming. The task facing many migrants to English-dominant countries is further hindered by lack of access to English-speaking communities, constrained choices in housing and employment, discrimination of various kinds, and an almost permanent shortage of adult ESOL classes. Yet at the same time the need for English and English qualifications is greater than ever. People who wish to become British citizens, who wish to practise their professions and even those who work in very unskilled jobs all need to prove their level of English in increasingly more formal ways.

In this chapter, and the rest of the book, our main focus has been on issues of language learning, both inside and outside the ESOL classroom. This inevitably means that our focus is often on teachers or their students and the struggles they face in their daily lives. What is missing from our picture, and from most narratives and discourse on migrants is, of course, the story from the other side, that is the expert speakers in majority communities who interact in different situations with people whose English is less expert than theirs. It is a common sense idea that the onus for communication rests entirely with the minority language speaker and not with his or her interlocutor. Some researchers have been aware of this for many years. Interactional sociolinguists such as John Gumperz in the USA and Celia Roberts in the UK have focused on miscommunication in cross-cultural interaction; they suggest that those from the dominant culture in unequal interactions need to understand the communication styles and linguistic differences of their interlocutors in order to avoid judgements which can fuel breakdowns and even racism. The report *Talk on Trial* (Roberts and Campbell 2006) is a recent version of this kind of work; it shows how interviewers are often responsible for communication breakdowns and misunderstandings in interviews, yet rarely realize this, thereby focusing the 'blame' on the linguistic minority candidate.

In today's climate, political and media discourse is often all too ready to reproach migrants for their failure to integrate, a failure to learn the language and for the perceived breakdown in social and community cohesion. They are upbraided for 'self segregating' and leading parallel lives; the focus of such criticism is invariably on what migrants lack, fail to do or are unable to do. But the same questions are rarely asked about homogenous white communities—especially wealthy ones—who could well be accused of the same 'self-segregation'. The cliché 'it takes two to tango' is truer nowhere than in oral communication. Some of the interactional work needs to shift onto the shoulders of the indigenous population.

Further reading

Analysing classroom interaction

Information and techniques on how to understand and analyse classroom talk can be found in these publications.

Seedhouse, P. 2005. *The Interactional Architecture of the Language Classroom: A Conversation Analysis Perspective.* Oxford: Blackwell.

Thornbury, S. and **D. Slade.** 2006. *Conversation: From Description to Pedagogy.* Cambridge: Cambridge University Press.

Tsui, A. B. M. 1995. *Introducing Classroom Interaction.* London: Penguin.

Walsh, S. 2006. *Investigating Classroom Discourse.* London and New York: Routledge.

Cross-cultural communication and interactional sociolinguistics

The first of these works is a publication from a large study of interaction between majority and minority speakers in five European countries. Roberts and Campbell's *Talk on Trial* is a study of real job interviews which shows how, due to largely hidden demands made upon them by the structure of interviews and expectations of interviewers, non expert speakers of English face a 'linguistic penalty' in the British job interview. Two DVDs have been produced based on the findings of *Talk on Trial*, the first for interviewers, the second for foreign-born students and their teachers.

Bremer, K., C. Roberts, M. Vasseur, M. Simonot, and **P. Broeder**. 1996. *Achieving Understanding*. Harlow: Longman.

Roberts, C. 2007a. *Successful at Selection: Fair Interviewing in a Diverse Society* (DVD). London: Department for Work and Pensions.

Roberts, C. 2007b. *F.A.Q.s Frequently Asked Questions and Quickly Found Answers* (DVD). London: Department for Work and Pensions.

Roberts, C. and **S. Campbell.** 2006. *Talk on Trial*. London: Department for Work and Pensions.

Listening

This book contains a range of activities for helping students learn to listen.

White, G. 1998. *Listening*. Oxford: Oxford University Press.

Testing

Lazaraton's book takes a discourse analysis approach to interaction recorded during Cambridge ESOL testing exams. McNamara and Roever look at the social aspects of language testing, placing the testing of migrants for language and citizenship in its historical and political context.

Lazaraton, A. 2002. *A Qualitative Approach to the Validation of Oral Language Tests. Studies in Language Testing 14*. Cambridge: University of Cambridge Local Examinations Syndicate/Cambridge University Press.

McNamara, T. and **C. Roever.** 2006. *Language Testing: The Social Dimension*. Oxford: Blackwell.

6 ESOL, LITERACY, AND LITERACIES

I've come back to study. What changed my mind? My writing was worse, and my spelling was worse as well. So I thought to myself, yeah, if you keep like this you are going to get worse, so you might as well study now.
Somali man, London

Introduction

If Chapter 5 concerned the vital importance of oral communication for ESOL students, so this chapter and the next (on electronic literacy) relate to written communication, to literacy, one of the most complex issues in ESOL. At the heart of this complexity is the difficulty in defining what literacy actually is or means. Is literacy principally a cognitive, a linguistic, or a social activity? Is it best understood as a set of reading and writing skills which can be taught, learnt, measured, and assessed? Or is it better thought of dynamically, as something that is done or performed in social contexts? How does its teaching relate to students' lives outside classrooms and beyond ESOL? How are educational policies shaped by ideas about literacy? And how does politics impinge on literacy teaching? These are some of the questions visited in this chapter. And, looking ahead to Chapter 7, how does the coming of electronic communication alter the ESOL literacy landscape?

This chapter has a central concern with contrasting theoretical approaches to literacy, and how they have an effect on practice. A fundamental distinction is between the notions of 'literacy as commodity' and 'literacy practices'. On the one hand, literacy has a narrow or conventional definition, as a finite set of skills that can be the focus of instruction. This interpretation of literacy is all about the decoding and encoding of linguistic texts, and allows a view of literacy as a store of knowledge that students can learn and be taught. Literacy rooted in this basic skills tradition will be familiar to many ESOL students and teachers today. On the other hand, literacy viewed as social practice, or rather, plural social *practices*, sees it as being done by people in various contexts. This broader notion of literacy is to do with how texts are both produced and used to fulfil social purposes. The distinction between these two views of literacy is crucial; subscription to one view or another positions ESOL students in very different ways.

This chapter opens with literacy for new readers and writers, considered by many teachers to be the most challenging area of ESOL pedagogy. This leads to theories of literacy which to an extent are in conflict, the literacy as commodity and the literacy practices views. We then draw the link between a functional view of literacy and 'employability', a notion that is current in much political and educational discourse, at least in English-dominant countries. This is a pertinent matter for ESOL, as language and migration are so often tied up with the question of employment. An investigation of functional literacy and employability brings us finally to discussion of a more questioning approach to literacy, 'critical literacy', itself allied to the literacy practices tradition.

ESOL students with basic literacy needs

Say if I get a letter from the immigration people today, I can't read that letter properly, I can't understand the meanings correctly and if I misread the words there'll be a lot of problems.
Kamal, Sri Lankan man, London

I would read my own letters. I would write my own letters. I would work. I think I would do many things.
Gulnaz, Turkish woman, London

In a survey of around 500 ESOL students, 12 per cent reported not being able to read or write in either their primary language or English (Baynham and Roberts, *et al.* 2007). The reasons for this vary. Some migrants come from countries and societies where there is no written form of their language or where a written form has existed for only a relatively short period of time. Others have faced social, economic, and cultural barriers to schooling. For example, Gulnaz, the Turkish woman quoted above, was prevented from going to school as a girl because of poverty compounded by gender. We return to her story later. The upheaval caused by military conflict and war is a further reason why people have found it impossible to become literate, even in societies where the literacy rate was previously relatively high; Kamal, also quoted above, is a Tamil refugee whose education has been seriously disrupted because of the civil war in Sri Lanka.

Low literacy can have serious repercussions and provoke strong feelings and anxieties for ESOL students. Migrants to societies such as the UK who had not previously regarded their literacy (or lack of it) as a problem are suddenly faced with a pressure to learn to read and write in English, their second or third language, sometimes at the very time when they are confronting the stresses of migration. Other people, who immigrated many years ago, may have worked in jobs which required little from them by way of literacy; now unemployed, however, they are facing new demands from potential employers in the increasing textualization of even the most unskilled manual work. That is, even menial jobs now entail employees having to negotiate with written texts. There are potentially serious problems for people unable to read English when they are faced with the bureaucratic demands made of migrants in English-dominant countries. This is particularly true for asylum seekers and refugees such as Kamal. Many people in his position have access to community networks and resources to help them process important bureaucracy such as letters from the immigration authorities; they also have recourse to official interpreters and translators provided by government offices and local councils. However, one of the reasons people attend ESOL classes in the first place is to break their sense of dependency on either official translators or friends and relatives. This dependency can occasionally provoke insulting treatment from street-level bureaucrats and functionaries, as Yasmin's story suggests:

> *I have no confidence in anything, no control. I went to the bank to open an account. I took my sister with me to interpret. The cashier said, 'You don't know English?' 'No, I don't.' 'You can't open the account.' I froze in my place. I said, 'What, don't I have any value or anything?' He says to me 'You don't know English. Go and get an interpreter.' My sister said she was interpreting. 'You must pay money for an interpreter.' So I said, 'Let's go.' The man shook me up. In my country my brother opened an account for me. Nobody said anything. You get a strange feeling when you come to a strange country. You've left everything, and then people talk to you like this.*
> Yasmin, Yemeni woman, Leeds

Apart from the serious immediate and day-to-day reasons for needing literacy in English, many students are motivated to become literate to fulfil their longer term aspirations for employment and further study. Although many migrants face barriers which are arguably greater than those created by their low levels of English language and literacy, such as poverty, racism, and other discrimination, they often see literacy as their main passport to greater personal and economic fulfilment. Some people, often women, regard their efforts to acquire literacy in English as attempts to redress many years of inequality and frustration. Gulnaz's story is an illustration of this.

CASE STUDY 1 Gulnaz's Story

My father sent all of my brothers to school but he did not send me. I studied in primary school until the fifth year. They did not send me after that because we were living in a village. Actually there was not even a school building in my village. There was a very old building where they used to teach children. There was not even any tables or chairs. We used to sit on the floor. Some people went to secondary school in towns because they had some relatives living there. People who did not have any relatives in towns, like me, had to work in the fields. The other reason was that I was a girl. They believed that girls should not need to study.

After a while I got married. After I got married I had family problems. My husband did not want me to go to college. If my father had sent me to school before I got married, everything would have been different. I worked for a while in a factory. I was cleaning the clothes after they sewed. There was work in the factory at that time. My husband did not support me to go to college in the first years of our marriage. He was a very jealous husband. He did not send me to college because there were male students. Now he is not like he used to be. He wants me to go to school now. He knows we are not young anymore. After three children I think he knows no one would want me.

I really want to learn to speak English. I really really want to learn. I will go to school and learn English, then I will work, and I will get out of the house. Like all other normal women I want to work in a normal job such as a hairdresser, in a job with other English people. Without working I feel useless, not worth anything. I am doing nothing but house work. If you stay at home all day you will go mad and start having depression. That is why I have to go to college or work, to not go mad. It is the best thing, going to college or work. When I see some women in a hurry to go to work I envy them really. I want to be like them.

I want my daughters to study. I do not want them to become one of my kind. I do not let them do any housework. I really want them to study. If they carry on studying this is a country full of opportunities. The government gives people the chance to study. It is up to them. At least I want them to have a decent job. What am I doing? Going home to cook, washing dishes, nothing else but cleaning the house.

(Abridged interview translated from Turkish)

As Kathleen Rockhill (1987) points out in her work on Latina women seeking literacy classes in the USA, literacy education is experienced by women such as Gulnaz as both a *threat*, that is, to her husband and her role in the home, and as a *desire* to change her own future and the future of her daughters. She sees learning English and acquiring literacy as an escape, and going to class as entering a world that holds the promise of change.

Teaching basic literacy to ESOL students

As the ESOL population expands there are growing numbers of students like Gulnaz and Kamal seeking to learn English and acquire English literacy. Meeting the needs of ESOL students with low literacy creates several challenges for teachers and providers. These include defining who is and who is not an ESOL literacy student, and deciding how provision should be organized. In their guide to teaching basic literacy to ESOL students, Marina Spiegel and Helen Sunderland define a basic literacy student as: 'Someone who is still learning to read a short simple text and struggles to write a simple sentence independently … Some students may have little or no print literacy in their own languages, while others may be able to read and write extremely well one or more languages' (2006: 15). Beyond this definition, Spiegel and Sunderland point to a number of factors which complicate matters for teachers of basic literacy to bilingual students. Some students come to ESOL classes with an ability to read and write another language which uses Roman script. Others might be familiar with an ideographic writing system, a syllabary, or a non-Roman alphabet. Others still may have little or no knowledge of any writing system at all. Thus all students of basic literacy arrive in their classes with different starting points, and classifying students according to their English literacy needs becomes problematic for teachers.

ACTIVITY 1 Basic literacy and ESOL

Consider the institution where you currently teach, or one you are familiar with.
How does the institution provide for ESOL students with literacy needs?
What are the literacy backgrounds of students in ESOL literacy classes?
How does the institution find out about the literacy of ESOL students?
What do you know about the literacy backgrounds of your students?

One helpful distinction made by adult literacy acquisition researchers is between those students with some foundational literacy in a primary or expert language and those with none. Those with some expert language literacy are viewed as having skills to transfer on to literacy in their new language, a point made by Tarone and Bigelow (2005) among others. In ESOL classrooms, teachers appreciate that progress is slower among those with no skills to transfer. As Jill Sinclair Bell (1995: 687) says, 'most ESL literacy teachers would agree that students who are literate in their native language make better progress than those without native language literacy'. ESOL teachers will also recognize the fundamental point about language transfer: people are able to transfer knowledge that they have about literacy, regardless of script; for example, as Spiegel and Sunderland (2006: 15) call it, an understanding: 'that there is a link between sound and symbol or that different genres have their own conventions'.

ESOL students with no literacy in a primary or expert language are better served in a class which is able to address basic literacy needs, while those who are literate in another language, especially one using the Roman script, can be catered for in mainstream ESOL beginner classes. However, in many institutions students not literate in any language are placed in beginner ESOL classes alongside those who are literate in their expert language. This may be because there are not enough literacy students to warrant special provision or because of a lack of awareness on behalf of the institution. The onus for dealing with this mix is usually placed with teachers who are required to respond to the diverse needs of their students through differentiation and individualized approaches to teaching and learning. People with very low literacy, though, often fare badly in mixed classes and the dropout rate among them is high. If most of the students in a class are literate they and their teachers can draw on resources for learning such as written texts, bilingual dictionaries, and so on. Lacking the skills possessed by most of the rest of the class can be very alienating for a low-literacy learner such as Yasmin, who we met earlier in this chapter:

> *Sometimes she says, 'Look in the dictionary. Open the dictionary.' But it is difficult for me because I don't know written Arabic. The others, if they don't understand they check in their dictionary. I am embarrassed. It's very difficult for me that they read and understand and I don't.*
> Yasmin, Yemeni woman, Leeds

Some students spend years without getting the intensive, specific literacy teaching they require, and remain in low-level classes as 'false beginners', failing to make any progress to higher levels. Kamal, who we also met earlier, upon being asked to compare his previous mixed classes with his current literacy class, said the following:

> *The teacher would try and put something into our head, to make us learn as much as she could teach us. But why didn't we understand even though she tried hard? Why can't we understand at least a bit? From the beginning she was trying her best to, so why did we still not understand? That was worrying me a lot. But in Linda's class, you feel like you can study in her class for a lifetime. It's like that for me. She makes me understand a lot.*
> Kamal, Sri Lankan man, London

Expert language literacy or English literacy?

Some researchers in bilingualism and biliteracy believe that adults acquiring literacy for the first time will learn more effectively if taught literacy in their primary or expert language. As there is little research done on the effectiveness of this approach for adults, this belief is based on a considerable body of research carried out on children in the early grades of school. Jim Cummins, an authority on bilingual education, states the following (1990: 7):

> *It makes sense to introduce literacy in the learners' stronger language. This lessens the complexity of the task since only the literate code is being acquired (rather than a second language and the literate code) and also permits learners to become more actively involved in their own learning since they are fluent in the language of instruction.*

Cummins and others believe that literacy skills are easier to acquire in a stronger language and once acquired, will transfer to a weaker language. Rather than hinder or slow down the acquisition of English, evidence from bilingual programmes in North America suggests that promotion of literacy in the primary language 'provides a conceptual foundation that sustains stronger growth in English literacy skills' (Cummins 1990: 8). Bilingual instruction would also make it easier for teachers to find out what their students' real-life concerns and interests are. Some writers on ESOL literacy believe that teaching beginner ESOL literacy students in English (rather than in their expert language) is very unlikely to be effective, as this quote from Elsa Auerbach suggests (1993: 18):

> ... the result of monolingual ESL instruction for students with minimal L1 literacy and schooling is often that, whether or not they drop out, they suffer severe consequences in terms of self-esteem; their sense of powerlessness is reinforced either because they are de facto excluded from the classroom or because their life experiences and language resources are excluded.

Bilingual literacy education for adults is controversial in the USA, where the 'English Only' movement lobbies fiercely against it. In the UK, despite some attempts to implement it in projects such as the Sheffield Yemeni literacy project (Gurnah 2000), it remains very much a minority approach. Teachers, however, are often aware of the massive task facing students who have low levels of oral English attempting to learn English literacy at the same time, and in areas of the country where there are large numbers of people from the same linguistic background it would seem sensible to at least consider bilingual instruction as an option. This would of course depend on the political will to fund such programmes, which is perhaps unlikely in a socio-political climate in which English is viewed as the primary linguistic tool of integration and community cohesion.

ACTIVITY 2   The challenge of basic literacy

Try to learn to read and write the days of the week in Korean or, if you are familiar with Korean, in a script with which you are unfamiliar. Return to the activity a week later, then a month later.

What existing knowledge did you draw on to help you do this?

How much did you rely on your visual memory? How much did you rely on knowledge of your own written language(s)?

How much more difficult might this be if you had no knowledge at all of the written form of your expert language?

While this section has focused on pedagogy, it has also implicitly raised questions of the nature of literacy. Literacy here has been considered variously as something that has a rate or level, something that people can have more or less of, a mental or cognitive learning process, and a powerful factor in self-fulfilment. Moreover, lack of literacy has been seen as a barrier to employment and access to services. The sections that follow look at some of these very different ideas of literacy and the theories which underpin them, illustrated with examples from ESOL and literacy classrooms.

Literacy theories in conflict: basic skills and literacy practices

The efforts of ESOL literacy educators such as Spiegel and Sunderland (2006) to train teachers to teach basic literacy to ESOL students has led to a greater awareness amongst practitioners and institutions as to what their needs might be, and it is increasingly the case that ESOL literacy students are placed in classes designed to cater specifically for them. The pedagogical challenge for teachers thus becomes that of deciding which approaches, strategies, and materials best suit the teaching of basic literacy to ESOL adults. The major debates in ESOL literacy reflect those in other fields of language and literacy education and are influenced in turn by larger questions about the definition of literacy itself. A key theoretical distinction is between literacy as a basic skill and literacy as socially situated practices.

Literacy as a basic skill

ACTIVITY 3   Definitions of literacy

Here are some sentences drawn from the British National Corpus, a 100-million-word database of samples of written and spoken English. Each sentence contains the words 'literacy' or 'illiteracy'. How is literacy understood in each case?

a   It has been suggested that literacy levels in these weaving villages were higher than they were to be in the industrial towns of south Lancashire a generation later.

b   Belorussia had the lowest literacy rate among all the peoples of European Russia.

c   Some lands were redistributed to landless peasants, literacy was raised.

d   She gave most of it to a charity promoting adult literacy, living instead on the £115,000 presidential salary.

e   The worsening condition is evident in the poor life expectancy and literacy statistics in Pakistan.

f   By the usual measures of third-world misery: infant mortality, unsafe water, calorie intake, illiteracy …

These instances of the words 'literacy' and 'illiteracy' reflect the dominant or prevailing view of literacy, at least in the West, as a commodity that has a rate, an abstract notion of free-floating matter that one can have more or less of. Sentences (a) and (b) talk of a literacy 'rate' and 'level'. In addition, sentences (c) and (d) imply that literacy is generally a good thing. Moreover, literacy has an antonym, illiteracy, invariably viewed as a bad thing. Lack of literacy (sentences (e) and (f)) is in fact widely seen as a scourge. This interpretation of literacy encourages it to be seen as a body of knowledge that people can and should learn; the learning of which will be generally beneficial to their lives. The British anthropologist and linguist Brian Street has called this view of literacy the 'autonomous' model (Street 1984); autonomous, that is, in as much as it can be thought of generally, without close reference to individual lives and concerns.

Subscription to an autonomous model of literacy encourages teachers and students to consider literacy as primarily a linguistic activity, the learning of which happens in individual people's minds. Literacy pedagogy can then be thought of as comprising basic reading and writing skills taught and learnt largely in isolation from the contexts of their use. This is the 'common sense' notion of literacy that many students and teachers of adult literacy draw on when talking about their literacy learning and teaching. For example, here is a monolingual English-speaking adult literacy student talking about her lessons:

> *I find it really helpful going right back to the beginning. Right back to basics. It's a bit boring sometimes thinking, 'Oh, oh it's only a comma', but I think that's what I needed, to go right back.*

The idea of going 'back to basics' is a very strong metaphor in everyday talk about adult literacy. Moreover, the student's mention of punctuation as a token of her literacy learning echoes a familiar theme in popular books promoting a highly prescriptive view of 'correctness', such as Lynne Truss' *Eats, Shoots and Leaves* (2003) and John Humphrys' *Lost for Words* (2004). An overriding concern with the technical skills of syntactical accuracy, punctuation and spelling is also common with adult ESOL and bilingual literacy students. In the example below, bilingual students in an adult literacy class in London are discussing with a researcher what, in their opinion, is appropriate lesson content. Among these students the crucial aspect of English literacy is again narrowly defined as spelling: 'It's good for us to know about spelling. Yeah, we write something we can't write a spelling mistake'. To equate literacy with a focus on spelling also corresponds with what happens in their literacy lessons:

I=interviewer, S=students

I   What do you actually do in this class? How are you improving? What are you doing?

S   We're doing spelling.

S   Dictation.

S   We have separate spelling books.

S   Everyday we do a spelling test. There has a different spelling book.

S   And dictation.

S   Dictation only and words beginning with the word. So I think this is good for us.

These students too have an idea of literacy which is rooted in the notion of literacy as a basic skill, associated with correctness in spelling, grammar, and punctuation.

ESOL literacy classes sometimes focus very narrowly on a limited set of 'skills' such as decontextualized word recognition, spelling, handwriting, or phonic awareness. Such attention on the level of the word, or even on individual sounds and symbols, situates ESOL literacy teaching at the extreme end of a basic skills notion of literacy. Debates about pedagogy which rage in other areas of literacy education are therefore also pertinent in ESOL literacy. The teaching of phonics in particular provokes strong feelings. There is some evidence to show that adults acquiring literacy for the first time in a new language benefit from intensive coaching in mastering sound/symbol relationships (Craats, *et al.* 2006), but to take such evidence as a basis for ESOL literacy pedagogy is a risky strategy. This is principally because it distracts the focus of literacy from the creation of meaning. Making this kind of tuition relevant to students' lives is probably impossible and can seem very alienating to adult students with pressing concerns outside the class. As one ESOL student on a phonics-based programme put it, in an interview translated from Kurdish (Campbell, *et al.* 2007):

> *I am more interested in sentences that I can use when I need to, making an appointment, phoning college saying I can't come. We learn things like cat, frog, which I don't need.*

Literacy practices

A basic skills view of literacy concentrates on an ability to read and write in ways that are measurable and easy to assess, and are relatable to a prescriptive standard. However, literacy can also be understood as plural, dynamic, socially and culturally situated and contextualized practices, comprising individual literacy events. This literacy practices view represents a challenge to classifications of literate or illiterate that assume a generalizable, autonomous literacy. It also allows us to think about literacy as embedded in everyday social practice, considering ESOL classrooms as one among many sites of language use.

A turn towards the social, cultural, and ethnographic has been influential in literacy theory in recent years, developing a body of work termed the New Literacy Studies. Socially- and culturally-oriented literacy is neither sterile nor context-free. Although it incorporates the technical skills involved in reading and writing, it encompasses more than this, and reading and writing are never decontextualized in a literacy practices approach. Early theorists in the tradition were anthropologists, who showed that the purposes of reading and writing arise from social and cultural needs and expectations. What is more, the uses which people make of literacy were seen to vary hugely across and between cultures and communities. So it is not appropriate to assume one single literacy, or to impose a view of literacy which arises from one specific cultural source. To take an example, a student of Qu'ranic Arabic at a madrasah in Algeria will have a very different understanding of the uses and purposes of literacy to a new migrant from Latin America in the US who is in the process of applying for a job.

ACTIVITY 4   Reflecting on literacy practices

Here is a list of literacy practices. What kind of reading or writing is involved? Why would some people have difficulties with these? Can you add to this list? If you are teaching at present ask your students to do this activity too, referring to English and to their expert languages. What do you find out?

- reading academic papers
- following instructions for putting together flat pack furniture
- reading the 'help' menu on a computer programme
- reading the financial section of a newspaper
- following signs to find your way around a large store
- writing a letter to a bereaved friend
- reading a spreadsheet
- reading a page on the social networking website *Facebook*.

Ethnographies of literacy practices in bilingual and multilingual communities show that even people with low levels of literacy participate in literacy events and practices in their daily lives. In his study of literacies amongst Panjabis in Southall, west London (1994) Mukul Saxena found that the grandmother of a family could not read in her expert language but nevertheless participated in literacy events at home, in the community, and at her place of worship.

The very narrow focus of some literacy classes, and the fact that teachers often do not talk to their students to find out about their daily lives, means that many literacy students are deemed to have lower skills and less knowledge about literacy than they exhibit in their lives outside the classroom. Tests used to assess a student's literacy abilities usually focus on the 'skills' aspect of reading and writing and result in a checklist of what the student cannot do, which is then addressed through learning plans and schemes of work which attempt to bridge the gaps. A different way to assess and to teach is to find out and work from the knowledge that even beginners at reading and writing have about literacy, such as the ability to recognize signs and to know what different texts are for.

A basic skills view of literacy tends to focus on the product of literacy, and on the reading and writing skills required to decode or encode such a product. In a literacy practices view, the status of written language as opposed to spoken language in terms of a 'divide' between the two is invalid. The role of oral language in literacy is clearly recognized, as is that of literate language in oral speech. Literacy in this broad view operates as cultural practices within particular contexts and communities. One does not even have to be reading, or even be able to read, to engage in literacy practices. The anthropologist Shirley Brice Heath, in her book *Ways with Words* describes how reading for the inhabitants of Trackton, a black, working-class community in the south-eastern USA, is 'a social activity' (1983: 196):

> … *when something is read in Trackton, it almost always provokes narratives, jokes, sidetracking talk, and active negotiation of the meaning of written texts among the listeners … The evening newspaper is read on the front porch for most months of the year … An obituary is read for some trace of acquaintance with either the deceased, his relatives, place of birth, church, or school; active discussion follows about who the individual was and who he might have known.*

Moreover, the great range of forms of both spoken and written language in their different contexts of use exposes the limits of a divide between speaking and writing. Speech is not always ephemeral or situation-bound any more than writing is always permanent or displaced. Much writing is impermanent: like a scribbled note 'back in 5 minutes', for example, or like electronic writing such as mobile phone text messaging. There is something typically speech-like as well about the note: we can imagine it being spoken. And much spoken language is very written-like: for instance the news on the radio, or a presidential address, both certainly composed in writing. As Brian Street says (1993: 4): '… spoken and written activities and products do not in fact line up along a continuum but differ from one another in a complex and multidimensional way both within speech communities and across them'.

Teachers who subscribe to a literacy practices approach maintain that if adopted in teaching, it enables them, and even obliges them, to take into account—and draw from—students' lives in their planning and teaching (for examples, see Kate Pahl and Jennifer Rowsell's *Literacy and Education* (2005)). They can look beyond the mechanics of decontextualized literacy learning and view what happens in lessons in terms of classroom literacy practices. Such classroom literacy practices should involve oral communication, but in ESOL literacy classes of all levels, teachers often focus on reading and writing to the exclusion of oral development. This is particularly detrimental to students who are beginning speakers of, as well as writers in, English. One ESOL literacy class observed in the research of Baynham and Roberts, *et al.* (2007) saw that, although students could write their names and some basic sentences, there was no improvement at all in their oral development over a six-month period. This is in marked contrast to progress in most beginner ESOL classes.

One way that teachers and classroom-based researchers can investigate classroom literacy practices is suggested by John Hellermann in an article in the journal *Applied Linguistics*, where he writes about how two adult ESL students develop second language literacy in their classroom. Rather than focusing on their test scores, or in fact paying very much attention at all to the particular materials and techniques the teacher uses in the class, Hellermann concentrates on what he calls 'the social processes which foster the development of classroom and interactional practices that characterize beginning literacy activities for adults in an L2' (2006: 377). In Hellermann's words, 'linguistic processing … is embedded within and inseparable from social practices or routines in which individuals are engaged' (2006: 379). Within these literacy practices there are identifiable and recurring events, for example, when the students are choosing a book to read, or are filling in their reading logs. Teachers can investigate the interaction around literacy events through observation of their own classrooms. This can help them understand the processes by which students develop an understanding of literacy in their classrooms.

ACTIVITY 5 Day-to-day literacy practices and events

Think back through the last 24 hours. Make a list of all the activities you engaged in where reading or writing was involved. Include literacy events where you might not have been actually reading or writing, or where other people were participating, for example, someone read aloud from a menu in a restaurant, or someone read you the bus number because it was too far away for you to read, or you looked at a web page with someone else.
• What was the context in which this happened?
• Did each activity involve the same kind of literacy?
• If possible, interview an ESOL literacy student about his/her literacy practices. What do you learn?

Functional literacy and employability

An extension of the established or traditional 'skills-based' approach to literacy is functional literacy. If a literacy practices view represents an opening-up of literacy, then functional literacy risks closing down literacy education, promoting a restricted, unquestioning literacy, and positioning ESOL students as subservient to the needs of business and industry. The idea of functional literacy is powerfully evident in the discourse of educational policy, as this quote from an Adult Basic Skills policy document from England (DfEE 1999) shows:

> *Some seven million adults in England—one in five adults—if given the alphabetical index to the* Yellow Pages, *cannot locate the page reference for plumbers. That is an example of functional illiteracy. It means that one in five adults has less literacy than is expected of an 11-year-old child.*

How the figure of seven million adults unable to find the page reference for plumbers in the phone book was actually calculated is not clear. It is also not suggested that people might use the alphabetical organization of the phone book, rather than its index, to find a plumber, or even to rely on word of mouth or a personal recommendation. The term 'functional literacy' is largely meaningless, therefore, until we stop to consider, as the literacy theorist David Olson does (1994: 11): 'functional for what or functional for whom'.

In educational policy, the 'function' of literacy, as with learning in general, is often economic. Literacy is widely assumed to have an economic impact, as part of a 'knowledge economy', where knowledge itself can be sold or exchanged. Students of literacy are cogs in the economic machine, and the overriding purpose of literacy education is to make students more economically productive. Applied linguist Randal Holme puts it in this way (2004: 12):

> *Education and training ... become a means to add value to the students who are its 'products' just as manufacturing increases the worth of raw materials by turning them into usable goods. ... Functional literacy consists of some of the basic skills that the individual needs to fulfil their economic and social potential. The concept of functional literacy should therefore be associated with that of education and training as adding value through training in basic skills.*

The case for a causal relationship between literacy and economic growth is not conclusive. If anything, argues Holme (2004: 22) 'the probability is that an increase in literacy rates is as much a product of economic development as a cause'. He cites the example of Sweden, whose economic development during its industrial revolution preceded a growth in literacy rates. Yet the motivation in policy of linking literacy and the economy continues to be to encourage economic activity through the development of individuals' capacity.

In functional literacy classes the emphasis is on the basic skills of reading, writing, grammar, spelling, and punctuation. In addition, functional literacy encompasses a limited set of core genres, for example, the formal letter, the CV, the job application form. These might relate more or less to what a teacher perceives as their students' literacy needs. This is not to say that teaching the skills of literacy is unimportant or that these core genres need not be taught. But the association of functional literacy with 'basic skills' and the core genres mentioned here risks a separation of how literacy is learnt and the reality of people's everyday literacy needs and experiences.

Literacy and employability

In educational policy literacy is often associated with employability, the ability and capability people have to gain employment. This requires an interpretation of literacy primarily as a basic skill (the conventional or 'common sense' definition), and relies on the questionable assumption that the economic value of the workforce can be increased through training in basic skills. ESOL students are often viewed in terms of how they can become more economically productive, and conversely are castigated for being a drain on the economy when they do not progress to a certain level. This corresponds with a broader discourse in education policy, which ties education to employability.

Quotations from politicians and educational policy makers provide evidence of this way of thinking. Here are two, from a UK Government education minister, and the authors of a government-commissioned review of skills.

> *I want a [Further Education] system … which helps employers of all shapes and sizes achieve their business goals.*
> Denham 2007

> *Nowhere is the UK's skills deficit more apparent than in basic skills. Today, more than five million adults lack functional literacy, the level needed to get by in life and at work.*
> HM Treasury 2006: 61

The dominant perspective in policy is thus that:
a   students in Further Education (which includes the majority of ESOL students in the UK) are there to service employers and their business needs;
b   functional literacy is a skill that can be measured or quantified;
c   if you do not have functional literacy, you, like five million others, cannot 'get by in life and at work'.

There are a number of pedagogic and ideological reasons why the development of literacy skills with a focus on 'employability' adequately addresses neither literacy pedagogy nor the needs of those seeking employment.

Functionality should not be, but frequently is, considered in isolation from individual circumstances, which is to say, people's particular reasons for learning. The complicating factor here is that these circumstances are just that—individual—and moreover, they change over time. This makes any attempt at pinning down the nature of the skills that constitute functional literacy very difficult to do. And even if the scope and nature of such skills are tightly defined in syllabuses, they may well not adequately cover students' broader literacy needs. David Olson's questions posed earlier still beg: Functional for what? Functional for whom?

It may be the case that the answer to Olson's questions are 'for employment' and 'for employers', and it is the case that for a good number of students the demands of work create their most urgent needs with regard to English language and literacy. For many workers, language training is an essential part of their socialization into a specific workplace or world of work. Doctors and nurses, for example, who are learning to do their job in an English-dominant country, need to follow very specific language training courses whose content relates closely to their needs in employment. On a general ESOL course they are not likely to encounter the language and literacy practices they need to perform specific activities in their jobs. For such students, it is appropriate to do a targeted English for Specific Purposes (ESP) course which may be provided at a college or in the workplace itself. Students who are already workers need a complex set of language and literacy competencies. These include the specific institutional and occupational discourses of their jobs. In addition, as the work of the UK Government-funded Industrial Language Training Unit (1974–1989) showed, workers need the interactional competence to form relationships with their colleagues and negotiate their rights. These issues are discussed in a book by Celia Roberts and her colleagues, *Language and Discrimination* (1992).

In many ESOL contexts, employment-focused courses provide only the most generic, decontextualized focus on the skills of employability such as writing letters of application and CVs, and preparing for interviews. This is reflected in the growing number of ESOL courses and qualifications which concentrate on ESOL for work. These courses can be contentious amongst teachers, who are resistant to teaching them because of their narrow generic focus and because of the associated shift of responsibility for funding adult ESOL courses away from colleges and towards employers. One ESOL manager, interviewed about her college's new ESOL for work programmes, observed the following problem for many ESOL teachers in the new turn towards the generic workplace:

We came into the public sector and we could all be earning more money if we were doing other things, but we had a belief in education, in colleges, in students or the politics of asylum or whatever it was, but this new agenda has nothing to do with that, it is all about being business focused, and we're not business focused people, that's why we're here.

Elsewhere in this book we criticize some ESOL courses for their attention to instrumental needs and 'survival English'. This criticism applies equally to ESOL for work qualifications and courses. English language students, whether jobseekers or not, should be exposed to as wide a range as possible of language, perhaps including the language of literature and storytelling, poetry and song, as well as the language skills needed in the workplace. Furthermore, not all ESOL students are actively looking for work, and some already have jobs which they are more than capable of performing. They therefore do not regard their ESOL course as essential to their increased efficiency as workers. Instead, many people are studying ESOL because they see an ability to communicate in English as a necessary and important aspect of living in an English-dominant country, for all the reasons outlined in Chapter 5. These people can feel excluded (and in some cases are in fact excluded) from ESOL classes with a predominant focus on developing generic work-related language skills.

It is certainly the case that literacy is becoming more and more important for work, even if the job does not, on the face of it, require high levels of literacy skills in English. Literacy now acts as a gatekeeper in employment contexts as never before. However, the association between functional literacy and work is a complex one, and one that can be explored through the example of an individual case, that of Abbas.

CASE STUDY 2 Abbas

Abbas is originally from Afghanistan and is a speaker of Dari. He was interviewed when he was on an ESOL course at a training centre in London whilst in the middle of a difficult period of unemployment. In Afghanistan his education was severely disrupted because of the civil war and the activities of the Taliban regime. He has acquired a high level of fluent spoken English but has serious problems with English literacy, particularly writing.

The story of how he came to England is complicated and very traumatic. He fled Afghanistan as an unaccompanied minor at the age of 15 or 16, becoming a displaced refugee in Tajikistan and then Pakistan. In Pakistan he was unable to make a living because there were so many refugees trying to do the same, so he paid a large sum of money to get out of Pakistan, arriving in England some time later after an arduous journey. He was sent by the authorities to several different English towns in succession and waited two years for a decision to be made about his claim for asylum. All the while his family had no idea where he was and he had no contact with them until the Taliban were ousted in 2001.

Abbas has had many jobs since he was given permission to work. He was determined to work at any cost in order to survive. He has a long work record, having had jobs in warehouses, factories, and shops. He began as a cleaner in a warehouse ('I was happy to do it') and while there informally learnt the trade of some of the other workers, such as driving a forklift truck. He has found work through several employment agencies, some of which are less scrupulous than others. The inefficiency of agencies has meant that he has lost jobs on occasions and has had to spend time with no work and no money. He has had a spate of bad luck recently and has been unable to get work either through the Job Centre or through agencies, so has been going around employers on foot and trying to get work through his contacts and word of mouth. His current job is delivering pizzas.

One of the problems facing Abbas now is that recently he has found that his low-level literacy is a barrier to employment. In an attempt to get a steady job he applied for training as a bus driver, a job which in England has serious recruitment problems which companies are addressing by recruiting in new EU countries such as Poland:

> The last job I applied was for bus driver. I've still got the letter from them. They called me to the Job Centre in Finchley, one person from the bus company was there and he was checking how we write and speak. So when I went he gave me a piece of paper and said, 'OK, you have to write something', and I said, 'Oh my God, this is the worst thing for me'. I asked them why, to drive a bus? They say that this is a new rule, sometimes if you have an accident or some passengers have a fight inside the bus if the police are involved you need to describe to the police what happened and you need to write a report to the company as well. So this is the new rule, you must be able to understand English but you must be able to write as well. They said I had to improve my writing. They said, 'Once you can write, call us again.'

More seriously, though, Abbas is also finding that jobs he could easily get previously are becoming less and less open to him because of the literacy demands of even menial jobs.

> Most of the companies now they are saying you must have reading and writing English so you need to know about safety and so on. Most of the warehouses they are saying you must have basic writing because they are saying sometimes we will give you the basic paperwork we don't have time so you have to write the reports. For example, where I used to work, when you are handling the goods for the customers, if the box is damaged they don't accept it they ask why it is damaged so they say they want compensation. So now they say you should write a report, what are the damages, what happened and what the customer is saying, what compensation he wants, so this is the kind of thing they want in all the warehouses. Writing is the most important thing now, it's everywhere. The first question when you apply for a job is this.

This case study throws up a lot of questions, about literacy, about employability, and about funding of adult education and skills. Abbas is a hard worker, prepared to do almost anything to get by. He has a young family to support and is very frightened by the thought of unemployment. Getting a job is proving increasingly difficult for him because it is very competitive (he says 'every job is a war') and because he is being asked more and more frequently for a level of literacy he does not have. Aware of this, he is doing his best to learn what he can at the training centre and to study at home. As he says though, acquiring literacy is a slow process:

> *My writing is getting better now. I think I can see the difference. It is not getting lots better but I feel better anyway. I know it is quite hard and it takes time.*

Abbas faces several problems, some of which may prove intractable and which may mean that he never gets the ESOL literacy education he needs. Firstly, he has to find a class which can provide the intensive, sustained instruction he needs to improve his literacy, which would involve consistent support and detailed feedback. This is not available to him at the training centre he attends because the tuition there is funded only for six months and because his teacher, although well qualified, has no experience of teaching people with low literacy, nor has she had training in how to support them. Aware of this, Abbas has made several attempts to get a place at the local college where literacy expertise is available, but each time has been put onto a long waiting list.

Even more serious is what might happen to Abbas in the future. Responsibility for who pays for training for adults rests not only with publicly-funded colleges but also with employers, who are encouraged to identify which skills they, as businesses, require their workforce to acquire, and train them accordingly. Companies tend to invest in narrow skills training which is tailored to their needs as employers; they are less likely to put long-term investment into the language, literacy, and general adult education needed by workers such as Abbas. In fact Abbas, despite his intelligence and keen work ethic, is finding it difficult to get into any workplace at all; if he does find a job it is likely to be in a firm which is either too small to be able to invest in training or too concerned with profit to care. Stories of extreme exploitation of foreign workers hit the news every day and give little cause for optimism. The union leader Frances O'Grady pointed out in a speech in 2006:

> *The migrant worker horror stories are sadly all too familiar, but that doesn't make them any less shocking. Like the two Filipino women being paid £75 for an 80-hour week at a Norfolk care home. The Portuguese man and his pregnant wife working on a farm in Lancashire, sharing a house with 17 others, and left with just £6 a week to live on after deductions. This is not some Dickensian nightmare—this is happening here and now, in Britain, in 2006.*

It can remain only an outside chance that employers who are unwilling even to ensure basic rights for their workers are ever likely to invest in training of any kind, let alone in what Abbas needs.

A critical take on literacy

Given cases such as that of Abbas, it could well be argued that ESOL practitioners can no longer see themselves as neutral instructors in the English language (if they ever could), and need to adopt a critical stance as never before. Critical literacy has been very influential in some parts of the world, though rarely explicitly so in ESOL in the UK. It is both a reaction against strictly functional literacy and a complement to the literacy practices view. If literacy is conceptualized as social practice, it is also critical in the sense of the tradition of critical pedagogy, a movement most closely associated with the Brazilian educational theorist Paolo Freire. Freire believed that literacy is emancipatory and transformative; the first step to critical reflection and action upon the forces that affect students' lives. His work strongly rejects the 'banking' notion of education, whereby knowledge is conferred by those who have it (teachers) upon those who do not (students). Freire writes (1970: 58):

> *In the banking concept of education, knowledge is a gift bestowed by those who consider themselves knowledgeable upon those whom they consider to know nothing. Projecting an absolute ignorance on others, a characteristic of the ideology of oppression, negates education and knowledge as processes of enquiry. The teacher presents himself to his students as their necessary opposite; by considering their ignorance absolute, he justifies his own existence.*

The banking notion of learning, where knowledge is transmitted from teacher to students, is connected to inequality, dominance of one group over another, and oppression. A critical take on literacy recognizes that literacy practices are far more than cognitive processes, and relate to other social constructions such as class, gender, ethnicity, and political status. In the words of the critical literacy educators Morgan and Ramanathan (2005: 151), literacy practices are:

> *at root social arrangements, embedded in and constitutive of issues relating to unequal distributions of power within communities and institutions ... In this respect, literacy can be seen as doing the work of discourse and power/ knowledge.*

Critical educators are aware that it is not only individual competences but also larger societal forces which shape the life possibilities of ESOL students. There is a danger, however, that literacy education in itself is held as the key to redressing political and socio-economic inequities. This caution is indicated by Michael James, a literacy educator in San Francisco working with young people on social issues such as health, employment, and drug use:

> *Many literacy educators and programs today would hope their programs were indeed transformative. The new interest [in literacy for transformation] has also generated an inclination to mystify literacy, to ascribe to it catalytic properties far beyond its actual utility. It has captured the imaginations of many activists and educators for whom it represents a panacea for social and political inequities.*
> 1990: 15

Most ESOL literacy programmes cannot be said to be emancipatory or transformatory in Freire's sense, a notable exception in the UK being the Reflect for ESOL programme instigated by the charity Action Aid. One notion which is a direct descendant of Freire's ideas is that to be effective, lesson content and materials have to be directly relevant to students' lives. Some educators working in the Freirean tradition have developed the concept of the participatory curriculum in which students bring along their own real-life concerns and texts to class, thus creating the curriculum according to their evolving needs (see Baynham 1988, Wallace 1989, Auerbach 1992). This is compatible with the approach proposed in Chapter 3, in which teachers are encouraged to look to their own classrooms when developing methodology. Elsa Auerbach and Nina Wallerstein (2005) take this further, advocating that literacy work be always at the service of students' larger political concerns, that it should be not educational work with 'relevant content' but rather, embedded in political processes in communities and workplaces which have an educational character.

Adopting a critical orientation towards ESOL literacy does not mean teachers have to disengage with the importance of the technical skills of literacy or with the core genres of formal letters, CVs, and the like. Students both want to and need to know how to write in certain genres and how to spell and punctuate their writing accurately. But it is also vital that they know *why* these functional and technical skills are important, and this is where a critical stance is important. If students do not write according to a prescriptive standard, they will be judged unfavourably and disadvantaged, particularly if they are looking for work or aspiring to education beyond ESOL. As the linguist Deborah Cameron points out in her book *Verbal Hygiene* (1995), judgements are constantly made about people based on the extent to which their writing conforms to a standard or norm. In fact public concern with accuracy can reach the level of obsession. This can be difficult for teachers to stomach, aware as they are of the arbitrariness of standard or prestige varieties of a language, of the confusing intricacies of punctuation, and of the quirks of English spelling. However, a critical approach to ESOL literacy education can put the skills and core genres of functional literacy in their place, by encouraging an awareness of pervasive prescriptiveness, and of why written accuracy is held to be so crucial.

Conclusion

Literacy for ESOL encompasses the teaching and learning of reading and writing skills, but for written communication to be effective it must go beyond skills development, taking into account the relationships between readers and writers, and the contexts (inside and outside classrooms) within which literacy is done. We conclude this chapter with an attempt at drawing together the various strands it has covered with a definition of the sociocognitive view of literacy which might be usefully adopted in ESOL literacy pedagogy. This definition, proposed by American applied linguist Rick Kern, marries together cognitive, sociocultural, and critical strands of literacy. Kern presents the definition as one which characterizes literacy in foreign or second language education (2000: 16):

> *Literacy is the use of socially-, historically-, and culturally-situated practices of creating and interpreting meaning through texts. It entails at least a tacit awareness of the relationships between textual conventions and their contexts of use and, ideally, the ability to reflect critically on those relationships. Because it is purpose-sensitive, literacy is dynamic—not static—and variable across and within discourse communities and cultures. It draws on a wide range of cognitive abilities, on knowledge of written and spoken language, on knowledge of genres, and on cultural knowledge.*

Drawing as it does on different kinds of knowledge and abilities, we can extend the sociocognitive view of ESOL literacy education and say that it is concerned with knowledge of the *what*, the *how* and the *why* of literacy.

Knowing what: The cognitive dimension of literacy is concerned with encoding and decoding written text, as well as gaining an understanding of what the relationships are between words and between longer stretches of discourse. Developing the cognitive processing abilities involved in reading and writing in a new language is fundamental in beginner ESOL literacy for people with little or no foundational literacy in their expert language. Those with literacy in other languages often find they have cognitive skills they can transfer over to their new language.

Knowing how: This dimension encompasses an understanding of how literacy practices are carried on in their social and cultural contexts. This is particularly challenging for ESOL literacy students, who might not have the same social and cultural background knowledge as those they communicate with. ESOL students know the importance of learning how to write for particular audiences, and when certain conventions should be followed. Teaching ESOL literacy therefore involves helping students gain an awareness of how literacy is done in various contexts and situations.

Knowing why: The critical dimension of literacy is a vital concern in ESOL. Critical literacy involves developing an appreciation through critical reflection of why the relationships between writing and contexts of the use of writing are as they are. Not only is it important to know how to write in certain ways, to follow certain conventions, but it is also vital to know why we write in such ways. Literacy is about more than autonomous skills. ESOL literacy pedagogy involves equipping students with an awareness of how literacy practices do the job of mediating power relations in societies.

It falls upon the shoulders of teachers to address this complexity in ESOL literacy lessons, and for this they need at the very least a grounding in what literacy comprises beyond skills, and what might be appropriate approaches to its teaching in ESOL classrooms. In the chapter that follows the theme of literacy continues, with a focus on electronic literacy and the literacy practices that ESOL students engage with when using new technology.

Further reading

Literacy practices

Barton's *Literacy* is an updated edition of his introduction to the interpretation of literacy as socially situated and plural practices. Papen's *Adult Literacy as Social Practice* also takes a socially situated view of literacy and describes its relevance to adult literacy teaching. Street's book is an early work developing the notion of an ideological literacy which subsumes, and goes beyond, an autonomous skills-based view of literacy.

Barton, D. 2006. *Literacy: An Introduction to the Ecology of Written Language* (second edition). Oxford: Blackwell.

Papen, U. 2005. *Adult Literacy as Social Practice: More than Skills*. London: Routledge.

Street, B. 1984. *Literacy in Theory and Practice*. Cambridge: Cambridge University Press.

Critical literacy and participatory curricula

Auerbach and Wallerstein's book promotes the notion of a participatory curriculum, one in which students and their broad political as well as educational concerns are central. Freire's book is the original text on emancipatory literacy. Reflect and ESOL describes a participatory approach to adult learning and literacy developed by Action Aid and adapted for ESOL.

Auerbach, E. R. and **N. Wallerstein.** 2005. *Problem-posing at Work: English for Action.* Edmonton, Alberta: Grass Roots Press.

Freire, P. 1970. *Pedagogy of the Oppressed.* New York: Seabury Books.

Reflect for ESOL (online) http://www.actionaid.org/main.aspx?PageID=128

Teaching and assessing ESOL literacy

Kern's book outlines an approach to language teaching that uses literacy as its organising principle. Spiegel and Sunderland's handbook is a practical and useful guide to teaching basic literacy to ESOL students. Wrigley's film shows an alternative way to assess the basic literacy of ESOL students. Pahl and Rowsell's book, though geared towards primary, secondary, and family literacy teaching, is a valuable handbook relating the New Literacy Studies to classroom practice.

Kern, R. 2000. *Literacy and Language Teaching.* Oxford: Oxford University Press.

Pahl, K. and **J. Rowsell.** 2005. *Literacy and Education: Understanding the New Literacy Studies in the Classroom.* London: Paul Chapman Publishing.

Spiegel, M. and **H. Sunderland.** 2006. *Teaching Basic Literacy to ESOL Learners.* London: LLU+.

Wrigley, H. S. 2003. (online) *The Reading Demonstration* (video). Available online at http://www.literacywork.com/readingdemonstration

7 ESOL AND ELECTRONIC LITERACY PRACTICES

I did not know anything about computers. So everything I do I enjoy. I didn't know the computer could be fun. I didn't know that I can watch news, I can communicate from abroad, I can research things on the computer, I can see a lot of images.
Somali woman, Leeds

Introduction

New technologies of literacy—networked computers, the internet, and the World Wide Web (www), various tools of computer-mediated communication—are associated with change and revolution. This chapter builds on the previous one, looking at how literacy is changing for ESOL students in and out of their classrooms with the coming of electronic communication. How is the literacy landscape changing with the advent of electronic literacy? And how do students experience the new technologies of literacy? That is, what are their electronic literacy practices?

This chapter is concerned with four themes of electronic literacy, as they relate to ESOL. The first is reading online and on the screen, a different matter from more traditional types of reading. Electronic literacy has brought some of the multiple modes of communication to the fore: online readers know that text can be integrated with graphics, video, and audio, and that reading can follow non-linear paths through links. Correspondingly, new technologies allow for new ways of learning, through the use of multimedia and multimodal texts. This enables teachers to cater for the visual and aural dimensions of students' learning.

The second theme is computer-mediated communication (CMC). While the range of CMC now encompasses video and audio communication, electronic writing—principally email and text chat using messenger programs—still plays a vital role in students' lives outside their learning environment as they attempt to maintain ties with distant friends and family.

It is difficult to consider information and computing technologies (ICTs) in isolation from processes of globalization, and the third theme is ESOL students' engagement with globally-spread virtual communities. Some ESOL students might sometimes be considered victims, or at least passive subjects, of globalization, migrating great distances to escape war, famine, and poverty. As refugees or asylum seekers in the West, their socio-political status can be quite marginal. Yet in the virtual world, the same students can have a very different status as core members of online communities.

The final theme links ESOL learning and teaching with barriers to access to the new technologies of literacy. ESOL students experience obstacles to ICT use—and consequently to the development of their electronic literacy—both within and outside their classrooms. A case study of one particular class, whose teacher is introducing ICTs into her teaching for the first time, illustrates some of the barriers experienced by ESOL students in gaining access to new literacy technologies.

Reading online: multimodality and web literacy

In the West, the introduction of the technology of printing eventually enabled mass literacy. What then of the introduction and widespread use of ICTs such as the internet and the www? If print literacy was dominated by the written word, so electronic literacy is characterized by the integration of multiple communicative modes, known as 'multimodality'—particularly visual and increasingly aural communication.

Multimodality

Language is and always has been multimodal. The effects of written language taken together with graphical aspects of language called 'paralanguage' have long been recognized. Artists and visual poets have at least since third century Greece experimented with form and the possibilities of the graphic aspects of text. In the visual poems or 'calligrammes' of Guillaume Apollinaire, for example, the idea of a message arrives via different modes, through a visual as well as a verbal communication channel. This effect can be seen in the calligramme *Il Pleut* (1916), reproduced on page 117.

The non-linguistic features of discourse are always extant, but in most traditional printed writing are not as obvious as in the poetry of Apollinaire or on the internet. Yet in the past there has been a tendency to treat aspects of language separately. For example, written text is normally studied and taught in isolation from its graphic aspects. Multimodality concerns the way that multiple communicative modes of communication are integrated. This may be, for example, text with graphics and pictures, or speech with gestures. Literacy theorists such as Gunther Kress and Theo van Leeuwen, in their book *Reading Images* (2006), argue that from the late twentieth century visual communication became more prominent, and the integration of multiple communicative modes became more explicit, particularly when compared to more traditional printed text.

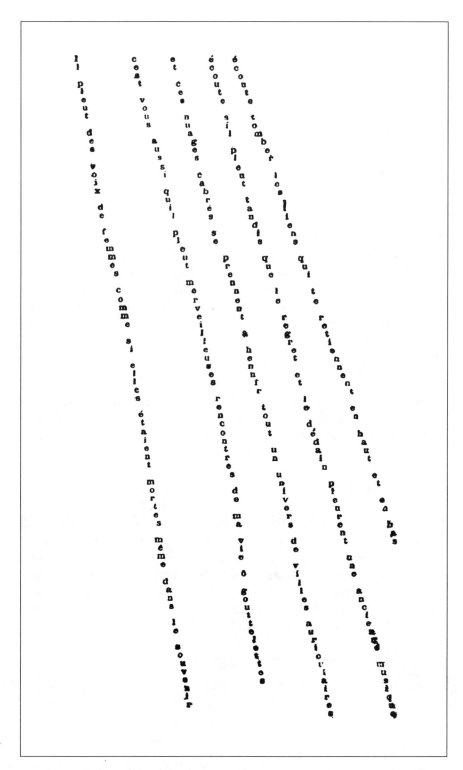

Il Pleut *(1916), by Guillaume Apollinaire*

ACTIVITY 1 Multimodality

Examine a page in a magazine or newspaper. The messages are communicated through written language but there are also non-linguistic features of communication. What are the particular effects of aspects such as:

- pictures
- typeface (font)
- print size
- layout and arrangement of the page
- colour?

Web literacy: reading in virtual space

Web literacy—reading online—is central to online communication. The www is an enormous database of written text, graphics, animation, video, sound, and other multimedia material. The content of the web is connected very differently from the linear sequencing of traditional print literacy, and is increasingly multimodal. Web page design, multimedia, and hypertext links all have an effect on reading, and on the choices which readers consequently have to make if they are to be web-literate. How students read the www is a branch of electronic literacy with implications for ESOL practice.

The structure of text on screen and the ways in which it can be used differ from traditional print literacy. Text is now adaptable, capable of being moved and copied, and of being linked with other text. The technology and its application allows integration of graphics, audio and video with text, enables screens to be split, icons to be clicked, menus to drop down, and help to pop up. On the computer screen, text coexists with visual images and sound, and these images are not simply used for illustration. There is a tendency to bring information and on-screen controls to the surface, and an associated tendency to display this information graphically and non-hierarchically. A quick look at any web page will show that instructions and information are often given with graphical or audio cues rather than with text-based commands. The capacity of text to make meaning is known as the 'functional load'. Much of the functional load once carried by writing is being shouldered by visual images and audio.

ACTIVITY 2 Reading on page and screen

Compare an article from a newspaper with the same article on that newspaper's website. What are the differences between the two? How does the layout differ? What information is included on screen and not on the page (and vice versa)? In what sequence do you read the information on the page? Do you read in a different way on the page/the screen?

Web navigation is quite dissimilar from traditional reading, even if you still read the text on a web page in linear fashion. And certainly browsing on the www is a different sensation from that of reading a traditional book. From one page, links can be followed in any number of directions to new pages, each with other links. Web readers can explore layer upon layer of pages, through a maze of links on a route of their own design. This presents a challenge to ESOL students and teachers. Choosing which pages to visit, which to read, and which further links to follow, is increasingly difficult as the number of sites and possible links grows. Also web readers must judge the quality of what they view for themselves. Material on the www might have passed through editors, but is just as likely not to have done. Students can also be tempted to follow irrelevant links and become lost in insignificant detail. So deciding what to read and what to attend to are essential skills of web literacy, just as they are for print literacy. Language teachers have begun to address the challenges of learning to read the web through techniques such as web quests, activities where students have to find certain information from web pages preselected by the teacher, to complete a project.

Multitasking and polyfocal attention

How some people actually carry on the process of doing literacy appears to be changing as well, with the emergence of new literacy technologies. The term 'polyfocal attention' was coined by Ron Scollon (1998). It refers to paying attention to a number of different media and/or people at once. A related concept is multitasking, carrying out different activities simultaneously, online and offline. Scollon writes (1998: 256): 'It is particularly important to note that this condition of multiple and competing media discourses is considered [by students] to be a good or desirable condition, not something to be avoided.'

ACTIVITY 3 Multitasking

What activities do you carry out when you are using a computer? List the things that you do simultaneously (for example, checking your emails, working on a report). List the things that you do at the same time but not on the computer (for example, listening to the radio, watching television, having a conversation). Are some activities more amenable than others to polyfocal attention?

Online, someone can have many different programs open simultaneously, so it is quite normal for electronic literacy practices to entail a number of activities at a time, perhaps viewing successive web pages by following hypertext links (surfing), and carrying out a word processing activity. And people do not just read the web: other simultaneous computer-related activity might involve any combination of text-based synchronous chat, email, audio, or video communication. Beyond the screen, there might be a CD or internet radio playing. And of course, there could be a face-to-face conversation going on as well. So in addition to *attention* being polyfocal, the *communication* may be multimodal. The case study below shows how one ESOL teacher exploits the multimodal possibilities of new literacy technologies in his teaching.

CASE STUDY 1   Classroom multimodal literacy practices

Simon teaches an ICT and literacy class for ESOL students. Some of the students have already dropped out of mainstream ICT classes because of their unfamiliarity with the individualized workshop approach to teaching taken by their former ICT teachers. Others have previously tried to enrol on such courses, but were not allowed to join, being told by their ICT teachers that they need to develop their literacy skills first. Part of the rationale for Simon's course is to enable students to gain the reading skills required to understand the instructions of the ICT examinations that are the assessment aim of the course. As Simon explains:

> It's not so much about ESOL and the kind of survival curriculum-esque English. It's about developing reading skills for the purpose, which is to read the kind of exam materials that are handed out by different examining boards.

Simon believes that there is a need to develop students' literacy skills while studying ICT, and to address the literacy needs to help people pass the ICT course. The American applied linguist Mark Warschauer, who has written much about literacy and new technology, describes how English is a tool for using computers and the internet, rather than ICTs being a tool for helping learners to learn English. In 2001, Warschauer said:

> Just ten years ago … it was very common for those involved in CALL [computer-assisted language learning] to say that 'A computer's just a tool; it's not an end in itself but a means for learning English.' … Yet earlier this year, an English teacher in Egypt told me this, and this is a real quotation from a real teacher: 'English is not an end in itself; it's just a tool for being able to use computers and get information on the Internet.'
> Warschauer 2001: 4

Simon's stance is subtly different from Warschauer's: he views English literacy and ICT learning as carrying on in parallel and in a complementary fashion. Yet like Warschauer, Simon knows that it is increasingly difficult to consider literacy separately from the technologies of electronic literacy.

Simon makes full use of multimedia and video in his lessons. He posts all the materials on to his college's web-based Virtual Learning Environment (VLE), accessible out of class, before the lesson; students prepare for the lesson by reading, watching, and listening to the materials that they are going to discuss in class. Materials are of a very high quality, and include a range of visual and audio multimodal resources in a variety of formats, and from an array of sources. Students' focus is clearly on the ICT side of the syllabus, as they all harbour ambitions to pursue careers in ICT. So while students are also aiming for a general literacy qualification, literacy has an ICT focus, and specifically, a focus on enabling students to cope with the demands of reading instructions on the ICT examination papers. The result of this approach is that these students' reading skills have developed in advance of their other skills. However, their reading ability is particularly strong only in the technical genres relating to ICT: they face the same difficulties that most ESOL students face when tackling context-specific and culture-bound reading material.

Simon's philosophy of learning is evident in his approach to ICT and the multimodal and multimedia materials used in his class. He takes the view that many people learn better through audio and visual channels. Multimodal learning in his view is a more effective route to learning, memorization, and retention of information than the monomodal input from textbooks, for example. His approach is influenced by reflection on the way he himself learns best, and by Richard Mayer's work on learning with multimedia (Mayer 2000, 2005). Mayer's central argument is that people can learn more deeply with words and pictures than with words alone. This view is reflected in what Simon himself says about learning:

> *Reading and writing are very much artificial skills as opposed to speaking and listening, and the traditional way in which we teach reading and writing does a disservice to a great number of people who don't naturally learn through paper-based means. Multimedia and multimodal methods seem to me to be a much more natural way of learning by exposing people to audio counterparts to written materials. There is a way to facilitate numerous learning cues, numerous paths into memory and memory retrieval. We tend to remember more what we see and what we hear than what we read. Me in particular, I forget a lot of what I read but if what I read is reinforced by audio and visual I find that personally that helps me to retain a great deal more. And I think that is typical of many people.*

This multimodal approach to teaching is very popular with students, who recognize that they might possess learning styles that are more oriented to the visual, and that the course caters for these. As two students in Simon's class say:

> *[Using ICT] is a very good idea because sometimes I like to watch something more than reading. It is exciting to see something and you can keep it in your mind more.*

> *Well the first time when I use computer I felt I can take just by eyes all of them. When I learnt before I didn't learn by writing and reading and studying, just learn by eyes, looking after teacher, and what he doing and I done also.*

Computer-mediated communication (CMC)

Susan Herring, a writer on computer-mediated communication, defines CMC as: 'communication that takes place between human beings *via* the instrumentality of computers' (1996: 1). That definition encompasses not only text-based communication such as email and text-based chat, but also visual and verbal modes of communication. In the early days of CMC, it was purely text-based, and there was quite a neat distinction between synchronous and asynchronous CMC. Asynchronous CMC, for example, in the form of email, does not require people to be online at the same time to interact, while synchronous CMC, for instance text chat, takes place in real time, with participants online simultaneously. With advances in technology, CMC now includes visual and verbal modes of communication, using web cams and microphones for video and audio chat. Mobile technology has meant a blurring of the distinction between computers and mobile phones, with the same gadget now capable of performing functions once requiring both devices. CMC also makes use of the interactive dimension of the www: CMC today includes communication on web logs (blogs), interaction on social networking sites such as *My Space* and *Facebook*, audio and video podcasting, as well as communication in graphics-based virtual worlds like *Second Life,* where textual or even verbal interaction is not necessarily paramount.

Because of their relative accessibility, email and synchronous text-based and audio chat are popular with ESOL students. These forms of CMC are particularly appropriate for the creation and maintenance of friendship ties. Communication via email has in many cases replaced letter writing, and the popularity of internet chat and messaging using text, voice, and video is not in doubt. So in language learning and teaching, the use of CMC is well-suited to quite informal activities which focus on the creation and maintenance of social and community ties, to discussions and debates, and to role play and other play-focused activities. Some ESOL teachers are involved in tandem learning and key pal (analogous to pen pal) projects, where students in geographically separate classes communicate with one another in online collaborative activities.

ESOL students' use of email and messenger out of class: two examples

Of course students' electronic literacy practices include the use of CMC out of class. Email and real-time text-based and audio chat programs are often used to maintain contact with people who are distant from them. Here, two part-time intermediate level ESOL students in England, Teuta and Olivia, use CMC to keep in contact with distant family and friends.

Teuta uses CMC with her friends and relatives in Kosovo. She and her parents left Kosovo when she was a teenager. They moved to England, where Teuta got married, aged 16, to a Kosovo-born British citizen. Her parents' claim for asylum was turned down soon after, and they were deported. She says: 'After I married, one year later, the Home Office sent my family back to country so just me in here now. With my husband and his family.' Teuta, now 23, lives with her three children, her husband, and his parents. Teuta has a demanding caring role; as well as young children to look after, she also cares for her aging and ill parents-in-law.

Teuta uses email and the synchronous CMC program *MSN Messenger* to keep in contact: 'I talk on MSN with my family, my friends.' She has a computer and broadband internet access at home, but access is more difficult for the friends and family in Kosovo, who rely on other friends and on visits to the internet café in their town. She and her friends use both English and Albanian when they use *MSN Messenger*. This reflects an interesting trend. It is not surprising that multilingual participants in online conversations might use English as a lingua franca, given the current status of English as a global language. What is more curious is why Teuta and her friends, all Albanian-speaking Kosovans, would also use English in their online communication. This online multilingualism is explained by Teuta's seven-year residence in an English-dominant country, and by her friends' association of English with online communication.

Olivia too has pressing personal reasons for using CMC and the internet. She is an asylum seeker from Zimbabwe, a single mother with a six-year-old son, who has lived in the UK for five years. She has another son, now aged 11, who she had to leave in Zimbabwe when she fled the country. Because of her immigration status in the UK, her eldest son is not allowed to join her. This son attends a boarding school in Zimbabwe, but spends the school holidays with a cousin in South Africa. In a discussion with a researcher she describes the situation concerning her eldest son.

I=interviewer, O=Olivia

I How often are you in contact with him?

O Only during school holidays, because my cousin who is in South Africa now, he took him to the boarding school to hide him. So when the school is closed they take him to South Africa, that's where I manage to contact him.

I So he spends his school holidays in South Africa, then goes back

O To the boarding school and I'm not allowed to phone the school.

I Is he OK?

O To me I think he's not OK because he's young, he needs a mother's love. He's eleven. He's been on his own for five years.

I And you haven't seen him?

O No.

Olivia describes a range of electronic literacy practices. For her, ICT and CMC have opened up many possibilities. She can watch the news, communicate with people abroad, and check for updates from the immigration authorities. Her only contact with her elder son is by phone and via email. She uses email with her cousin in South Africa who looks after her son during the school holidays:

I And what about email? Who do you email?

O Oh, my cousin, I tried to send email to my cousin he's in South Africa, in Lesotho, and he replied and said, oh I can send email.

I Have you emailed anyone in Zimbabwe? Can you email there?

O I haven't emailed anyone in Zimbabwe, only my cousin in South Africa.

Although both Olivia and Teuta are in a different country from other members of their families, they still manage to maintain a connection through an electronic network, however tenuous. Email, messenger programs, and internet telephony using audio chat programs and Skype, as well as more traditional letter writing, enable the maintenance of important ties, even when people are radically separated from friends and family. Unlike letter writing, however, CMC creates new globally-spread social spaces. Users can inhabit these virtual spaces through their electronic literacy practices. Thus they are separate and distant in real life, but in the online world they can share an intimate and real-time connection.

ESOL, ICTs, and globalization

Chapter 1 commented on the spread of English as a global language. The current importance of English as the language of online communication could be said to have an economic basis associated with the commodification of language, just as a functional view regards literacy in general (see Chapter 6). The dominance of English online is actually on the wane, however. David Graddol (2006: 45) suggests that the proportion of English online has been overestimated. He says: 'What began as an Anglophone phenomenon has rapidly become a multilingual affair.' While in the 1990s, an estimated 80 per cent of internet traffic was in English, this figure had fallen to 50 per cent in 2007 as internet access grew in other parts of the world, as English-dominant countries became more multilingual, and as technological advances allowed for the expansion of operating systems and web page authoring software in non-Roman scripts. Such figures are of course difficult to estimate accurately; on one hand, non-native speakers increasingly use English and combinations of English and other languages online, and on the other hand, electronic translation tools become ever more sophisticated.

A slightly different position is argued by Mark Warschauer, who suggests that as short-term advantages of English as the language of the internet decrease, so the long-term position of English becomes more entrenched and established.

This is because English was already the de facto global language before the creation of the internet. The internet, maintains Warschauer, requires a global language by the very fact that it enables global communication. Furthermore, he says (2003: 98) that: 'A mutually reinforcing cycle takes place, by which the existence of English as a global language motivates (or forces) people to use it on the Internet, and the expansion of the Internet (and online English communication) thus reinforces English's role as a global language.' People will use their own language for local communication, but will be obliged to use English for global communication.

An example of contemporary global English language use lies in the literacy and language learning experiences of an individual ESOL student who has moved from one geographical area to another and has gained competence in the skills of electronic literacy.

CASE STUDY 2   Reza

Reza is an Iranian student in an intermediate ESOL class who also follows an ICT course. Still aged only 19, he left Iran alone in his mid-teens, and after a year in Greece, came to the UK three years ago. He did not learn to read and write his primary language, Farsi, but did learn some Greek. His first engagement with formal literacy learning was when he enrolled in a beginners' ESOL class on his arrival in England. He has progressed remarkably quickly; although he is still only in his third year of study, he has passed ICT and literacy exams at intermediate and upper-intermediate level. He has now enrolled on a course to prepare him for university entrance, and his ultimate aim is to study architecture.

Computers play an important role in Reza's life. He uses them a lot at college, and to do college-related work at home. He is particularly interested in website development and computer-aided design. His social internet use is also highly developed, and he is heavily involved in a range of socially-oriented electronic literacy practices. Computer technology, and what it allows for, is in fact central to his way of life:

> I have a computer at home. I use for study, I use for chat and for Photoshop to change the picture and to get design or something like that, I use Microsoft Office for writing a letter, I use email also to send an email for friends family or any teacher, I use internet to get for sport, news, a lot of things.

Exactly how central ICTs and electronic communication are in his life can be seen from this comment:

> Sometimes when I sit on the computer I forgot to go to eat. I spend five or six hours on the computer, just to go there and come here and open that one, you go deep, deep.

Because some of his electronic literacy practices relate to his college courses, he emails friends, teachers, and his student colleagues to get information or to help with problems associated with his work. But most important for him are the relationships he has developed while engaging with CMC, particularly in the chat rooms of the internet chat service *Paltalk*. In these chat rooms and other virtual spaces, he makes and maintains close friendships, often sharing and chatting about music, using voice and video technology as well as text-based chat. He and his friends coordinate their meetings in *Paltalk* using *MSN* and *Yahoo Messenger*. His online friends are globally spread, many of them in the United States, and communication is normally in English. He regards his online communication as being beneficial to his English language learning.

> We have a chat room to listen to each other and to asking them questions and making new friends in chat room. Typing and voice also. I have a lot of friends in United States as well [laughs]. I saw them as well because you can open video camera web cam. I have a web cam. For example I like music I cannot find here. They gave me the music or pictures and this is good for improving English. That's very good. It help me. I spend a lot of time on the internet. They are my best friends. I cannot leave. You can meet the people from Leeds or the people from Canada or London or everywhere.

His internet use is typically polyfocal, attending as he does to more than one thing at a time. His CMC use is also at times beyond the capabilities of his computer and internet connection.

I=interviewer, R=Reza

I When you are using the computer you have messenger and Paltalk. Do you have other things at the same time?

R Yahoo, Skype. Skype is new and sometime I listening music. If I don't like this music I have Real Player and Media Player.

I All going on at the same time maybe five or six different things?

R And sometimes my computer is stop. What can he do now? I have to switch off the computer and restart the computer.

As a refugee who arrived in the UK as an unaccompanied teenager, and whose political status has yet to be fully determined, Reza's status could be regarded as quite marginal. But online, he is a central participant in a globally-spread web-based community.

Eva Lam (2000) writes about Almon, a migrant from Hong Kong to the USA. In her case study, she notes that Almon's electronic literacy skills advanced to the extent that they '… enabled him to develop a sense of belonging and connectedness to a global English-speaking community' (Lam 2000: 76). The same could be said for Reza. The examples of Reza and Almon raise questions of the very nature of 'nativeness' and what it is to be a 'native speaker' of English on the internet. Reza's electronic literacy skills are clearly ahead of those of many native speakers. In this respect he is a more competent communicator as a 'non-native speaker', than a 'native speaker' would be under the same circumstances. Case studies such as Reza's also raise questions about the relative status of English in online and offline communication. In 'real life', Reza struggles to overcome the gatekeeping devices of an assessment framework and literacy tests as well as the political hurdles of naturalization, and he is thus still somewhat marginalized. Yet in the virtual world, his status as an ESOL student and a migrant is no hindrance to his playing a central role in an English-speaking online community.

ACTIVITY 4   Electronic literacy practices

Carry out a survey of your students' out-of-class electronic literacy practices.

What range of activities do they participate in? These might include:

- surfing the www for news and information
- writing letters using Word
- using internet chat and messenger
- sending and receiving emails
- Skype-casting, and using video and audio CMC
- blogging
- social networking using sites such as *My Space*
- communicating in virtual worlds such as *Second Life*
- playing online and video games

What languages do they use?

Inequality and the information poor

Whether the motivation to participate in online communication in English is primarily economic or social, ultimately questions of access inevitably arise. For ESOL students, simple access to the hardware of ICTs and to connections to global networks is frequently denied, through cost and a lack of availability. There is concern, says David Graddol (1997: 39) that: '… unequal access to information technologies will create new distinctions between the information poor and the information rich'. Such distinctions are commonly termed the 'digital divide'. The concept of a digital divide between those who have access and those who do not is superficially a helpful one. The situation is often more complex than it is painted, however. Commentators on access to new technology propose a shift of focus away from the question of simple access to technology and towards the social circumstances of its use.

Mark Warschauer, in his book *Technology and Social Inclusion*, suggests five ideological reasons for criticizing the dichotomy implied by the concept of a digital divide, which can be summarized below:

1 The concept of a digital divide attaches overriding importance to the physical availability of computers and connectivity.

2 The implication of a digital divide is of a bi-polar split (the *haves* and the *have nots*).

3 The concept is patronizing: it encourages a stereotyping of disconnected social groups by characterizing them as being on the wrong side of a digital divide.

4 The concept implies a chain of causality: lack of access harms life chances.

5 The overemphasis on computers and connectivity provides a poor roadmap for using technologies to promote social development.

Warschauer proposes an alternative and more participatory framework to that of the digital divide. Rather than attempting to lessen a digital divide which emphasizes hardware and connectivity, he argues for a consideration of ICTs as they relate to social inclusion, whereby: '… individuals, families, and communities are able to fully participate in society and control their own destinies, taking into account a variety of factors related to economic resources, employment, health, education, housing, recreation, culture, and civic engagement' (2003: 8). Access to new knowledge using ICTs (rather than access to ICTs themselves) is seen as vital for social inclusion. But it remains the case that to gain access to new skills and knowledge using ICTs, students have to have some sort of access to those ICTs themselves.

The case study below shows how one ESOL teacher and her students use ICTs in their lessons. It demonstrates some of the barriers that have to be overcome for the effective development of the students' electronic literacy skills, and their full engagement in electronic literacy practices.

CASE STUDY 3 ICTs and the myth of autonomy

Teachers may wish to integrate ICTs into their lessons in response to a perception that this is useful and important in the modern world, and also to promote the idea of self-access learning and the promotion of learner autonomy. Claire, an ESOL teacher and manager, is introducing ICTs into her teaching for the first time, and an outline of some of the difficulties she and her intermediate level students experienced illuminates many of the barriers to access which ESOL teachers and students face more generally.

Claire is by no means an ICT expert. However, she wishes to systematically integrate ICT use into her lessons, wanting to 'lead by example'. This has been possible because her centre has a suite of computers, she has access to a mobile computer and data projector, and also to high quality technical assistance from another ESOL teacher who happens to be the ICT facilitator at her college. ICTs are mainly used as a revision tool in her lessons. Work introduced and practised in class over the past week or two is integrated into teacher-authored computer-assisted language learning (CALL) materials that Claire herself writes for revision and practice during the hour or so a week the students are using the ICT suite at the centre. Claire has modified her approach to CALL material design through trial and observation of students at work. With the help of the ICT coordinator, she made a principled decision to keep her own CALL materials as simple as possible. She describes a tendency among students not to read the text on the screen, preferring to navigate quickly through the pages:

> *One of the things is the screen, they won't always read it very carefully. You can have this great descriptor about what you want them to do, very clearly, and I know they could understand it but they don't read it. And it's the same with me, you know, you just don't, do you? So if they're not going to read it all there's no point having it, and I can't personally run round eighteen computers getting them to read it all. So it's got to be really really basic and clear.*

Students in Claire's class are motivated to work with ICTs, enjoy and appreciate being able to use ICTs in their English language learning, and see the value of computers in their lives. This Palestinian student's experience will be familiar to any computer novice who has school-aged children:

> *I like computer because it's very important for me and for my family. Now my son is 11 year. And he should know them for information for computer. But I didn't have any chance to learn for computer. We do many practice, you know, to computer class, here, with Claire, and I think I do well, you know, and because of this I like it.*

Claire's experience shows that for integration of ICTs in class, it helps for students to be within some sort of structured learning environment, and at a centre with a high level of ICT provision.

> *Here we are in a college with quite a lot of equipment and all sorts of technical wizardry and it's not been that easy for us, has it? And put yourself in a community centre, I mean any of the community centres that we work out of, there's no technical support on site and the hardware just is not up to it.*

Despite the difficulties of using ICTs in ESOL teaching, teachers might also wish to encourage ICT use among their students out of class, for example to access distance or support materials, to do research on a topic using the internet, or to use email or a messenger program to contact their teacher and colleagues. Activities such as these are often carried out in the name of promoting student autonomy. There is, however, a big difference between students wanting to access the technology for learning out of class time, and actually being able to. Out-of-class access is problematic for Claire's students on a number of levels. Teachers often find that students cannot get online to gain access to material, and the reasons for this can be complex. Barriers to access include simply logging on to a site, which in some cases is very demanding—perhaps too demanding—for many students. The interface design may be difficult to navigate, the site students are trying to gain access to could be unavailable, or they might enter their login details incorrectly. Access to technology depends heavily on literacy skills, including the ability to copy and type correctly. Most frustratingly, there is no one there to support them when things do go wrong. A result is that students, trying unsuccessfully to gain access to internet sites and web-based virtual learning environments, have lost confidence, as Claire describes:

> *They need classic things like logging on. Another of them came to me yesterday, she'd tried to log on from home onto Blackboard and she couldn't and that's a total of six or seven of them have tried, I'm delighted that they've tried, one or two of them regularly do now. Other people have had problems and it's a real shame because they've gone away with enthusiasm, they've gone away identifying it as something that might help them to learn, they've identified it as something they've wanted to do, they've had the energy to turn on the computer, and then it's blipped and they haven't got on. And they may not have got on because the site might have been down, you know, and they won't have known that. They may have struggled because the interface was not one that they were familiar with. They may not have got on because they'd put in their password incorrectly. Each of those things, there's so many things that could go wrong, aren't there? That's really sad, that's really awful. And there's nobody at home to say 'try this, try that.'*

Students might feel they are under pressure to buy their own computers. Claire however discourages this, knowing as she does the levels of poverty and destitution many of them suffer. She describes how shocked she was when she found out that one of the students in the class had bought a computer, and suggests strategies which avoid having to do this:

> *I was appalled when she said she'd bought a computer. And I knew that it wouldn't work. I knew. I mean if I tried to get onto it at home without anybody to help me and without knowing what I was doing it wouldn't work. I was absolutely appalled. So I knew that the next time the thing to do was just to say to students, 'Do not go out and buy a computer.' It's incredible. 'Just don't do it. Go to a library, try to access it from a library, go to the learning centre at the college, just try in a few different places and practice. Go to a friend's house and do it from a friend's house.' Because you know, it's not so essential, it's not so critical.*

There are clearly a number of obstacles to the use of ICTs by ESOL students in and out of classrooms. Many teachers do not possess the competence (or the confidence) to use ICTs systematically and usefully in their teaching. Compounding this is the lack of access to an expert guide when trying to integrate ICTs into their teaching. Not every teacher can call on the help of a more knowledgeable or experienced colleague who can guide them through the difficult early stages of classroom ICT use. Some students are unable to sit in front of the screen for long periods of time; many complain of headaches when they do. And simply logging on and getting started with computers in class can take some time, time which for many ESOL students is precious and limited.

Conclusion: electronic literacy and communicative competence

Chapter 6 described different ways of thinking about literacy: as a set of autonomous skills and as literacy practices situated in their social contexts. In this chapter we have seen that networked computers play a role in reshaping the terrain of literacy for ESOL, both in the skills needed and in recognition of the range of literacy practices that electronic communication now allows. It has become common to refer to electronic literacy: the range of skills and abilities needed to use the new technologies underpinning learning and life in the modern world. However, if the broader view is taken of literacy as extendable situated practices, electronic literacy practices, or electronic literacies, should be considered as elements of a person's and a community's communicative repertoire.

The skills involved in order to read and write are changing. The literacy education theorist Naz Rassool suggests (1999: 202) that:

> … in a world increasingly driven by (a) the need for innovation through research and development (R&D), (b) the multileveled changes brought about in our everyday lives as a result of the nature and speed of technological developments, (c) the volume and range of information available, and its open accessibility, (d) the multimodal features of electronic text as well as (e) its interactive nature, we require significantly more than just the ability to read and write in a functional way.

Communication in general is undergoing remarkable changes, and is becoming ever more complex and multifaceted. In the introduction to her book on electronic literacy Ilana Snyder (2002: 3) calls the current period a 'new communication order'. The new communication order is shorthand for the communicative milieu within which literacy practices, including those associated with screen-based technologies, now exist. Some salient features of the new communication order are the emergence of new types of discourse (for example, email and internet chat), new practices (such as the predominance of polyfocality and multitasking), new types of community (for instance the virtual community which Reza belongs to), and new ways of teaching and learning (as shown in Simon's and Claire's classes). As Snyder (2002: 5) puts it: 'We are learning to read, write, speak, listen and view in different ways as new forms of communication are made possible by technological development.'

Further reading

Technology, teaching, and learning

Levy and Stockwell aim to give information on modern CALL for teachers, researchers, and software designers. Richard Mayer's edited collection of papers explores various aspects of learning with multimedia. Warschauer and Kern's book is an early collection of papers on network-based language teaching.

Levy, M. and **G. Stockwell.** 2006. *CALL Dimensions: Options and Issues in Computer-Assisted Language Learning.* London: Routledge.

Mayer, R. E. (ed.). 2005. *The Cambridge Handbook of Multimedia Learning.* Cambridge: Cambridge University Press.

Warschauer, M. and **R. Kern.** (eds.). 2000. *Network-Based Language Teaching: Concepts and Practice.* Cambridge: Cambridge University Press.

Literacy and technology

Crystal's book is a synthesis of a large amount of research on online English language use. Olson's and Ong's books are both influential and readable accounts of literacy and its relationship with mental processes. Warschauer's book is a critique of the notion of the digital divide, drawing on Warschauer's research on ICTs and education around the world.

Crystal, D. 2001. *Language and the Internet.* Cambridge: Cambridge University Press.

Olson, D. 1994. *The World on Paper: The Conceptual and Cognitive Implications of Writing and Reading.* Cambridge: Cambridge University Press.

Ong, W. 1982. *Orality and Literacy: The Technologizing of the Word.* London: Routledge.

Warschauer, M. 2003. *Technology and Social Inclusion: Rethinking the Digital Divide.* Cambridge, MA: The MIT Press.

Multimodality and new literacy

Three books by pioneers in the study of contemporary literacy and multimodality. These works stress the centrality of visual design in meaning-making.

Kress, G. 2003. *Literacy in the New Media Age.* London: Routledge.

Kress, G. and **T. van Leeuwen.** 2001. *Multimodal Discourse: The Modes and Media of Contemporary Communication.* London: Edward Arnold.

Kress, G. and **T. van Leeuwen.** 2006. *Reading Images: The Grammar of Visual Design* (second edition). London: Routledge.

8 LEARNING ABOUT TEACHING

I don't feel jaded about teaching. I'm still interested and even though I've been teaching all these years I still really like it. I'm still learning and thinking 'that's a good idea'.
ESOL teacher, London

Introduction

Throughout this book we have described the complexity of the work of ESOL teachers and the range of qualities, skills, and knowledge they draw on to respond both to their students and to the demands of their professional contexts. In this final chapter we look at how teachers continue to develop after they have completed their initial teacher training. In particular, we discuss classroom observation—how teachers are judged on their performance—but also how they can learn from each other through peer observation, how teachers engage with theory about language teaching and learning (and how research engages with teachers), and finally, how teachers can investigate their own classrooms through action research. Continuing to develop knowledge about language acquisition and pedagogy is crucial if ESOL teachers are to understand both their immediate teaching contexts, and the wider social and political world in which their work is situated.

For most teachers, the point at which they begin to learn about teaching is in their initial teacher training. New teachers need to develop both a knowledge of pedagogy and the linguistic and discourse features of English. Those who are training for the public sector also need to learn about current policy-driven stipulations which will impinge on their practice. Initial teacher training schemes carry a heavy burden of expectations. Not only do they require new teachers to acquaint themselves with the basic tenets of pedagogy and, in the case of ESOL, the rudiments of English language and literacy, they also need to ensure that teachers are equipped to carry out the particular bureaucratic and politically-motivated demands of the current government or administration. Teacher training programmes are unable to offer more than an introduction to the complexity of ESOL teaching; as most teachers would testify, much of what they come to know about their field they gain *after* their initial training.

Standardized teaching qualifications

As we saw in Chapter 3, teachers of ESOL come from a wide range of backgrounds and have followed different routes into their current posts; this diversity is reflected most obviously in the range of different teaching qualifications they possess. Some teachers have high-level qualifications gained from a background teaching English overseas or in the private sector; others have adult ESOL qualifications, and others hold secondary or primary teaching credentials. This diversity is regarded by many as a strength. However, in the case of England, Wales, and Northern Ireland, inspection results seemed to show that many ESOL teachers were performing poorly or inadequately. Since the inception of the national Skills for Life policy at the turn of the century, there has been a government-led drive to standardize the teacher qualification framework with a view to improving teaching in the post-compulsory sector as a whole. A new set of standards was produced which set out general requirements for teachers as well as subject specifications for literacy, numeracy, and ESOL. This led to the creation of one standard qualification for all teachers in post-compulsory education in England, Wales, and Northern Ireland (see DfES 2004, 2005 for more background on this policy).

Although welcomed by some, the reforms created confusion in the ESOL sector, as teachers were already variously qualified to different levels. For some it meant retraining after many years of teaching and for others their old qualifications had to be validated through recognition schemes. The centralizing tendency of a single qualification brings with it other problems. Any standards created centrally will inevitably reflect the concerns of the current government. As we have shown throughout this book, one of the main concerns of governments in the West with regard to adult learning is the connection between qualifications, employment, and greater economic productivity. Another concern is accountability, evident in practices emanating from 'individualized' learning and the extensive testing of even low-level students. A further concern for governments in recent times is the vaguer notion of integration and social cohesion, which politicians of every hue claim can be brought about by adults engaging in learning. Standardized qualifications run the risk, therefore, of focusing too closely on current political and economic matters at the expense of subject knowledge and pedagogy.

Developing professional vision

Government reforms come and go, as ESOL teachers who have spent time in the sector well know. One thread running through much reform is a discourse of 'professionalism' and 'professionalization'. Such notions, when transmitted 'top down' via policy and reinforced through inspection, tend to view professionalism as an ability to behave in a normative way. That is, the definition of professional behaviour rests on an imposition defined from above and ratified by inspectorial evaluation. Yet, as seen in Chapter 3, as their careers unfold teachers develop their own notions of professionalism and their own values. Thus there is an alternative conception of being a professional, which invokes the notion of 'professional vision', originally developed by the American linguist and anthropologist Charles Goodwin (1994). Baynham and Roberts and their colleagues (2007) describe teachers with professional vision as those who are 'reflective about their practices and work in a contingent and responsive way. They are self-critical, critical of demands that undermine their professional practice and confident in trying out potentially risky activities in the classroom' (2007: 63).

Developing a professional vision requires time and experience, but experience is not in itself a basis for development; in order to trigger a deeper understanding of teaching, practitioners need to expand their knowledge base, explore their practice, and reflect critically upon it. Exploratory or reflective practice helps teachers to see aspects of their teaching which are not necessarily intuitively obvious and helps them make sense of the complex activity that takes place in their classrooms. In the remainder of this chapter we consider several ways that teachers expand their knowledge, reflect on their own practice, and forge their own professional vision, beginning with classroom-based observation.

Observation in ESOL

ACTIVITY 1 Observation of teaching

Here are some situations in which ESOL teachers are being observed. What is the purpose of the observation in each case? Who is learning from the observation? Can you sort these situations into categories?

a   A teacher is observed by her colleague as she teaches the ESOL class they share, as part of a teacher-initiated classroom-based action research project.
b   An ESOL teacher observes a more experienced colleague, hoping to find out new ways of eliciting meaningful talk from students.
c   An ESOL lesson is scrutinized by an inspector during a formal inspection.
d   A manager from another department observes an ESOL class as part of a college-wide self-appraisal process.
e   A teacher trainer watches an ESOL class being taught by a new trainee ESOL teacher.
f   A small group of trainees watch a lesson being taught by an experienced ESOL teacher.

g A researcher studying students' use of ICTs observes a group of ESOL students working in their college's ICT suite.

h An experienced ESOL teacher who is a part-time student on an MA course observes and records a lesson to collect data for a project on the use of ESOL students' expert languages in class.

The examples in the activity above fall into four broad groups. The categories are suggested by the language teacher educator Angi Malderez, in an article on observation in *ELT Journal* (2003).

Teacher development: In this category, teachers observing each others' practice use the opportunity of a shared lesson to talk to each other about particular aspects of teaching. Both the observer and the observed teacher can be the learners here: the observee might benefit from the observer's perspective to develop an area of practice; the observer might benefit more immediately from observing a colleague teach. Examples (a) and (b), and other forms of peer observation, action or exploratory classroom-based research, fall into this group.

Evaluation: Here the observer, often with a managerial or inspectorial responsibility, is watching the class in order to make a judgement: the purpose is for evaluation. The observed teacher's behaviour is right or wrong, or (more usually) graded on a scale of adequacy. Examples (c) and (d) are in this category. The purpose is not primarily to aid the teacher's development, and any learning that might take place is done by the observer and passed on to a higher authority. Example (e) may also fall into this group if the observation is for assessment, as the basis for deciding whether a trainee should pass a course.

Training: The focus of observation here is to help trainees, perhaps on initial teacher training courses, develop 'skilled practitioner behaviour' as they become teachers. The nature and definition of the desired behaviour is decided by someone other than the trainee teachers, perhaps according to teacher training standards. Trainees observe experts or are themselves observed by experts as they attempt skilled practitioner behaviour themselves. This is part of the process by which trainees are taught to 'do it as we do it'; that is, they are encouraged to behave and look like teachers. Feedback will focus on descriptions, interpretations, and evaluations of the lesson led by the trainer, possibly involving other trainees. Examples (e) and (f) belong to this type of observation.

Research: The purpose here is for the observer, a researcher, to generate data which will contribute to the creation of theories. In this case the researcher is the main learner, and 'the focus is initially on generating descriptions and plausible explanations of educational phenomena' (Malderez 2003: 181).

Developmental feedback is not normally given or expected here. Examples (g) and (h) fall into this group.

Observation for 'outside' research (as opposed to practitioner-led action research or exploratory research) is not covered here, but there are some references to research handbooks in the suggestions for further reading at the end of this chapter. Our main concern is with the first two types of observation, for teacher evaluation and development, though much of what follows on observation for teacher development will be useful for teachers of teachers.

Critical issues in observation for evaluation

Observation for the purposes of evaluation in inspections or quasi-inspections can overshadow ESOL teachers' experience, to the extent that these are the only types of observation with which the word is associated. Many ESOL teachers find observations for inspection a time-consuming and stressful activity, and feel that it dominates their teaching and their students' learning to an unreasonable extent. Beyond this, there are a number of significant problems inherent in observations that are carried out as part of an inspection or other evaluative process.

The difficulty of observing teacher behaviour

Observations for inspection focus quite naturally on the observable detail of lessons. Yet much teacher behaviour is either too global or too subtle to be easily observed. 'Global' teaching behaviour relates to a teacher's stance towards their teaching, factors such as their rapport with their students, and the extent to which the students and the teacher understand each other. These qualities may well be missed in an inspection or an evaluation, particularly one which involves a checklist of predefined categories, or one which focuses overly closely on the teacher's lesson plan. Other teacher behaviours are particularly subtle, may happen in the course of ongoing classroom talk, and might not have been noted on a lesson plan submitted to the observer. These behaviours are not easily observed, particularly if the observer is not an ESOL specialist, or does not have deep knowledge of language classroom discourse.

ACTIVITY 2 Observing teacher behaviour

Study this transcript of a stretch of interaction from an ESOL lesson. What is the purpose of the teacher's talk? What learner language is generated by the teacher's talk? How easily would an inspector who is not a language expert find it to notice the nuances of the teacher's use of language evident here?

The lesson is with a low-intermediate ESOL group. This discussion takes place during a pre-reading activity after which students are going to read a text about family life in Morocco. In this discussion a student, Leila, has been explaining that in her country, Somalia, children are expected to look after old people.

T=teacher, L=Leila, S=other student

T what about, I mean, what about the child? Does your child want to do that? Are they happy to do that?

L yes, yes

T yeah? They are?

L my mum

T did you look after her or did she look after you?

L yes

T or did you look after each other?

L each other

T it's quite a difference.

L but it depends, you know how is the er you know very old, no child can look after her, the mum goes, not grandchildren, the old people, I look after her when very old, but when it's a normal person.

S in my country it's

L when she's sixty or fifty-five she's quite young still but she needs some help so she got grandchildren, they help her.

In this extract, the teacher asks the student Leila a series of questions, which at first elicit short one-word or other minimal responses. But by continuing to question the student, she eventually elicits a longer turn. As mentioned in Chapter 5, the output hypothesis in SLA, as developed in particular by Merrill Swain (1995, 2000), supports the idea that this type of longer turn is needed for learning to take place. Since talk is work in the ESOL classroom, criteria for observing talk require an understanding of language processes by inspectors and those who observe and evaluate teachers. Yet very often, particularly in cross-institution inspections, ESOL classes are observed by people whose knowledge of the role of talk in ESOL teaching is minimal. Would a non-expert notice the way the teacher eventually elicited a longer turn from the student? Would they even understand the important pedagogic purpose for her doing so? Moreover, the behaviour here is so unobtrusive and so much part of the contingent minute-by-minute unfolding of classroom talk that it could not have been noted in advance on a lesson plan.

Inspections encourage prescription

A second critical point concerns the criteria that inspectors and other evaluators use to appraise ESOL teaching. What are the bases for their judgements? An insight into this matter was given in an article by an ESOL inspector which appeared in a practitioners' magazine, *Reflect* (Julka 2005). The article notes the types of behaviours and factors which an inspector of an

ESOL lesson in England or Wales would expect to see in a 'Grade 1' (that is, 'outstanding') lesson. These include:

- learners are in charge
- there is a detailed, thought-through lesson plan, with clear aims and objectives shared with the learners
- teachers start by questioning the learners about their previous learning
- the tutor is quick to correct, albeit subtly, errors of grammar and pronunciation
- assessment of written work is rigorous
- grade 1 lessons have a logical structure
- learners are not even aware of language learning
- the lesson is tutor-directed but learner-led
- outstanding teaching methods totally engage all the learners.

Julka 2005: 18–19

In outstanding lessons, then, 'learners are in charge': a bald statement in which is inherent a set of contradictions. Elsewhere in these comments, there is heavy prescription at the level of planning and of lesson structure. For example, outstanding lessons have 'a detailed, thought-through lesson plan, a logical structure', and 'start by questioning the learners about their previous learning'. The 'aims and objectives are shared with the learners' ('shared with' presumably means 'told to' in this case). In an outstanding lesson 'the tutor is quick to correct, albeit subtly, errors of grammar and pronunciation'. Assessment of written work is 'rigorous'. Under such conditions, students are unlikely either to be in charge or to feel they are in charge. Nor are they likely to be 'not even aware of language learning' in lessons which are described paradoxically as 'tutor-directed but learner-led'.

The prototypical Grade 1 lesson in fact orients to a high level of teacher control. Moreover, the emphasis on structure and rigour in planning and 'delivery' hardly allows for the responsiveness to student contributions that learner-led interactions demand. Flexibility and intuitive reactions are frequently required in real ESOL lessons: teachers are often not sure who will attend, and what psychological state they will be in when they do. Perhaps they will be amenable to 'outstanding teaching methods' which 'totally engage all the learners'. Perhaps, however, the fact that they have even managed to come to class at all is to be applauded: total engagement with the lesson is not realistic for all students at all times. Sometimes thorough planning and logical progression of activities must take second place behind the imperatives of students' lives.

On a more abstract level, the article implies a high level of domination by inspectors, an attempt from the outside to control and interfere with what happens within ESOL lessons. In many cases centres are dependent on good grades at inspection to secure funding, and managers and teachers alike are tempted to look to inspection criteria to guide them in their approach to teaching. But should the tail wag the dog in this way? The role of the inspector is not to embark on ESOL lesson observations with preconceived notions of what constitutes 'outstanding'. Rather, they should judge lessons on their merits according to the exigencies of the situation as they find them. There is more than one way to teach a good lesson, just as there is more than one way to learn one. The idea that certain characteristics must exist for a lesson to be considered outstanding gives quite the opposite message. *A priori* decisions by those in an inspection role about what constitutes outstanding teaching behaviour need to be treated with caution. What is more, prescriptive sets of 'outstanding' characteristics may work against the very imagination which draws talented and skilled individuals to ESOL teaching in the first place.

Peer observation for teacher development

Observation of a different kind—peer observation—is one through which teachers can learn from each other. Peer observation has particular benefits. Ruth Wajnryb says in her book *Classroom Observation Tasks*: 'Being an observer in the classroom, rather than the teacher … affords us the freedom to look at the lessons from a range of different perspectives outside that of the actual lesson plan of the teacher' (1992: 7). Addressing the observee, Angi Malderez and Martin Wedell in their book *Teaching Teachers* (2007: 118) say: 'There is nothing more useful for you, when you are trying to improve a particular aspect of your work, than to invite another pair of eyes in (or into) the room to "notice" one or more aspects of what is going on.'

There are many possible patterns and scenarios where peer observation might be useful, the most effective being those in which the motivation for engaging in the activity comes from the teachers themselves:

- A teacher observes another teacher (a peer or a more experienced colleague) 'in response to a perceived need to develop in a particular area' (Wajnryb 1992: 3).
- A teacher in development might ask to observe a more experienced teacher. The less experienced teacher would be the main learner in this case.
- A teacher on an in-service development programme takes part in peer observation as a requirement of their course.
- Two or more teachers together identify an area of their practice which they would like to know more about. They take turns observing each others' classes in a collaborative effort. In this case they swap roles of observer/ observee.
- A teacher has a general interest in processes of teaching and learning, and asks to make some informal observations of a series of colleagues' lessons. The focus of the observations may become refined as they progress.

- Teachers in a department take part in semi-informal but structured peer observations as part of an ongoing action research initiative supported by their centre management.

Peer observation: the pitfalls

Peer observation is part of being a reflective practitioner; teachers reflect and explore each others' practice in a mutually supportive way and with an eye on development. For people new to peer observation, however, there is a danger that they will draw on other observations they have experienced and approach the activity in a judgemental way. It is impossible to avoid some evaluation when observing a lesson but the role of the observer in peer observation is *not* to be evaluative or judgemental. Peer observation should not involve the formal recording and passing on of the observer's judgement; Malderez and Wedell (2007: 118) give four clear reasons why it is crucial not to do this, which are summarized here:

1 You can destroy a trusting relationship a lot more easily than you can build one, and judgements may be perceived as harmful.
2 Your judgement is an outsider's viewpoint and not necessarily helpful.
3 Your judgement may be wrong because you may lack much relevant information. You will not know what is on the teacher's mind, you might not understand the relationships between the teacher and their students, and you might have missed some crucial detail.
4 Neither you nor the observee will know whether the session has been effective until later. That is, until the opportunity arises to observe the impact of some teaching upon students' language behaviour.

Doing peer observation

The ability to see with acuity, to select, identify and prioritise among a myriad of co-occurring experiences is something that can be guided, practiced, learned and improved.
Wajnryb 1992: 1

A fundamental concept in observation is 'noticing'. Whatever the purpose of observation, it involves 'obtaining, and often recording, what we notice, in order to support the elaboration of starting points for further work' (Malderez 2003: 179). Noticing is a skill: people do not generally enter classrooms for the first time and know either what to look for, what to look at, or how to notice. It is difficult to see what is going on in a lesson; classrooms are complex places with many activities co-occurring. It could be said that the main difficulty of observation is the problem of not being able to notice, yet if observers are unable to notice, they are unable to think about what they have observed and therefore cannot learn from their observations. However, as the quote by Wajnryb points out, noticing is something which can be learnt; the references at the end of the chapter give some suggestions of guides which help to do this.

ACTIVITY 3   Peer observation

What would be the implications of inviting a colleague to observe one of your classes? The following sentence completion exercise will help to focus your ideas:

- I would feel OK about having an observer in my class if …
- The aspects of my teaching I would like to know more about are …
- I would like a sympathetic observer to give me feedback on the way I …
- I would prepare for the observation by …
- The most useful way the observer could give me feedback would be …

(Head and Taylor 1997)

Teachers engaging with research

To understand language learning and acquisition, researchers need to know about the cognitive processes involved, about the contexts in which learning takes place and about how language functions in social practice. Most researchers focus on one or two of these aspects and it is unusual for research to cover all aspects of language acquisition. Consequently there is a bewildering array of theories and evidence which language teachers and those who train them can draw on to inform their practice.

The theory/practice 'gap'

There is a persisting belief that a gap exists between language teachers and researchers in SLA. Teachers have certain well-founded reasons to subscribe to this position. The most common reason they give for not engaging with research is lack of time; reading research is hard to fit into busy workloads. Teachers also find that their institutions are not 'research friendly', that is, a lot of their professional development consists of learning about college systems or implementing government initiatives. Therefore those who do wish to read, discuss, and try to act on research often find themselves doing so in isolation. Another cause of the gap is that researchers do not always write in a way which is accessible to people who are not used to reading academic writing. This is not just a question of style, or of an inability of academics to write in readable ways. Researchers and teachers belong to very different domains, each with their own discourses, practices, and demands. For example, researchers have to fulfil requirements imposed by their universities to publish in peer-reviewed academic journals. Most of these are not written for teachers, although they may be about teaching, and are more often than not literally inaccessible to teachers because they are available only through university library subscriptions. In his article 'Revisiting the gap between SLA researchers and language teachers', David Block writes that we should not ignore:

> *the physical and psychological space which separates practitioners around the world from academics who are currently not teachers of English as a foreign or second language themselves and above all who do not live and work in conditions which are even remotely similar.*
>
> 2000: 133

Many researchers share an anxiety about the theory/practice divide and believe that it is essential to close it wherever possible. There are signs that bridges are being built between research and practice and that the gap is not as wide as it sometimes seems. More SLA researchers are concerned with producing theories which are of some value to the 'real' world, or at least the worlds of language classrooms. In her paper 'Classroom SLA research and second language teaching' (2000), Patsy Lightbown recalls that in 1985 she had concluded that SLA research at that time 'could not serve as the basis for telling teachers what to teach or how' because 'most of the research had not been designed to answer pedagogical questions' (2000: 431). Revisiting her 1985 paper in 2000, however, she found much research had been published in the interim which did address both SLA theory and its pedagogical application. There has recently been a move in SLA away from the narrow confines of the classroom towards researching language learning in its social, cultural, and political contexts (see Block 2003, for an overview). This body of research is particularly interesting and useful for teachers of migrants to English-dominant countries in that it deals with issues of identity and inequality and how language learning is affected by these.

Research and practice: a mutual dialogue

There are many vital reasons why researchers and practitioners need to bridge the gap and communicate with each other in a mutual dialogue. For a start, despite what we have said above, most SLA researchers are not interested in producing theories which have no application in the real world; they need to know whether and how their theories translate to classroom settings and whether theories claiming universality apply in diverse contexts. On the other hand, teachers need to know about research in order to understand what underpins the teaching methodologies and classroom practices they encounter in their teacher training and in their text books and curricula. Although most SLA theories are still evolving, and are therefore contested, there are some basic tenets about which much research seems to be in agreement. Knowledge of these can inform teaching on a very practical level.

Take, for example, the theory that 'there are predictable sequences in L2 acquisition such that certain structures have to be acquired before others can be integrated' (Lightbown 2000: 442). It seems that many linguistic features are acquired according to a developmental sequence and that 'although learners' progress *through* a sequence may be speeded up by form-focused instruction, the sequence which they follow is not substantially altered by instruction'. It follows then that there is little point in focusing too much on accurate production of forms which learners are not yet ready to acquire. Despite this, many ESOL teachers still concentrate anxiously on verb morphology, drilling their students to produce, for example, the 's' on the end of third person present tense verb forms or '-ed' endings in the past simple tense, and become frustrated when their students seem to forget them from one lesson to the next. There are several other strong generalizations derived from SLA which ESOL teachers should be aware of, summarized in Patsy Lightbown's (2000) paper or in the book *How Languages are Learned* (2006), co-authored with Nina Spada. Chapter 1 of Kathy Pitt's *Debates in ESOL* (2004) also includes a discussion of the search for universal language learning characteristics.

Research as 'common sense'

It is also informative and helpful for ESOL teachers to know when and how current theories came about and what came before them. Often, teachers' knowledge about their work seems like 'common sense'; in fact this is a frequent response from teachers to much SLA or classroom-based research (and indeed from many people to research in general). However, most knowledge was not always just common sense but emerged from theory building at the level of research, entered into a particular domain, and gained currency as more and more people subscribed to it. Teacher trainers need to place current theories about teaching in their historical context to show that what is regarded as old fashioned or outmoded today was at one time itself common sense. Thus, in the beginning of the last century it was common sense that people learnt languages through translation and studying literary texts. In the 1960s it was common sense that people learnt languages through drilling and repetition in methods such as audiolingualism, an idea which was contested a decade later by the rise of Communicative Language Teaching (CLT), in which it seemed absolute common sense that people learn languages by exposure to comprehensible input and plenty of opportunities to interact.

Of course, there are ideas which are common sense to some people and not to others and in some settings and not others. One example of this is the use, or not, of students' expert languages in the language classroom. Some people—teachers and students—believe that English should be the only language used in class because in this way the amount of time using the language is maximized. Others believe that expert languages are a valuable resource and that judicious use in the classroom aids comprehension of the target language. There is evidence for both these arguments in different fields of research; for example in some versions of CLT there is support for exclusive use of the target language, whereas in the field of bilingual education this is clearly not the case. This example points to the need to read and evaluate research critically and from more than one source.

Another issue to bear in mind is that theories do not necessarily become 'common sense' even when the evidence for them is solid and reliable. Most knowledge is disputed, and the theories and knowledge that come to prominence and gain prestige as common sense sometimes do so because those who espouse them have the power and influence to make them dominant. In fact some ideas which have currency in education seem to ignore the complexity of academic debates altogether, as the case study on SMART targets (below) suggests.

It follows that knowledge of the main theories underpinning their practice will help teachers and teacher trainers evaluate and critique new policies which are imposed upon them from above, especially those which seem to have little grounding in empirical research. In fact one of the frustrations for many ESOL teachers is not that they lack knowledge of theory but that their knowledge is undermined by policies introduced by politicians and civil servants who know less about their field than they do.

CASE STUDY 1 Not so SMART

The example we use here is one which stirred controversy in ESOL teaching in the years after the inception of Skills for Life in England, Wales, and Northern Ireland, that of the Individual Learning Plan (ILP), in particular the imposition of what are known as SMART targets. ILPs have become a central part of ESOL teaching since 2001, and how to write one now features on all teacher training programmes. They have been promoted tirelessly by the Government and inspectorates for years, but are far from accepted as 'common sense'. The reason for this is that many ESOL teachers know they have no basis or standing in theories of language learning and acquisition. There is no evidence to show that students learn more and better with an ILP or without one. As one ESOL educator and writer commented:

> It is this idea that, somehow, that they are good practice, and I feel—and I am sure that everybody around this table is thinking the same—that there is no evidence to show that they improve learning or don't. I mean, they might, but do we know? And I think that is what really exasperates me, the way that they have been kind of taken on as the gold standard, for no reason.

The ILP has been the subject of considerable controversy and resistance in the form of letters to journals, workshops and debates at conferences, and across

ESOL networks. Strikingly, teachers in these debates have drawn consistently on their own knowledge of how languages are learnt to resist the ILP, in particular the frequent requirement that students' aims be expressed in the form of SMART targets. SMART is an acronym from the world of management training. It stands for Specific, Measurable, Achievable, Relevant, and Time bound (or, in some formulations, Trackable); to some, this is an acronym that is just too neat to be credible. Most criticism of SMART targets amongst ESOL teachers has been that they encourage disproportionate focus on atomistic aspects of language which are easily observed, at the expense of less tangible, more profound language needs.

Despite the many and varied debates in SLA, there is agreement that language learning is neither unidirectional, nor linear, nor uniformly paced. As Patsy Lightbown and Nina Spada say in *How Languages are Learned* (2006: 189):

> *Learners may use a particular form accurately at stage x (suggesting they have learned that form), fail to produce that form at stage y, and produce it accurately again at stage z ... Language development is not just adding one rule after another. Rather, it involves processes of integrating new language forms and patterns into an existing interlanguage, readjusting and restructuring until all the pieces fit.*

It is also clear that the rate at which development takes place is highly idiosyncratic and varies greatly from person to person. Two teachers here appeal to their theoretical knowledge, as well as knowledge gained through observation of their own students' learning, when making criticisms of SMART targets:

> *Language is a sort of organic, holistic thing. If you work on ten past tenses a week how is that going to help the whole breadth of the language? It's very difficult to pick out little itty bitty measurable targets for a language in general.*

> *Learners are quite inconsistent with their mistakes. So, you know I get three pieces of writing, and I think I could make some SMART targets according to these pieces of writing. But if I look back at the previous ones, they didn't make the same mistakes then, and they keep changing.*

Evidence alone does not make change happen, neither in education nor elsewhere. We are not suggesting that knowledge of theory is sufficient to resist practices such as ILPs, which are imposed by forces representing more powerful interests than those of ESOL students and teachers; indeed there is a strong case to be made for mass resistance to this kind of policy, perhaps aided by union activity. The tension between what ESOL teachers know and the dismissal of their expertise by ministry officials can create a feeling amongst teachers that they are not trusted to carry out their work and that their professional knowledge is of the wrong sort. This risks causing a crisis in the teaching profession as a whole, as well as radical changes in teacher identity. Responses amongst teachers vary from rejection to resignation (of both kinds), or to a kind of 'strategic compliance'. However, what we hope to show through this example is that a knowledge of theory can go some way to helping teachers forge a strong professional vision, form a critical mass with others, identify the sources of their dissent, and so perhaps make their resistance more convincing when they are able to make their voices heard.

ACTIVITY 4 Attitudes towards research

Read these statements about teaching and research. Choose the statement which is most similar to your own attitude to research. Why did you reject the other two?

- Research is not particularly useful. Researchers don't understand my teaching context, and the only way to improve my teaching is through my own experience with students.
- Research can be useful, if it is presented in the form of specific and practical strategies, techniques, and approaches I can readily use in the classroom.
- Research is useful, but I don't need it to give me practical strategies. I want it to challenge my assumptions and help me build my theories about teaching.

Zeuli and Tiezzi 1993

Exploratory teaching and action research

One of the most powerful ways that teachers can bridge the theory/practice divide is by doing their own classroom research in their own contexts, sometimes with academic support and informed by theory, with an aim to expanding their knowledge and forging their own professional vision. When practitioners research their own practice in their own workplace it is known as 'action research'. Action research in education has a long history and its roots can be traced to the work of John Dewey, who argued against the separation of theory and practice in education. There are various types of action research and various approaches to it, and throughout its history it has come in and out of vogue. A useful overview of the history of action research in language education can be found in Anne Burns' (2005) paper 'Action Research, an evolving paradigm?' Proponents of 'grassroots' action research believe that in order for it to be valid, action research must emanate from the real local concerns of teachers. So when action research is implemented 'top down', it risks being viewed by managers as a cheap way of meeting teacher development commitments, or of getting teachers to implement policy efficiently. A further caveat regards the use of action research as part of initial teacher training (ITT); criticism here centres on the fact that many initial teacher training programmes rely heavily on 'reflection' at the expense of theoretical knowledge. Shirley Lawes makes the following point in her paper 'What, when, how and why? Theory and foreign language teaching':

> *ITT today is prescribed by a framework of mandatory competence-based standards, largely of a practical orientation, which places theoretical knowledge on the margins of beginner teachers' professional knowledge. ... Questions of theory are easily ignored because the notion of 'reflection' is seen as key to effective professional development. Reflective practice is the guiding principle in teacher professional development and this signals a shift in the way 'theory' is understood. It is reflective practice rather than theory that underpins both policy and practice in initial training and education of teachers.*
> 2003: 22

These caveats aside, however, there are many reasons why action research remains valuable to teachers. Action research can be a more effective way for teachers to engage with research processes and theory than simple exposure to research findings, and can also lead to changes in the field at a local level and (given the right support) beyond. Some proponents of action research, such as Kincheloe (2003), believe that it should always be carried out as a form of critical practice. He believes critical teacher-researchers have the potential to 'move to a new conceptual terrain, as they raise questions about the situation itself so as not to be confined by the assumptions embedded within it' (2003: 19–20). The point of critical teacher-led research is not just to implement policy more effectively but, where appropriate, to become a form of critical resistance to some of that policy making.

The features of action research

As we have said, there are several models and approaches to action research, and a lot has been written about it; at the end of the chapter we recommend books and articles for those who would like to read more. Some common, basic features of action research are as follows:

- Action research involves problem-posing, as well as problem-solving. It is motivated by a desire to improve and understand practice by changing it. Teachers identify problems or puzzles, that is, gaps 'between the ideal and the reality that people in the social context perceive as in need of change' (Burns 2005).
- Teachers explore and examine their own practice systematically and carefully using the techniques of research, and where possible the support of researchers as mentors.
- Teachers need to collect evidence on which to base rigorous reflection. This reflection should be informed by other academic research in the particular field.
- Action research goes through stages of reflection, planning, action, and analysis which are often cyclical, i.e. the findings of one action research cycle can lead to another.

The stages of action research

Various models of action research propose different stages and label the stages in different ways. Here we represent four stages as if they were rather clear-cut; they are not as fixed and predictable in the real life of the classroom:

Stage 1 Explore and reflect: the process starts with a period of reflection on teaching. This will include discussion, reflection on practice, self- or peer-observation and collection, and analysis of some kind of data. At the end of this stage teachers will identify puzzles which they might wish to explore further.

Stage 2 Plan: teachers then decide on how they are going to explore the puzzle they identified in Stage 1. At this point they need to plan the action they are going to take. This might mean planning whole lessons, trying out new activities, rearranging the classroom, or any other action they want to try.

Stage 3 Act: teachers then start to carry out their plan from Stage 2, for example, teach the first lesson or lessons. They should observe what happens as a result of the changes they are making and modify their plans as necessary. At this stage teachers should collect some kind of data for the next stage.

Stage 4 Analyse and reflect: this stage involves analysis and evaluation of the changes that have happened as a result of the action. At this point teachers can reflect on the puzzles arising from their new data, and (if feasible) start the process again.

CASE STUDY 2   ESOL teachers doing action research: the 'Turning Talk into Learning' project

To illustrate how action research might be done, we draw here upon a project called Turning Talk into Learning (TTL) (Cooke and Roberts 2007a, 2007b). TTL was carried out by five teachers with the support of two university-based researchers. The starting point for the action research was a particular finding from the ESOL Effective Practice project (Baynham and Roberts, et al. 2007) which related to the teaching of speaking. The researchers had seen little work in classrooms which focused on speaking at the level of discourse—that is a stretch of language that is perceived as meaningful and unified (Cook 1989). This provided the team with their first puzzle: how could ESOL teachers focus on students' talk and best help them become more effective at producing longer utterances and at participating in conversations and other interactions? A further, and more challenging question then followed: once students start producing longer utterances, what can teachers do to help them become more effective at communicating what they are struggling to say, that is, how can they turn their talk into learning? Thus the action research was rooted very much in academic work directly relevant to the practitioners, and supported by researchers. The collaboration between practitioners and researchers was a close one, and included teachers in the 'action' and the 'research' parts of the project as well as the writing up and dissemination stages.

Stage 1 Explore and reflect

The team began their action research by reflecting generally on what happens in ESOL speaking lessons. Initial reflections centred on questions such as these:

- In our experience as teacher trainers/managers/observers/colleagues, what kind of work do teachers do in class to get students to talk?
- How do teachers get students to expand their turns at talk/produce longer utterances? (i.e. how can teachers encourage more talk through question, elicitation, and so on?)
- How can talk be turned into learning opportunities? (i.e. what is important about what students are trying to communicate? What would make them sound more understandable? When is the right time for the teacher to turn talk into learning (on-the-spot or later)? What linguistic knowledge and pedagogic know-how comes into play when these decisions are being made?)

Discussion and reflection was an opportunity to explore teachers' knowledge, experience, and intuition about ESOL practice. Among the topics covered during these discussions was the challenge of responding to student initiated talk when teachers have a lesson plan which they feel the need to stick to. This topic became an important theme in the rest of the project. One teacher put it like this:

> *Some tutors miss golden opportunities to extend discussions. As an observer it can be easier to see how you can exploit this but as a tutor you may be worrying about getting through the content, finishing on time, and making sure it fits in.*

Observation of own practice

Then the team moved to analysing data from their own classrooms. They set up speaking activities in their ESOL lessons which took place over a period of two or three weeks and reflected upon what happened. Here the observation moved to specific classroom practices, asking questions such as:

- When did student talk happen in the lesson? What kind of talk was it? (i.e. planned, unplanned, part of another exercise). What was the talk about?
- What opportunities did I provide to my students to produce talk, especially extended utterances? Did they make their own opportunities?
- What were the students trying to communicate?

Stage 2 Plan

In addition to written reflections on lessons the team recorded and transcribed their lessons, or the parts of their lessons in which speaking took place. These were then analysed and used to help the team decide which classes to work with and which puzzles to focus on. For example, for the exploratory stage of the action research, Michael, the teacher of an upper-intermediate ESOL class, set up a series of activities in which students engaged in discussions and debates. He recorded these activities during lessons, and transcribed and analysed some of them. One of the main puzzles for Michael which emerged from his analysis of his lesson transcripts was how to teach his students about argumentation and rhetorical styles, especially arguments in the western tradition. So he settled on the question of how to improve students' argumentation. He then planned a series of lessons focusing on the issues arising from his discussion with the team and from his reading about argumentation. Rather than attempt to get students to change their rhetorical style, which he felt was neither possible nor desirable at this stage, Michael decided to use the actual tape scripts from his exploratory lessons as an awareness raising exercise. In order to guide the students through their analysis, Michael produced a worksheet which included prompts to reflection such as:

* Do you use examples or evidence to support your argument?
* Do you use what other people say to help you argue?
* How do you try to persuade somebody of your point of view in your own language and culture? Are there any rules? Is it different from how people do this in Britain?

Stage 3 Act

Michael found that his students were able to notice different modes of argumentation such as use of hypothesis, generalization, and giving evidence in the form of examples: 'I use examples to develop what I am saying.' They were able to reflect and discuss their own rhetorical styles as well as compare them with other, different styles. There was a discussion about argumentation based on passionate assertion and appeal to authority. Paralinguistic features such as increasing volume, finger pointing, and so on were also commented upon.

Stage 4 Analyse and reflect

Rather than expecting students to adopt a style which is alien to them, or to turn into model 'westerners', the aim of Michael's lessons was to begin a process of awareness about discourse structures and rhetorical styles, thereby arming his students with analytic tools to better understand the interactions they engage in and to better develop their argumentation styles on their own terms. He went on to develop this theme with lessons on argumentation in the 'real world', especially in scenarios in which rhetorical style might be a factor in communication breakdowns with people such as street level bureaucrats.

ACTIVITY 5   Action research

Here are some possible puzzles from ESOL classrooms that might usefully be explored through action research. Reflect on your own teaching and try to add to the list:

- whole class discussions are always dominated by the same students
- students don't wish to read longer texts
- students are over-focused on their exam
- you don't see eye-to-eye with the teacher you share your class with
- you encourage students to use their expert languages to work together but they don't wish to do so.

Conclusion

The Turning Talk into Learning project produced many findings and conclusions about working with student talk, which are discussed in the guides published as a result of this work (Cooke and Roberts 2007a, 2007b). From the point of view of the practitioners, the most important aspects of the experience were the opportunity to work closely with other teachers and be supported by researchers, and the chance to spend a fairly prolonged period of time on one project. The benefits expressed by the team on this project are well documented in the literature on action research (see for example, Burns 2005 for a summary). A lament among ESOL teachers in England, particularly those working in the state sector, is that since they first trained, they have had little time to develop academically as teachers, spending most of their non-teaching time on bureaucracy or training connected to institutional requirements. This is frequently at the expense of attention to the real problems and concerns of teachers and of the fostering of a culture of rigorous practitioner inquiry.

In this chapter we have discussed various ways in which teachers develop their professional vision; we have stressed the importance of their work being grounded in knowledge of the research and theories which underpin it. We have also described some of the obstacles facing teachers in their attempts to expand their knowledge and develop their pedagogy. We end with a message about why it is important to build on that knowledge, however difficult it may seem. Although this chapter has focused on research related to SLA and pedagogy, teachers—in ESOL and in all sectors of education—need to widen their knowledge to include broader principles of education and society. Such knowledge should include 'wider social, political and philosophical issues in education' without which teachers 'will develop a narrow, functional perception of professional knowledge' (Lawes 2003: 24). With a breadth to their knowledge, teachers will understand more clearly that many of the issues affecting them affect others in education and beyond. This will surely strengthen their ability to evaluate critically the policies and frameworks they become subject to in the course of their careers.

Broader knowledge of this kind must begin at initial teacher training, and continue throughout a teacher's career. Without it there is a danger that training and development will not progress beyond the level of classroom competence and teachers will become mere technicians; this is a major feature of the de-professionalization of teaching which leads inevitably to the poor pay and conditions which blight ESOL in many countries. We hope that this book has served in some degree as both a warning against this and as an inspiration for ESOL teachers to draw on their many strengths and qualities to resist it.

Further reading

Observation for teacher development and research

Ruth Wajnryb's book is a collection of activities for observation in teacher development, teacher training, and trainer training. The activities focus on seven areas: learners, language, learning processes, lessons, teaching skills and strategies, classroom management, and materials. It includes guidance on how to record observations. Head and Taylor's resource book also includes sections on observation, as does Malderez and Wedell's book for teachers of teachers.

Head, K. and **P. Taylor.** 1997. *Readings in Teacher Development.* Oxford: Heinemann ELT.

Malderez, A. and **M. Wedell.** 2007. *Teaching Teachers: Processes and Practices.* London: Continuum.

Wajnryb, R. 1992. *Classroom Observation Tasks: A Resource Book for Language Teachers and Trainers.* Cambridge: Cambridge University Press.

Reflective practice and action research

Burns' paper is an overview of the history of action research in language education. Mason presents noticing as a key skill to develop when researching classroom practice. Pollard's textbook for reflective classroom practice is for trainees, mentors, new teachers, and more experienced teachers undergoing continuing professional development. Richards and Nunan's collection of papers emphasizes language teacher education (rather than training), in particular where teachers are involved in developing their own theories.

Burns, A. 2005. 'Action research: An evolving paradigm?' *Language Teaching* 38: 57–74.

Mason, J. 2002. *Researching Your Own Practice: The Discipline of Noticing*. London: RoutledgeFalmer.

Pollard, A. 2005. *Reflective Teaching* (second edition). London: Continuum.

Richards, J. C. and **D. Nunan.** 1990. *Second Language Teacher Education*. Cambridge: Cambridge University Press.

Doing research

These are well-known and very useful handbooks for new researchers. Chapter 11 of Bell's perennial favourite among new researchers covers observation studies. Cohen, Manion, and Morrison's book is now into its sixth edition. Chapter 17 covers observation from a research viewpoint.

Bell, J. 2007. *Doing Your Research Project: A Guide for First-time Researchers in Education, Health and Social Science* (fourth edition). Buckingham: Open University Press.

Cohen, L., L. Manion, and **K. Morrison.** 2007. *Research Methods in Education* (sixth edition). London: Routledge.

APPENDIX
Overseas contexts

Australia and the Adult Migrant English Program (AMEP)

The provision of English to adult speakers of other languages in Australia is described by one of its leading researchers, Anne Burns (2006: 98), as 'privileged on a world scale'. This comment refers to the fact that the provision of English language education in Australia has been guaranteed in law as a right of settlement for new arrivals. The Adult Migrant Education Program (AMEP) provides 510 hours of free tuition to immigrants and refugees in a variety of modes, from formal courses to distance learning, from home tutoring to self-paced learning through Independent Learning Centres. Some providers have also developed online learning programs. Through the Special Preparatory Program, refugees and humanitarian entrants are offered a further 100 hours of provision if they have suffered torture or trauma which could affect their learning. For those between the ages of 16 and 24 years, with fewer than seven years' formal schooling, an additional 400 hours of tuition is available.

ESL in Australia has a national curriculum framework, the Certificates in Spoken and Written English (CSWE) developed by the New South Wales Adult Migrant English Service (NSW AMES), one of the main AMEP providers, and a national research centre which conducts research across the Program, often in close collaboration with teachers. Unlike some other curricula the Australian curriculum is 'text-based'; its theoretical grounding is in systemic functional linguistics and the work of Michael Halliday, which has been highly influential across the Australian education system. Anne Burns writes: 'the overarching orientation is towards the discourse competencies required to undertake a range of spoken and written genres taught through a curriculum cycle based on the notion of explicit or "visible pedagogy" ' (2006: 102).

The AMEP has undergone several major changes over the years. In the 1950s and 1960s it was a textbook-based programme with materials issued centrally from the Commonwealth Government. In the 1970s and 1980s it moved to a classroom-centred negotiated programme with teachers acting as curriculum managers, developing individualized programmes to cater for students' local needs. The 1990s and beyond have seen a move to an overarching articulated curriculum with syllabuses planned at a local level within learner 'pathways'. The pathways differentiate between learning for vocational purposes, further study, and 'community access'. The aim is to keep the pathways flexible so that students can switch between strands. This change came through providers' responses to student demands for greater clarity in their learning programmes and from teachers who were finding the individualized system time-consuming and difficult to implement. Students are placed in the Certificates framework according to their language level, their learning pace, and their educational background. The curriculum was developed through teacher working groups and is reaccredited every five years in response to feedback from across the nation. Students can also undertake courses in language required for citizenship as part of their AMEP learning. The curriculum is now used broadly in corrective services, indigenous education, private providers, and high schools.

Despite its reputation, the Australian system is not immune from the influences and concerns caused by larger global trends. The CSWE curriculum framework was 'developed in a climate of economic restructuring where competency-based training, focused on outcomes, was seen as a way of making education more responsive to the changing demands of labour markets and more accountable to funding authorities' (Burns 2006: 102). The success of the curriculum lies in its flexibility. It states broad learning outcomes but leaves the contextualization of these outcomes in the hands of local providers. However some centralized syllabuses have been developed, including resources to teach language through the topic of citizenship.

The AMEP has problems reaching some sectors of the migrant population and suffers from obstacles familiar to other countries, such as a shortage of bilingual teachers and assistants. There is also the issue that most migrants and refugees do not complete their full entitlement of hours' tuition. New arrivals in Australia are increasingly obliged to obtain employment as soon as possible and AMEP is under pressure to prepare students for the workplace, losing its original focus on settlement.

Further reading and information

For more information on AMEP:

www.immi.gov.au/living-in-australia/help-with-english/learn-english

For information on the research centre of AMEP, based at Macquarie University in Sydney:

www.nceltr.mq.au

Work by Susan Feez explains the Australian curriculum in more detail:

Feez, S. 2002. 'Heritage and innovation in second language education' in A. M. Johns (ed.). *Genre in the Classroom. Multiple Perspectives.* Mahwah, NJ: Lawrence Erlbaum Associates.

ESL in Canada: LINC and Benchmarks

Canada is a country familiar with inward migration: one in five Canadians were born in another country. Each year about 230,000 immigrants arrive in Canada, which has a population of 33 million. In Canada's largest city, Toronto, 42 per cent of the population are immigrants from approximately 170 countries speaking more than 100 languages. This background is reflected in a well-developed English programme for adult new arrivals, who can join English language (ESL) classes under the LINC programme, Language Instruction for Newcomers to Canada. LINC classes are funded by the national government, are available up to intermediate level and are offered through public boards of education, community agencies, and colleges. There are eligibility criteria, however; LINC classes are only available to permanent residents, not refugees or people with Canadian citizenship. ESL classes for refugees and for citizens are coordinated at a provincial or local level, and many people with ESL needs are taught in adult literacy classes.

LINC comes under the umbrella of Citizenship and Immigration Canada (CIC), thereby connecting ESL in law with immigration and citizenship. The fact that LINC classes are federally funded also demonstrates that the national government recognizes its responsibility to provide English (or French) language education for new arrivals, though only those with 'permanent residence' status. There is also a language requirement for citizenship, described in the Canadian Citizenship Act as 'an adequate knowledge of one of the official languages of Canada', and further glossed by the CIC: 'Canada has two official languages—English and French. You need to be able to speak one of these two languages well enough to communicate with people. In other words, you must know enough English or French to understand other people and for them to understand you.'

ESL under the LINC programme faces funding crises familiar to ESOL in other countries; waiting lists for classes can be long, provoking criticism of CIC and its financial investment into language and settlement programmes. For example, in a report entitled 'A system in crisis' (Friesen and Hyndman 2004), researchers at Simon Fraser University in British Columbia had this to say about language provision for migrants:

> ... *immigrants are ... facing growing wait-lists for services thus hindering their settlement and integration process. Being able to speak one of Canada's official languages is one of the most pressing needs consistently identified by*

immigrants. Without being able to speak one of Canada's official languages, immigrants are doomed for underemployment while increasing their chances of facing abject poverty.

ESL class levels are matched against the curriculum for ESL in Canada, the Canadian Language Benchmarks (CLB). These were published in 2000 (Pawlikowska-Smith 2000), and have been used since 1992 in various draft forms (see Norton Peirce and Stewart 1997; Norton and Stewart 1999). The French equivalent in this bilingual country is called *Niveaux de compétence linguistique canadiens*. The CLB is a 12-point scale of language proficiency descriptors, and is widely used to guide ESL teaching and assessment.

The CLB are common across Canada, recognized between provinces. There are global performance descriptors, similar to 'band' descriptors in assessment documents, complemented by a series of 'can do' statements of communicative language ability, broken down into four skills, and framed as items on a checklist. The 'can do' checklist for reading at Level 1 (Stage 1, Basic Proficiency Level 1) has the following descriptors:

I can read the alphabet;
I can read some words that I see often;
I am learning the sounds of letters;
I can read a short sentence with the help of a picture;
I can read name, address, phone number.

As well as being used as a curriculum framework for LINC classes, the CLB are also employed in certain professions. At the school level, different provinces and territories have diverse approaches to language education for children and young adults, some of which are particularly innovative, for example the Multiliteracies Project (see Cummins, *et al.* 2005). Research into ESOL literacy for schoolchildren is forming the basis of a Literacy Framework for the New Economy, which is accompanied by a set of principles for a pedagogy that brings a broad understanding of literacy to children's education and which encompasses multiliteracies and multimodal literacy practices. This move in children's literacy is expected to have a follow-through effect into adult ESOL literacy pedagogy.

Further reading and information

For information on the CLB, visit the Centre for Canadian Language Benchmarks (CCLB) website:

http://www.language.ca

For the CLB itself, refer to:

Pawlikowska-Smith, G. 2000. *Canadian Language Benchmarks 2000 English as a Second Language for Adults*. Ottawa: Centre for Canadian Language Benchmarks. Available online at http://www.language.ca/pdfs/clb_adults.pdf

The theoretical framework underpinning the CLB (2002):

Pawlikowska-Smith, G. 2002. *Canadian Language Benchmarks 2000: Theoretical Framework*. Ottawa: Centre for Canadian Language Benchmarks. Available online at http://www.language.ca/display_page.asp?page_id=257

The new experience of ESOL in the Republic of Ireland

ESOL in Ireland is a relatively new experience. Due chiefly to periods of high unemployment, Eire has been a country of emigration. Piaras Mac Éinrí of the Irish Centre for Migration Studies says (2001):

> *Historically, Ireland has not … received any significant immigration flows. As a relatively poor peripheral European country with strong and sustained emigration, limited employment opportunities and no traditional colonial ties to majority world countries (unlike several other EU member states), little consideration was given to a formal immigration policy.*

In contrast to some countries with a longer history of inward migration, not only was there no immigration policy, but there is no migrant settlement scheme. However, Ireland's population is growing by two per cent a year, attributable to both inward migration and a high birth rate. Figures from the 2006 census show that the largest group of immigrants comes from the UK (over 112,000), followed by Poland (63,000), Lithuania (25,000), Nigeria (16,000), and Latvia (13,000). While ESOL became a concern only relatively recently, it has now reached the attention of policy. On a broad level, the Irish government's *White Paper on Adult Education: Learning for Life* (2000) encompasses ESOL students, and reflects a situation that is similar if not identical to that in England, Wales, and Northern Ireland. Residents, EU citizens, and refugees are eligible for the same access to education and training as Irish citizens. Asylum seekers are not entitled to work but are, however, allowed to join free ESOL and literacy classes. In recognition of the need to address policy issues concerning immigration and social inclusion, Eire now has a Minister for Integration.

Responsibility for coordinating state provision of ESOL as well as research and teacher training rests with NALA, the National Adult Literacy Agency, positioning ESOL firmly within adult education and associating it closely with adult literacy. For example, ESOL students and teachers use the same curriculum framework as literacy students and teachers, a loose student-centred and voluntary instrument called *Mapping the Learning Journey*

(NALA 2005). In response to the *White Paper on Adult Education*, NALA's ESOL Executive Working Group produced a report in 2002 entitled: *Supports and Guidelines for Practitioners in the Literacy Service Working with ESOL Learners*. This document sets out an agenda for ESOL policy and practice, recommending a community-based approach, free ESOL and ICT lessons, a minimum of four hours' ESOL provision per week, and an assessment framework specifically for ESOL. A number of groups contribute to the English language teaching policy and framework, including the Vocational Education Committees (VECs), which are responsible for Further Education provision countrywide. Many VECs now provide teacher training in ESOL.

Other than ESOL classes provided by NALA and the VECs, a number of language schemes for refugees and asylum seekers exist. Notable among these is the provision by Integrate Ireland Language and Training (IILT) (formerly the Refugee Language Support Unit), which has been running intensive language classes for adult refugees since 1997.

Further reading and information

National Adult Literacy Agency (NALA) coordinates Adult ESOL provision in Ireland:

http://www.nala.ie/

NALA's guidelines for ESOL:

National Adult Literacy Agency ESOL Executive Working Group. 2002. *Supports and Guidelines for Practitioners in the Literacy Service Working with ESOL Learners*. Available online at http://www.nala.ie/publications/listing/20030624160824.html

Integrate Ireland Language and Training (IILT) is the foremost provider of ESOL for refugees:

http://www.iilt.ie/

New Zealand: the early stages of a strategy

New Zealand is a country of 4.1 million people, more than one in five of whom were born in other countries. Historically, European migration, principally from Britain and Ireland, has been accompanied by policies which discouraged or prevented immigration from non-English-speaking countries, leading to a population that claimed an English-speaking European or a Maori heritage. A demographic change in the 1950s and 1960s followed a desire for cheap labour; a rise in migration from other parts of the world meant New Zealand became more diverse. Yet the language needs of adult migrants have only recently attracted the attention of policy makers, with the *Adult ESOL Strategy* (2003).

The *Adult ESOL Strategy* is separate from the *Adult Literacy Strategy*, which preceded it by two years, but likewise makes a clear connection between literacy in English and economic development. The Strategy is motivated by the twin concerns of unemployment among non-English-speaking adults and of the language needs of refugees. It draws on the report *Breaking the Language Barriers* (DfEE 2000) which in England and Wales heralded the introduction of a national curriculum for adult ESOL. In New Zealand as yet there is no adult national curriculum framework for English or for Maori, its other official language. *The Adult ESOL Strategy* maintains a traditional distinction made in New Zealand between English for migrants and English for refugees, stating that 'the needs of refugees and migrants differ to such an extent as to warrant strands of their own' (2003: 8). Provision for both groups remains ad hoc, and reliant on the private and voluntary sectors.

Potential migrants wishing to enter the country through 'skilled' or 'business' migration routes face significant language-related barriers. Immigration acts in the 1980s and 1990s brought in a 'points', and then a 'pass-mark' system for migrant eligibility, attached to annually reviewed quotas. And although New Zealand actively encourages migration, English language requirements are stringent. Since a policy review in 2002, principal applicants have to meet a minimum standard of English before they arrive, which for some groups is 6.5 on the IELTS scale, as high as that for university entrance. As with Australia, some categories of migrant with lower levels of English may 'pre-pay' for ESOL classes, which they are expected to attend upon arrival.

The strict English language requirement makes it particularly difficult for non-English speakers to migrate to the country, and since 2002 there has been a downturn in successful applications from countries such as China, Taiwan, and Korea. As the historian Ann Beaglehole (2007) says of the 2002 policy changes, 'New Zealand's immigration regulations remained blind to race or nationality. But there was some evidence that the focus on skills and the high level of English language requirements were leading to a reduction in the number of immigrants from Asia.'

Ten per cent of migrants to New Zealand are refugees arriving via an agreement with the UNHCR, asylum seekers who make claims upon arrival (the vast majority of which are rejected), and Pacific Islanders. Traditionally these groups have relied on voluntary services for English classes. The biggest ESOL provider for refugees is the volunteer-run Home Tutor Service, established in 1992 as a non-government service for Pacific Island immigrants and refugees, which provides one-to-one tuition, group learning, literacy classes, and teacher training.

Adult ESOL provision in New Zealand is characterized, therefore, by wide variation, reliance on the private sector, and for refugees, on volunteer tutors.

And though the Adult ESOL Strategy brings welcome attention to the varied and diverse needs of ESOL migrants to New Zealand, developments from the strategy are in their early stages.

Further reading and information

Information about ESOL in New Zealand can be found on the Literacy Portal:

http://www.nzliteracyportal.org.nz/ESOL/

The ESOL Home Tutor Service website:

http://esolht.org.nz/about/about-us/

An informative article on refugees to New Zealand in the online encyclopaedia *Te Ara*:

Beaglehole, A. 2006. 'Refugees'. *Te Ara - The Encyclopedia of New Zealand* (updated 26 September 2006). http://www.TeAra.govt.nz/NewZealanders/ NewZealandPeoples/Refugees/en

New Zealand Ministry of Education. 2003. *Adult ESOL Strategy* is available online at http://www.minedu.govt.nz/web/downloadable/dl7577_v1/adult-esol.pdf

ESOL for 'New Scots'

There have long been settled ethnic minority communities in Scotland, with corresponding ESOL provision. For several reasons the demand for ESOL classes for adults in Scotland has experienced something of a boom in recent years. Scotland, particularly Glasgow, became host to a sizeable number of refugees and asylum seekers who were removed from London and the south east of England under a programme of dispersal after 2000. The other major rise in numbers came after the extension of the EU in 2004 when workers started to come to Scotland from the new accession states. In addition, the introduction of the citizenship test in the UK applies equally to residents in Scotland and has led to an increase in demand for classes. Finally, the Scottish Executive has an official attitude of actively welcoming inward migration with such policies as the Fresh Talent Initiative.

Since 2000 there has been a growing effort in Scotland to respond to the rising demand for ESOL for the 'New Scots', particularly in the urban centres. Since the extension of the EU in 2004, there has also been increased demand outside the cities in areas such as the Highlands and Islands, where ESOL is less well developed. The Scottish Qualification Authority (SQA) has ratified a full suite of qualifications which, unlike the Skills for Life curriculum in England and Wales, come under the same framework as mainstream Scottish education, with levels entitled Access, Intermediate and Higher. In theory this avoids the connotations of 'second class citizen' which are attached to the supposedly parallel qualification for Skills for Life in England and Wales and the Certificates in Spoken and Written English in Australia. Importantly, the ESOL Higher qualification is accepted as a university entrance level language qualification, which is particularly helpful for school-age ESOL students. In 2004 the Scottish Executive commissioned a survey of all aspects of ESOL demand and provision in the whole of Scotland. The resulting report gave the first national picture of who and where ESOL students are, the potential size of the demand, and the quality of existing provision. This was followed in 2005 by a consultation exercise on the feasibility of a national ESOL strategy for Scotland which cumulated in 2007 with *The Adult ESOL Strategy for Scotland*. The main work of the Strategy initially is to set up a national ESOL panel representing ESOL teachers, students, the main funding bodies, the SQA, employers, and the Scottish Executive. This panel will be responsible for two major policy reviews: a Best Practice in ESOL framework and a national ESOL curriculum group, which will prepare a national curriculum for Scotland.

With its different tradition of education and 'social practices' approach to adult literacy, Scotland has the chance to forge a curriculum which is different in conception and principle to the ESOL core curriculum in England and Wales, and which avoids some of the problems that have attracted criticism there, namely that it is prescriptive and too skills-based. Although Scotland and its government face similar challenges in its ESOL provision when deciding how best to provide adequate education for employment and citizenship, its approach has been generally regarded as 'holistic, inclusive, flexible and learner-centred' (from the analysis of responses to the consultation on the ESOL strategy). Scotland has also the chance to combine its ESOL Strategy with its general language strategy, which covers the maintenance of Gaelic and Scots as well as 'community languages' such as Urdu and British Sign Language (BSL) and the teaching and learning of foreign languages.

This is not to say that some practitioners do not see clouds on the horizon, or that more could not be done. *The Adult ESOL Strategy* places a strong emphasis on individual learning plans as a mode of assessment, which is a concern amongst some teachers who already feel these are too bureaucratic and unwieldy for large classes. Most serious though are the fears over funding and the doubts that this will be adequate to meet the large need in cities such as Glasgow where waiting lists are already very long.

Further reading and information

Information about all aspects of *The Adult ESOL Strategy for Scotland* and the *Strategy for Scotland's Languages* are available on the Scottish Executive website:

www.scotland.gov.uk

Details of Scottish ESOL qualifications are available on the SQA website:

www.sqa.gov.uk

The United States: complexity and fragmentation

The statistics on migration, of both documented and undocumented immigrants, and the need for provision of English for speakers of other languages (ESL in the USA) reveal a picture which is almost overwhelming in its size and complexity. It is estimated that between 1970 and 2005 the foreign-born population in the US tripled, and currently accounts for 12.4 per cent of the population, slightly fewer than 40 million people. Of these, 17 million report themselves to be 'Limited English Proficient' (LEP, a term commonly used in the USA), saying they speak English 'less than very well'. Interestingly, a certain proportion who report as speaking English 'less than very well' is native born. These are people from communities such as Puerto Rican, Native Hawaiian, Pacific Islander, and Native American. Classification as LEP is subjective and self-reported, so is not entirely reliable, but it is safe to say that the number of people needing and wanting to learn English in the US is very high indeed.

Funding for English language classes comes from a mixture of federal, state, local, and private sources and is widely regarded as woefully inadequate to meet the demand; despite rhetoric from US leaders in recent years that people must learn English to be American, federal funding has actually declined since the beginning of the Bush administration in 2000. In 'gateway' states, such as California, which have traditionally received high numbers of new arrivals, more money is provided by the state than from federal funds. In other states, however, where inward migration on a large scale is a new phenomenon, funding and knowledge about ESL is patchy and sometimes non-existent.

On top of the funding crisis, the provision of English language education in the US is generally regarded as fragmented, unstable, and marginalized even within adult education. At state level English language education for adults is spread across a number of sectors and there is no nationally agreed policy or approach to planning or organization or to the qualifications of ESL teachers. Many involved in ESL believe that if it is to be properly funded and achieve higher status professionally, it needs to be organized nationally. A lack of central control is, of course, seen by some as an advantage and there are many examples in the USA of innovatory and progressive programmes rooted in communities which cater to the specific needs of local people. The funding that does exist on a federal level must be accounted for through the National Reporting System for Adult Education. ESL programmes are not funded separately and are therefore subsumed in adult education more generally. This has meant that in order to secure funding ESL programmes have had to adopt a model which is amenable to current trends in adult basic education, which is currently strongly influenced by a skills and phonics orientation towards literacy.

The huge problems facing the ESL sector in the USA must of course be considered against the larger political backdrop in which immigration is one of the most contentious issues of the day and in which language is often a byword for race, class, or ethnicity. There is a widespread public misunderstanding of the length of time it takes to learn a new language and of the obstacles in the way of learning for immigrants who have little access to English-speaking communities. At the same time, public opinion is firmly of the belief that immigrants have a patriotic duty to learn English (which many believe, wrongly, is the national language of the country). People striving to learn English do so in this contradictory climate.

Further reading and information

The Center for Adult English Language Acquisition (CAELA) at the Center for Applied Linguistics:

www.cal.org/caela

For an overview of proposals for a national approach to English language education:

Teachers of English to Speakers of Other Languages (TESOL). 2000. *Adult ESL Language and Literacy Instruction: A Vision and Action Agenda for the 21st Century.* Available online at http://www.cal.org.ncle/vision

National Center for ESL Literacy Education. 2003. *Adult English Language Instruction in the 21st Century.* Washington, DC: Center for Applied Linguistics.

BIBLIOGRAPHY

This list of books, articles, and web resources brings together the works cited in this book and those which have been suggested for further reading.

Adamson, B. 2004. 'Fashions in language teaching methodology' in A. Davies and C. Elder (eds.). *The Handbook of Applied Linguistics*. Oxford: Blackwell.

Apollinaire, G. 1916. 'Il Pleut.' *Sic* 12, December 1916.

Auerbach, E. R. 1986. 'Competency-based ESL: One step forward or two steps back?' *TESOL Quarterly* 20/3: 411–27.

Auerbach, E. R. 1992. *Making Meaning, Making Change: Participatory Curriculum Development for Adult ESL Literacy*. McHenry, IL: Center for Applied Linguistics and Delta Systems.

Auerbach, E. R. 1993. 'Re-examining English Only in the ESL classroom.' *TESOL Quarterly* 27/1: 9–32.

Auerbach, E. R. 1995. 'The politics of the ESL classroom: Issues of power in pedagogical choices' in J. W. Tollefson (ed.). *Power and Inequality in Language Education*. Cambridge: Cambridge University Press.

Auerbach, E. R. and D. Burgess. 1985. 'The hidden curriculum of survival ESL.' *TESOL Quarterly* 19/3: 475–95.

Auerbach, E. R. and **N. Wallerstein.** 2005. *Problem-posing at Work: English for Action*. Edmonton, Alberta: Grass Roots Press.

Barton, D. 2006. *Literacy: An Introduction to the Ecology of Written Language* (second edition). Oxford: Blackwell.

Baynham, M. 1988. 'Action and reflection: The Freirean argument in ESL.' *Language Issues* 2/1: 6–12.

Baynham, M. 2006. 'Agency and contingency in the language learning of refugees and asylum seekers.' *Linguistics and Education* 17/1: 24–39.

Baynham, M., C. Roberts, M. Cooke, J. Simpson, K. Ananiadou, J. Callaghan, J. McGoldrick, and **C. Wallace.** 2007. *Effective Teaching and Learning: ESOL*. London: NRDC. Available online at http://www.nrdc.org.uk

Beaglehole, A. 2006. 'Refugees.' *Te Ara—The Encyclopedia of New Zealand* (updated 26 September 2006). Available online at http://www.TeAra.govt.nz/NewZealanders/NewZealandPeoples/Refugees/en

Beaglehole, A. 2007. 'Immigration regulation.' *Te Ara—The Encyclopedia of New Zealand* (updated 13 April 2007). Available online at http://www.TeAra.govt.nz/NewZealanders/NewZealandPeoples/ImmigrationRegulation/en

Bell, D. M. 2007. 'Do teachers think that methods are dead?' *ELT Journal* 61/2: 135–43.

Bell, J. 2007. *Doing Your Research Project: A Guide for First-Time Researchers in Education, Health and Social Science* (fourth edition). Buckingham: Open University Press.

Bell, J. S. 1995. 'The relationship between L1 and L2 literacy: Some complicating factors.' *TESOL Quarterly* 29/4: 687–704.

Bloch, A. and **L. Schuster.** 2005. 'At the extremes of exclusion: Deportation, detention and dispersal.' *Ethnic and Racial Studies* 28/3: 491–512.

Block, D. 2000. 'Revisiting the gap between SLA researchers and language teachers.' *Links and Letters* 7: 129–43.

Block, D. 2003. *The Social Turn in Second Language Acquisition*. Edinburgh: Edinburgh University Press.

Block, D. 2006. *Multilingual Identities in a Global City: London Stories*. London: Palgrave.

Block, D. and **D. Cameron.** (eds.). 2002. *Globalization and Language Teaching*. London: Routledge.

Borg, S. 2003. *Teacher Cognition in Language Teaching: A Review of Research on What Language Teachers Think, Know, Believe, and Do*. Cambridge: Cambridge University Press.

Bourdieu, P. 1986. 'The forms of capital' reprinted in S. Ball (ed.). 2004. *The RoutledgeFalmer Reader in Sociology of Education*. London: RoutledgeFalmer.

Bremer, K., C. Roberts, M. Vasseur, M. Simonot, and **P. Broeder.** 1996. *Achieving Understanding*. Harlow: Longman.

British National Corpus. Available online at http://www.natcorp.ox.ac.uk/corpus/index.xml

Brown, G. and **G. Yule.** 1983. *Teaching the Spoken Language*. Cambridge: Cambridge University Press.

Burns, A. 2005. 'Action research: An evolving paradigm?' *Language Teaching* 38: 57–74.

Burns, A. 2006. 'Surveying landscapes in adult ESOL research.' *Linguistics and Education* 17/1: 97–105.

Byram, M. and **C. Morgan.** 1994. *Teaching-and-Learning Language-and-Culture.* Clevedon: Multilingual Matters.

Callaghan, J. 2006. 'Methodological reflections on a study of how ESOL teachers construct professional identities.' Unpublished MSc dissertation, University of Leeds.

Cameron, D. 1995. *Verbal Hygiene.* London: Routledge.

Campbell, H., M. Hepworth, and **J. Simpson.** 2007. 'Foundations of literacy.' Presentation at ESOL Research Group, University of Leeds, 20 March.

Campbell, S. 2008. 'Trauma and learning–uptake of ESOL by female victims of trafficking.' *Language Issues* 19/1 (winter): 14–25.

Canagarajah, A. S. 2002. 'Globalization, methods, and practice in periphery classrooms' in D. Block and D. Cameron (eds.). *Globalization and Language Teaching.* London: Routledge.

Canale, M. and **M. Swain.** 1980. 'Theoretical bases of communicative approaches to second language teaching and testing.' *Applied Linguistics* 1/1: 1–47.

Carrier, K. 1999. 'The social environment of second language listening: Does status play a role in comprehension?' *Modern Language Journal* 83/1: 65–79.

Chomsky, N. 1965. *Aspects of the Theory of Syntax.* Cambridge, MA: The MIT Press.

Clarke, J. and **M. Clarke.** 1990. 'Stereotyping in TESOL materials' in B. Harrison (ed.). *ELT Documents 132: Culture and the Language Classroom.* London: Macmillan.

Cohen, L., L. Manion, and **K. Morrison.** 2007. *Research Methods in Education* (sixth edition). London: Routledge.

Colley, H., D. James, and **K. Diment.** 2007. 'Unbecoming teachers: Towards a more dynamic notion of professional participation.' *Journal of Education Policy* 22/2: 173–93.

Cook, G. 1989. *Discourse.* Oxford: Oxford University Press.

Cook, G. 2000. *Language Play, Language Learning.* Oxford: Oxford University Press.

Cook, G. 2003. *Applied Linguistics.* Oxford: Oxford University Press.

Cooke, M. 2000. 'Wasted opportunities: A case study of two ESOL programmes in a Further Education college in central London.' Unpublished MA dissertation, Institute of Education, University of London.

Cooke, M. and **C. Roberts.** 2007a. *Developing Adult Teaching and Learning: Practitioner Guides – ESOL.* Leicester/London: NIACE/NRDC.

Cooke, M. and **C. Roberts.** 2007b. *Reflection and Action in ESOL Classrooms.* Leicester/London: NIACE/NRDC.

Cooke, M. and **C. Wallace.** 2004 'Inside out/outside in: A study of reading in ESOL classrooms' in C. Roberts, *et al. English for Speakers of Other Languages (ESOL): Case Studies of Provision, Learners' Needs and Resources.* London: NRDC.

Craats, I. van de, J. Kurvers, and **M. Young-Scholten.** 2006. 'Research on low-educated second language and literacy acquisition' in I. van de Craats, J. Kurvers, and M. Young-Scholten (eds.). *Low-Educated Second Language and Literacy Acquisition: Proceedings of the Inaugural Symposium Tilburg 2005.* Utrecht: LOT.

Crystal, D. 2001. *Language and the Internet.* Cambridge: Cambridge University Press.

Cummins, J. 1990. 'When a learner attempts to become literate in another language, what is he or she attempting?' in J. Bell (ed.). *TESL Talk 20.* Toronto: Ministry of Citizenship.

Cummins, J., V. Bismilla, P. Chow, S. Cohen, F. Giampapa, L. Leoni, P. Sandhu, and **P. Sastri.** 2005. 'Affirming identity in multilingual classrooms.' *Educational Leadership* 63/1: 38–43.

Denham, J. 2007. 'Letter to the sector.' Available online at http://www.niace.org.uk/documents/letter-to-the-sector-from-John-Denham-July-2007.doc

Department for Education and Employment. 1999. *A Fresh Start— Improving Literacy and Numeracy* (The Moser report). London: Basic Skills Agency. Available online at http://www.dfes.gov.uk/readwriteplus/Skills_for_Life_policy_documents

Department for Education and Employment. 2000. *Breaking the Language Barriers: The Report of the Working Group on English for Speakers of Other Languages (ESOL).* Available online at http://www.lifelonglearning.dfee.gov.uk/esol/index.htm

Department for Education and Skills. 2001. *Adult ESOL Core Curriculum.* London: Basic Skills Agency/DfES. Available online at http://www.dfes.gov.uk/curriculum_esol/

Department for Education and Skills. 2003. *Skills for Life ESOL Learning Materials*. London: Basic Skills Agency/DfES. Available online at http://www.dfes.gov.uk/readwriteplus/LearningMaterialsESOL

Department for Education and Skills. 2004. *Equipping Our Teachers for the Future: Reforming Initial Teacher Training for the Learning and Skills Sector*. London: DfES.

Department for Education and Skills. 2005. *Further Education: Raising Skills, Improving Life Chances*. London: DfES.

Eggins, S. and **D. Slade.** 1997. *Analysing Casual Conversation*. London: Continuum.

Evans, Y., J. Herbert, K. Datta, J. May, C. McIlwaine, and **J. Wills.** 2005. *Making the City Work: Low Paid Employment in London*. Department of Geography, Queen Mary College, University of London. Available online at http://www.geog.qmul.ac.uk/globalcities

Feez, S. 2002. 'Heritage and innovation in second language education' in A. M. Johns (ed.). *Genre in the Classroom. Multiple Perspectives*. Mahwah, NJ: Lawrence Erlbaum Associates.

Freire, P. 1970. *Pedagogy of the Oppressed*. New York: Seabury Books.

Friesen, C. and **J. Hyndman.** 2004. *A System in Crisis: 2004 Inter-provincial Report Card on Language and Settlement Services in Canada*. Ottawa: Canadian Immigrant Settlement Sector Alliance. Available online at http://www.cissa-acsei.ca/admin/uploaded_documents/Report_Card-_Exec_Summary-Feb_2_version_1.pdf

Goldstein, T. 1996. *Two Languages at Work: Bilingual Life on the Production Floor*. Berlin: Mouton de Gruyter.

Goodwin, C. 1994. 'Professional vision.' *American Anthropologist* 96/3: 606–33.

Gordon, D. 2004. ' "I'm tired. You clean and cook." Shifting gender identities and second language socialization.' *TESOL Quarterly* 38/3: 437–57.

Government of Ireland. 2000. *Learning for Life: White Paper on Adult Education*. Dublin: Stationery Office.

Graddol, D. 1997. *The Future of English?* London: The British Council.

Graddol, D. 2006. *English Next*. London: The British Council. Available online at http://www.britishcouncil.org/learning-research-englishnext.htm

Gray, J. 2002. 'The global coursebook in ELT' in D. Block and D. Cameron (eds.). *Globalization and Language Teaching*. London: Routledge.

Gurnah, A. 2000. 'Languages and literacies for autonomy' in M. Martin-Jones and K. Jones (eds.). *Multilingual Literacies: Reading and Writing Different Worlds*. Amsterdam: John Benjamins.

Halsey, A. H. 1972. 'Political ends and educational means' in A. H. Halsey (ed.). *Education Priority 1*. London: HMSO.

Harmer, J. 2001. *The Practice of English Language Teaching* (third edition). Harlow: Longman.

Harris, R. 1997. 'Romantic bilingualism: Time for a change?' in C. Leung and C. Cable (eds.). *English as an Additional Language: Changing Perspectives*. Watford: NALDIC.

Harris, R. 2006. *New Ethnicities and Language Use*. Basingstoke: Palgrave Macmillan.

Hartley, B. and **P. Viney.** *Streamline English* series. Oxford: Oxford University Press.

Head, K. and **P. Taylor.** 1997. *Readings in Teacher Development*. Oxford: Heinemann ELT.

Heath, S. B. 1983. *Ways with Words: Language, Life and Work in Communities and Classrooms*. Cambridge: Cambridge University Press.

Hedge, T. 2000. *Teaching and Learning in the Language Classroom*. Oxford: Oxford University Press.

Hellermann, J. 2006. 'Classroom interactive practices for developing L2 literacy: A microethnographic study of two beginning adult learners of English.' *Applied Linguistics* 27/3: 377–404.

Herring, S. (ed.). 1996. *Computer Mediated Communication: Linguistic, Social and Cross-cultural Perspectives*. Amsterdam: John Benjamins.

HM Treasury. 2006. *Leitch Review of Skills: Prosperity for all in the Global Economy—World Class Skills*. London: HM Treasury. Available online at http://www.hm-treasury.gov.uk/leitch

Hodge, R. 2004. ' "This is not enough for one's life": Perceptions of living and learning English in Blackburn by students seeking asylum and refugee status' in C. Roberts, *et al. English for Speakers of Other Languages (ESOL): Case Studies of Provision, Learners' Needs and Resources*. London: NRDC.

Hoffman, E. 1989. *Lost in Translation: A life in a New Language*. New York: Dutton.

Holliday, A. 2005. *The Struggle to Teach English as an International Language*. Oxford: Oxford University Press.

Holme, R. 2004. *Literacy: An Introduction*. Edinburgh: Edinburgh University Press.

Howatt, A. P. R. with **H. G. Widdowson.** 2004. *A History of English Language Teaching* (second edition). Oxford: Oxford University Press.

Humphrys, J. 2004. *Lost For Words: The Mangling and Manipulating of the English Language*. London: Hodder and Stoughton.

Hymes, D. 1972. 'On communicative competence' in J. B. Pride and J. Holmes (eds.). *Sociolinguistics*. Harmondsworth: Penguin.

Hymes, D. 1974. *Foundations in Sociolinguistics: An Ethnographic Approach*. Philadelphia, PA: University of Pennsylvania Press.

James, M. 1990. 'Demystifying literacy: Reading, writing, and the struggle for liberation.' *Convergence* 23/1: 14–25.

Jenkins, J. 2000. *The Phonology of English as an International Language*. Oxford: Oxford University Press.

Jenkins, J. 2006. 'Current perspectives on teaching World Englishes and English as a Lingua Franca.' *TESOL Quarterly* 40/1: 157–81.

Julka, N. 2005. 'Characteristics of a Grade 1 lesson.' *Reflect* 4: 18–19.

Kachru, B. 1985. 'Standards, codification and sociolinguistic realism: The English language in the outer circle' in R. Quirk and H. G. Widdowson (eds.). *English in the World*. Cambridge: Cambridge University Press.

Kern, R. 2000. *Literacy and Language Teaching*. Oxford: Oxford University Press.

Kincheloe, J. L. 2003. *Teachers as Researchers: Qualitative Inquiry as a Path to Empowerment* (second edition). London: RoutledgeFalmer.

Kouritzin, S. 2000. 'Immigrant mothers redefine access to ESL classes: Contradiction and ambivalence.' *Journal of Multilingual and Multicultural Development* 21/1: 14–32.

Kramsch, C. 1998. *Language and Culture*. Oxford: Oxford University Press.

Krashen, S. 1985. *The Input Hypothesis: Issues and Implications*. London: Longman.

Kress, G. 2003. *Literacy in the New Media Age*. London: Routledge.

Kress, G. and **T. van Leeuwen.** 2001. *Multimodal Discourse: The Modes and Media of Contemporary Communication*. London: Edward Arnold.

Kress, G. and **T. van Leeuwen.** 2006. *Reading Images: The Grammar of Visual Design* (second edition). London: Routledge.

Kumaravadivelu, B. 1994. 'The postmethod condition: (E)merging strategies for second/foreign language teaching.' *TESOL Quarterly* 28/1: 27–48.

Kumaravadivelu, B. 2002. *Beyond Methods: Macrostrategies for Language Teaching.* New Haven: Yale University Press.

Kyambi, S. 2005. *Beyond Black and White: Mapping New Immigrant Communities.* London: Institute of Public Policy Research.

Labov, W. 1972. *Language in the Inner City.* Oxford: Blackwell.

Lam, W. S. E. 2000. 'L2 literacy and the design of the self: A case study of a teenager writing on the internet.' *TESOL Quarterly* 34/3: 457–82.

Lantolf, J. P. (ed.). 2000. *Sociocultural Theory and Second Language Learning.* Oxford: Oxford University Press.

Lawes, S. 2003. 'What, when, how and why? Theory and foreign language teaching.' *Language Learning Journal* 28: 22–28.

Lazaraton, A. 2002. *A Qualitative Approach to the Validation of Oral Language Tests. Studies in Language Testing 14.* Cambridge: University of Cambridge Local Examinations Syndicate/Cambridge University Press.

Levy, M. and **G. Stockwell.** 2006. *CALL Dimensions: Options and Issues in Computer-Assisted Language Learning.* London: Routledge.

Lightbown, P. M. 2000. 'Classroom SLA research and second language teaching.' *Applied Linguistics* 21/4: 431–62.

Lightbown, P. M. and **N. Spada.** 2006. *How Languages are Learned* (third edition). Oxford: Oxford University Press.

Lin, A. M. Y. and **P. W. Martin.** (eds.). 2005. *Decolonisation, Globalisation: Language-in-Education Policy and Practice.* Clevedon: Multilingual Matters.

Lumley, T. and **Brown, A.** 2005. 'Research methods in language testing' in E. Hinkel (ed.). *Handbook of Research in Second Language Teaching and Learning.* Mahwah, NJ: Lawrence Erlbaum Associates.

Mac Éinrí, P. 2001. 'Immigration into Ireland: Trends, Policy Responses, Outlook.' Irish Centre for Migration Studies, National University of Ireland, Cork. Available online at http://migration.ucc.ie/irelandfirstreport.htm

Malderez, A. 2003. 'Key concepts in ELT: Observation.' *ELT Journal* 57/2: 179–81.

Malderez, A. and **M. Wedell.** 2007. *Teaching Teachers: Processes and Practices.* London: Continuum.

Maslow, A. H. 1943. 'A theory of human motivation.' *Psychological Review* 50: 370–96.

Mason, J. 2002. *Researching Your Own Practice: The Discipline of Noticing.* London: RoutledgeFalmer.

Mayer, R. E. 2000. 'The promise of multimedia learning: Using the same instructional design methods across different media.' *Learning and Instruction* 13/2: 125–39.

Mayer, R. E. (ed.). 2005. *The Cambridge Handbook of Multimedia Learning.* Cambridge: Cambridge University Press.

McNamara, T. and **C. Roever.** 2006. *Language Testing: The Social Dimension.* Oxford: Blackwell.

Merriman, N. (ed.). 1993. *The Peopling of London: Fifteen Thousand Years of Settlement from Overseas.* London: The Museum of London.

Moder, C. L. and **G. B. Halleck.** 1998. 'Framing the language proficiency interview as a speech event: Native and non-native speakers' questions' in R. Young and A. W. He (eds.) *Talking and Testing: Discourse Approaches to the Assessment of Oral Proficiency. Studies in Bilingualism 14.* Amsterdam: John Benjamins.

Morgan, B. and **V. Ramanathan.** 2005. 'Critical literacies and language education: Global and local perspectives.' *Annual Review of Applied Linguistics* 25: 151–69.

National Adult Literacy Agency. 2005. *Mapping the Learning Journey User Guide.* Dublin: NALA. Available online at http://www.nala.ie/download/pdf/mlj_user_guide_section_1.pdf

National Adult Literacy Agency ESOL Executive Working Group. 2002. *Supports and Guidelines for Practitioners in the Literacy Service Working with ESOL Learners.* Available online at http://www.nala.ie/publications/listing/20030624160824.html

National Center for ESL Literacy Education. 2003. *Adult English Language Instruction in the 21st Century.* Washington, DC: Center for Applied Linguistics.

New Zealand Ministry of Education. 2003. *Adult ESOL Strategy.* Available online at http://www.minedu.govt.nz/web/downloadable/dl7577_v1/adult-esol.pdf

Norton, B. 2000. *Identity and Language Learning: Gender, Ethnicity and Educational Change.* Harlow: Longman.

Norton, B. 2006. 'Not an afterthought: Authoring a text on adult ESOL.' *Linguistics and Education* 17/1: 91–6.

Norton, B. and **G. Stewart.** 1999. 'Accountability in language assessment of adult immigrants.' *Canadian Modern Language Review* 56/2: 223–44.

Norton Peirce, B. and **G. Stewart.** 1997. 'The development of the Canadian Language Benchmarks Assessment.' *TESL Canada Journal* 14/2: 17–31.

O'Neill, R. 1972. *Kernel Lessons Plus.* London: Eurocentres.

Olson, D. 1994. *The World on Paper: The Conceptual and Cognitive Implications of Writing and Reading.* Cambridge: Cambridge University Press.

Ong, W. 1982. *Orality and Literacy: The Technologizing of the Word.* London: Routledge.

Pahl, K. and **J. Rowsell.** 2005. *Literacy and Education: Understanding the New Literacy Studies in the Classroom.* London: Paul Chapman Publishing.

Papen, U. 2005. *Adult Literacy as Social Practice: More than Skills.* London: Routledge.

Pawlikowska-Smith, G. 2000. *Canadian Language Benchmarks 2000 English as a Second Language for Adults.* Ottawa: Centre for Canadian Language Benchmarks. Available online at http://www.language.ca/pdfs/clb_adults.pdf

Pawlikowska-Smith, G. 2002. *Canadian Language Benchmarks 2000: Theoretical Framework.* Ottawa: Centre for Canadian Language Benchmarks. Available online at http://www.language.ca/display_page.asp?page_id=257

Pennycook, A. 1994. *The Cultural Politics of English as an International Language.* Harlow: Longman.

Phillipson, R. 1992. *Linguistic Imperialism.* Oxford: Oxford University Press.

Pitt, K. 2004. *Debates in ESOL.* London: Routledge.

Pollard, A. 2005. *Reflective Teaching* (second edition). London: Continuum.

Rampton, B. 1990. 'Displacing the "native speaker": Expertise, affiliation and inheritance.' *ELT Journal* 44/2: 97–101.

Rassool, N. 1999. *Literacy for Sustainable Development in the Age of Information.* Clevedon: Multilingual Matters.

Richards, J. C. and **D. Nunan.** 1990. *Second Language Teacher Education.* Cambridge: Cambridge University Press.

Richards, J. C. and **T. S. Rodgers.** 2001. *Approaches and Methods in Language Teaching* (second edition). Cambridge: Cambridge University Press.

Roberts, C. 2001. 'Language acquisition or language socialisation in and through discourse? Towards a redefinition of the domain of SLA' in C. N. Candlin and N. Mercer (eds.). *English Language Teaching in its Social Context.* London: Routledge.

Roberts, C. 2007a. *Successful at Selection: Fair Interviewing in a Diverse Society* (DVD). London: Department for Work and Pensions.

Roberts, C. 2007b. *F.A.Q.s Frequently Asked Questions and Quickly Found Answers* (DVD). London: Department for Work and Pensions.

Roberts, C. and **M. Baynham.** 2006. 'Where talk is work: The social contexts of adult ESOL classrooms.' *Linguistics and Education* 17/1 (special issue).

Roberts, C., M. Baynham, P. Shrubshall, D. Barton, P. Chopra, M. Cooke, R. Hodge, K. Pitt, P. Schellekens, C. Wallace, and **S. Whitfield.** 2004. *English for Speakers of Other Languages (ESOL): Case Studies of Provision, Learners' Needs and Resources.* London: NRDC.

Roberts, C. and **S. Campbell.** 2006. *Talk on Trial: Job Interviews, Language and Ethnicity.* London: Department for Work and Pensions.

Roberts, C., E. Davies, and **T. Jupp.** 1992. *Language and Discrimination: A Study of Communication in Multi-ethnic Workplaces.* London: Longman.

Rockhill, K. 1987. 'Gender, language and the politics of literacy.' *British Journal of Sociology of Education* 8/2: 153–67.

Rosenberg, S. 2007. *A Critical History of ESOL for Adults Resident in the UK 1870–2005.* Leicester: NIACE.

Ross, S. 1998. 'Divergent frame interpretations in language proficiency interview interaction' in R. Young and A. W. He (eds.) *Talking and Testing: Discourse Approaches to the Assessment of Oral Proficiency. Studies in Bilingualism 14.* Amsterdam: John Benjamins.

Saxena, M. 1994. 'Literacies among Panjabis in Southall' in M. Hamilton, D. Barton, and R. Ivanič (eds.). *Worlds of Literacy.* Clevedon: Multilingual Matters.

Schellekens, P. 2007. *The Oxford ESOL Handbook.* Oxford: Oxford University Press.

Scollon, R. 1998. *Mediated Discourse as Social Interaction: A Study of News Discourse.* London: Longman.

Scottish Executive. 2007. *The Adult ESOL Strategy for Scotland.* Available online at http://www.scotland.gov.uk/Publications/2007/05/09155324/0

Seedhouse, P. 2005. *The Interactional Architecture of the Language Classroom: A Conversation Analysis Perspective.* Oxford: Blackwell.

Seidlhofer, B. 2002. '*Habeas corpus* and *divide et impera*: "Global English" and applied linguistics' in K. Spelman Miller and P. Thompson (eds.). *Unity and Diversity in Language Use. British Studies in Applied Linguistics 17*. London: BAAL and Continuum.

Simpson, J. 2006. 'Differing expectations in the assessment of the speaking skills of ESOL learners.' *Linguistics and Education* 17/1: 40–55.

Simpson, J., M. Cooke and **M. Baynham.** 2008. *The Right Course? An Exploratory Study of Learner Placement Practices in ESOL and Literacy*. London: NRDC.

Skehan, P. 1989. *Individual Differences in Language Learning*. London: Edward Arnold.

Snyder, I. (ed.). 2002. *Silicon Literacies: Communication, Innovation and Education in the Electronic Age*. London: Routledge.

Soars, J. and **L. Soars** *New Headway English Course*. Oxford: Oxford University Press.

Spiegel, M. and **H. Sunderland.** 2006. *Teaching Basic Literacy to ESOL Learners*. London: LLU+.

Street, B. 1984. *Literacy in Theory and Practice*. Cambridge: Cambridge University Press.

Street, B. (ed.). 1993. *Cross-cultural Approaches to Literacy*. Cambridge: Cambridge University Press.

Sunderland, J (ed.). 1994. *Exploring Gender: Questions and Implications for Language Education*. Hemel Hempstead: Prentice Hall.

Swain, M. 1995. 'Three functions of output in second language learning' in G. Cook and B. Seidlhofer (eds.). *Principle and Practice in Applied Linguistics*. Oxford: Oxford University Press.

Swain, M. 2000. 'The output hypothesis and beyond: Mediating acquisition through collaborative dialogue' in J.P. Lantolf (ed.). *Sociocultural Theory and Second Language Learning*. Oxford: Oxford University Press.

Swain, M. 2005. 'The output hypothesis: Theory and research' in E. Hinkel (ed.). *Handbook of Research in Second Language Teaching and Learning*. Mahwah, NJ: Lawrence Erlbaum Associates.

Tarone, E. and **M. Bigelow.** 2005. 'Impact of literacy on oral language processing: Implications for second language acquisition research.' *Annual Review of Applied Linguistics* 25: 77–97.

Taylor, C. 2007. *ESOL and Citizenship: A Teacher's Guide*. Leicester: NIACE.

Teachers of English to Speakers of Other Languages (TESOL). 2000. *Adult ESL Language and Literacy Instruction: A Vision and Action Agenda for the 21st Century.* Available online at http://www.cal.org.ncle/vision

Thornbury, S. and **D. Slade.** 2006. *Conversation: From Description to Pedagogy.* Cambridge: Cambridge University Press.

Tollefson, J. W. 1986. 'Functional competencies in the US Refugee Program: Theoretical and practical problems.' *TESOL Quarterly* 20/4: 649–64.

Truss, L. 2003. *Eats, Shoots and Leaves: The Zero Tolerance Approach to Punctuation.* London: Profile Books.

Tsui, A. B. M. 1995. *Introducing Classroom Interaction.* London: Penguin.

Tsui, A. B. M. 2003. *Understanding Expertise in Teaching: Case Studies of ESL Teachers.* Cambridge: Cambridge University Press.

van Lier, L. 1989. 'Reeling, writhing, drawling, stretching, and fainting in coils: Oral proficiency interviews as conversation.' *TESOL Quarterly* 23/3: 489–508.

Vertovec, S. 2006. *The Emergence of Super-diversity in Britain.* Oxford: University of Oxford Centre on Migration, Policy, and Society. Working Paper No. 25.

Vygotsky, L. S. 1978. *Mind in Society: Development of Higher Psychological Processes.* Cambridge, MA: Harvard University Press.

Wajnryb, R. 1992. *Classroom Observation Tasks: A Resource Book for Language Teachers and Trainers.* Cambridge: Cambridge University Press.

Wallace, C. 1989. 'Participatory approaches to literacy with bilingual adults.' *Language Issues* 3/1: 6–12.

Wallace, C. 1992. *Reading.* Oxford: Oxford University Press.

Wallace, C. 2003. *Critical Reading in Language Education.* Basingstoke: Palgrave.

Wallace, C. 2006. 'The text dead or alive: Expanding textual repertoires in the adult ESOL classroom.' *Linguistics and Education* 17/1: 74–90.

Walsh, S. 2006. *Investigating Classroom Discourse.* London and New York: Routledge.

Walter, C. and **Swan, M.** 1984–87. *The New Cambridge English Course.* Cambridge: Cambridge University Press.

Ward, J. 2007. *ESOL: The Context for the UK Today.* Leicester: NIACE.

Warschauer, M. 2001. 'The death of cyberspace and the rebirth of CALL' in P. Brett (ed.). *CALL in the 21st Century* (CD-ROM). Whitstable: IATEFL.

Warschauer, M. 2003. *Technology and Social Inclusion: Rethinking the Digital Divide.* Cambridge, MA: The MIT Press.

Warschauer, M. and **R. Kern.** (eds.). 2000. *Network-Based Language Teaching: Concepts and Practice.* Cambridge: Cambridge University Press.

Wei, L. 2000. 'Extending schools: Bilingual development of Chinese children in Britain' in M. Datta (ed.). *Bilinguality and Literacy: Principles and Practice.* London: Continuum.

White, G. 1998. *Listening.* Oxford: Oxford University Press.

Winder, R. 2004. *Bloody Foreigners: The Story of Immigration to Britain.* London: Abacus.

Wrigley, H. S. 2003. *The Reading Demonstration* (video). Available online at http://www.literacywork.com/readingdemonstration

Zetter, R., D. Griffiths, N. Sigona, D. Flynn, T. Pasha, and **R. Beynon.** 2006. *Immigration, Social Cohesion and Social Capital: What are the Links?* York: Joseph Rowntree Trust.

Zeuli, J. S. and **L. J. Tiezzi.** 1993. *Creating Contexts to Change Teachers' Beliefs about the Influence of Research.* Report 93 National Center for Research on Teaching and Learning. Available online at http://www.ncrtl. msu.edu/http/rreports/html/pdf/rr931.pdf

Zuengler, J. and **K. Cole.** 2005. 'Language socialisation and second language learning' in E. Hinkel (ed.). *Handbook of Research in Second Language Teaching and Learning.* Mahwah, NJ: Lawrence Erlbaum Associates.

INDEX

Action Aid 111, 113
action research 147–52, 153–4
  features 148
  stages 149
  'Turning Talk into Learning' project 149–51
Adamson, B. 46
Adult Migrant English Program (AMEP)
  155–7
agency 74–5, 76
Apollinaire, G. 116, 117
asylum 17, 20–1, 27, 93, 107; *see also* policy
  and politics
audit culture 38–9
Auerbach, E. R. 51, 64, 97, 111, 113, 114
Australia 155–7, 163

Barton, D. 113
Baynham, M. 33, 75, 103, 135, 149
Beaglehole, A. 161, 162
Bell, D. M. 44
Bell, J. 154
Bell, J. S. 95
Bigelow, M. 95
bilingualism 15, 18, 19, 96–7
Blair, Tony 8
Bloch, A. 27
Block, D. 12, 143
Borg, S. 46
Bourdieu, P. 22
Breaking the Language Barriers 161
Bremer, K. *et al.* 69, 90
Brown, A. 83
Brown, G. 87
Brown, Gordon 9
Burgess, D. 51, 64
Burns, A. 147, 148, 152, 153, 155, 156
Byram, M. 65

CALL *see* computer-assisted language
  learning
Callaghan, J. 7
Cameron, D. 12, 111
Campbell, H. *et al.* 100
Campbell, S. 22, 79–81, 89, 90
Canada 157–9

Canadian Language Benchmarks (CLB)
  168–9
Canagarajah, A. S. 45, 46
Canale, M. 47
Carrier, K. 69
chat rooms 126
childcare 17–18
Chomsky, N. 42
citizenship 4, 9–11, 50, 157, 162
Citizenship and Immigration Canada
  (CIC) 157
classroom ecology 36–7
CLB (Canadian Language Benchmarks)
  168–9
CLT *see* Communicative Language
  Teaching
CMC (computer-mediated
  communication) 122–4
Cohen, L. *et al.* 154
collaborative learning 35, 36, 47
Colley, H. *et al.* 39
communicative competence 42, 47, 131
Communicative Language Teaching (CLT)
  42–3, 144, 145
communicative stress 87
community-based classes 25–6
computer-assisted language learning
  (CALL) 129, 132
computer-mediated communication
  (CMC) 122–4
constative speech 43
conversations 83
Cook, G. 47, 53, 63, 64, 149
Cooke, M. 53, 61, 77, 149–52
coursebooks *see* materials
Craats, I. *et al.* 100
critical literacy 110–12, 113–14
Crystal, D. 132
cultural capital 22
Cummins, J. *et al.* 96–7, 158
curriculum 54–7, 111, 113–14

Denham, J. 105
Dewey, J. 147
digital divide 127–8, 132

education 17, 18, 72, 93–4
EFL (English as a Foreign Language) 51
Eggins, S. 83
electronic literacy practices 115–32
    and communicative competence 131
    computer-mediated communication
        (CMC) 122–4
    ICTs and globalization 124–7
    inequality and the information poor
        127–31, 132
    reading online 116–21, 126, 132
ELF *see* English as a Lingua Franca
ELT *see* English Language Teaching
email 122–4
employment
    interviews 22, 79–82
    and literacy 92–3, 105–10
    motives and desires 22–3, 68–9
    and oral communication 68–9, 71, 82
    rights 55
England, Wales, and N. Ireland 5–12
    citizenship and language 9–11
    curriculum and materials 54–7
    ESOL and the economy 11
    ESOL as a 'Skill for Life' 6–8
    evolution of ESOL 5–6
    immigration 5
    literacy education 97
    London 2, 15, 162
    northern England 2, 8–9, 15
    policy and politics 8–10, 49–50, 105, 134,
        145–7, 162
    teaching qualifications 134
English as a Foreign Language (EFL) 51
English as a global language 3, 124–7
English as a Lingua Franca (ELF) 3, 55, 123
English as a Second Language (ESL) 5, 50–1
English for Specific Purposes (ESP) 106
English Language Teaching (ELT) xi, 3, 12, 50
ESOL (English for Speakers of Other
    Languages) xi, 4
Evans, Y. *et al.* 22
expert languages: use of 96–8, 144–5

family relations 18–20
Feez, S. 157
Freire, P. 37, 110, 111, 113, 114
Fresh Start, A 7, 104
Friesen, C. 157–8

gender 17–18, 27, 51, 71–2, 93–4
globalization 2, 12, 124–7
Goodwin, C. 135
Gordon, D. 27

Graddol, D. 3, 12, 124, 127
Gray, J. 52, 64
group learning
    affective benefits 36–8
    communicative approach 43
    group dynamics 35–6, 38
Gumperz, J. 89
Gurnah, A. 97

Halleck, G. B. 84
Halliday, M. A. K. 155
Halsey, A. H. 12
Harmer, J. 47
Hartley, B. 51
Head, K. 142, 153
Heath, S. B. 102
Hedge, T. 47
Hellermann, J. 103
Herring, S. 122
HM Treasury 105
Hodge, Margaret 9
Hodge, R. 27, 37
Hoffman, E. 70
Holliday, A. 3, 43
Holme, R. 104
Howatt, A. P. R. 47
Humphrys, J. 99
Hymes, D. 42, 87
Hyndman, J. 157–8

identity 70, 125–6
Individual Learning Plans (ILP) 33, 145–6,
    163
Industrial Language Training Unit 106
initial teacher training 133, 136, 147–8
input 67, 76
inspections 137, 138–40
Integrate Ireland Language and Training
    (IILT) 160
interactional sociolinguistics 67, 69, 76–7,
    80–1, 89–90
interactional space 76
interviews 22, 79–82, 84–5, 89
Ireland, Republic of 159–60

James, M. 111
Julka, N. 138–9

Kachru, B. 3
Kern, R. 112, 114, 132
Kincheloe, J. L. 148
Kouritzin, S. 27
Kramsch, C. 65
Krashen, S. 67

Kress, G. 116, 132
Kumaravadivelu, B. 44–5
Kyambi, S. 27

Labov, W. 77
Lam, W. S. E. 126
language and culture 65, 87–8
language play 53, 61–3, 64
language teaching 41–6
  principled pragmatism 44–5
  systemic forces 46
  teaching methods 41–5, 47–8
  see also practice challenges
language transfer 95, 112
Lantolf, J. P. 47
Lawes, S. 148, 152
Lazaraton, A. 90
learner autonomy 128–9
learning styles 121
lesson content 49–65
  curriculum 54–7, 111, 113–14
  language and culture 65
  materials 50–7
  playfulness 53, 61–3, 64
  principled pragmatism 63–4
  student-generated content 57–60, 64,
    74–6
  'survival English' 51, 55, 64
  taboo subjects 60–1
  tensions 49–50
Levy, M. 132
Lightbown, P. 143, 144, 146
Lin, A. M. Y. 12
LINC (Language Instruction for
  Newcomers to Canada) 157–8
linguistic imperialism 3, 51
listening 69, 90
literacy 91–114
  assessing literacy 114
  basic needs 92–8
  as basic skill 91, 98–100, 105, 112
  critical literacy 110–12, 113–14
  dependency 93
  and educational background 17, 18, 72,
    93–4
  and employability 92–3, 105–10
  expert language or English literacy? 96–8
  functional literacy 104–10
  and gender 18, 72, 93–4
  language transfer 95, 112
  phonics 100
  practices 91, 100–3, 110, 112–13
  punctuation 99
  sociocognitive view 112–13

spelling 99–100
student diversity 17, 18, 32
teaching basic literacy 94–6, 114
writing systems 95
see also electronic literacy practices
Lumley, T. 83

Mac Éinrí, Piaras 159
McNamara, T. 90
Malderez, A. 136, 140, 141, 153, 154
Martin, P. W. 12
Maslow, A. H. 36
Mason, J. 153, 154
materials 50–7
  CALL materials 129
  EFL coursebooks 51
  ELT coursebooks 50, 51–2
  ESOL materials 54–7
  'global' coursebooks 53–4
  ideology 51–2, 64
  inappropriacy 52–3
  inclusivity 52
Mayer, R. E. 121, 132
migrants and migration 2, 3–4, 5, 17–18,
  20, 27; *see also* policy and politics
Moder, C. L. 84
Morgan, B. 110
Morgan, C. 65
MSN Messenger 123, 126
multilingualism 15, 18, 123
multimodality 116–18, 120–1, 132

narrative structure 77
National Center for ESL Literacy
  Education 165
Nationality, Immigration, and Asylum Act
  (2000) 9
'native speakers' 126–7
New Literacy Studies 101
New Zealand 160–2
Northern Ireland *see* England, Wales, and
  N. Ireland
Norton, B. 4, 21–2, 27
noticing 140, 141–2
Nunan, D. 153, 154

O'Grady, F. 109
O'Neill 51
observation of teaching 135–42, 153
  for development 136, 140–2, 154
  for evaluation 136, 137–40
  inspections 137, 138–40
  peer observation 140–2
  purposes 135–7

for research 136–7
teacher behaviour   137–8
Olson, D. 104, 106, 132
Ong, W. 132
oral communication 67–73, 89
   and identity 70
   listening 69, 90
   in literacy practices 102–3
   miscommunication 89
   outside class 68–73
   and power relations 69–70, 73, 84, 87,
      89, 126–7
   and social cohesion 70, 72, 89
   see also speaking in ESOL classrooms;
      testing oral communication
output hypothesis 67, 76, 138

Pahl, K. 103, 114
Paltalk 126
Papen, U. 113
Pawlikowska-Smith, G. 159
peer observation 140–2
Pennycook, A. 3, 12, 42–3
personalized learning 33
Phillipson, R. 3, 12, 51
Pitt, K. 144
policy and politics
   Australia 155–7, 163
   Canada 157–9
   England, Wales, and N. Ireland 8–10,
      49–50, 105, 134, 145–7, 162
   literacy 104–6
   New Zealand 160–2
   Republic of Ireland 159–60
   Scotland 162–4
   teacher education and development 46,
      134, 153
   United States 164–5
Pollard, A. 153, 154
post-method condition 44
power relations 69–70, 73, 84, 87, 89, 126–7
practice challenges 29–30
   audit culture 38–9
   group learning 35–8
   professional identity 39–41
   student diversity and needs 32–3
   students' changing needs and attitudes
      33–5
principled pragmatism 44–5, 63–4
private sector 11
professionalism 39–41, 46, 134–5, 152–3

Ramanathan, V. 110

Rampton, B. 16
Rassool, N. 131
reading online 116–21
   multimodality 116–18, 120–1, 132
   multitasking and polyfocal attention
      119–21, 126
   web literacy 118–19
   see also literacy
Reflect for ESOL 111, 113, 114
reflective practice 134–5, 147–8, 153–4
refugees 2, 17, 20, 91, 93, 107; *see also* policy
   and politics
research 142–52, 153–4
   action research 147–52, 153–4
   as 'common sense' 144–7
   observation of teaching 136–7
   and practice: mutual dialogue 143–4
   theory/practice 'gap' 142–3
Richards, J. C. 48, 153, 154
rights 3–4, 55, 73, 106
Roberts, C. 22, 33, 69, 77, 80–1, 89, 90,
   103, 106, 135, 149–52
Rockhill, B. 72
Rockhill, K. 27, 94
Rodgers, T. S. 48
Roever, C. 90
Rosenberg, S. 5
Ross, S. 87
Rowsell, J. 103, 114

Saxena, M. 101
Schellekens, P. 48
Schuster, L. 27
Scollon, R. 119
Scotland 162–4
second language acquisition (SLA) 67–8,
   76; *see also* research
second language socialization 67
Seedhouse, P. 89
settings for ESOL 24–6, 30
shyness 73
Simpson, J. 82
Skills for Life 6–8, 79–80
SLA *see* second language acquisition
Slade, D. 83, 89
SMART targets 145–6
Snyder, I. 131
Soars, J. 52
Soars, L. 52
social cohesion 8–9, 20, 50, 55, 70, 72, 89
Spada, N. 144, 146
speaking in ESOL classrooms 73–82
   agency 74–5, 76

classroom interaction 89
contingency 75
encouraging learners to talk 76–8
and literacy practices 103
opening up and closing down 74–6
real-world challenges 78–82, 89–90
see also oral communication; 'Turning
  Talk into Learning' project
Spiegel, M. 94–5, 98, 114
Stockwell, G. 132
Street, B. 99, 102, 113
students 13–23
  agency 74–5, 76
  aspirations and obstacles 21–3
  asylum seekers 17, 20–1, 27, 93, 107
  diversity 2, 13–21, 26, 32–3, 35–6
  education 17, 18, 72, 93–4
  family relations 18–20
  gender 17–18, 27, 51, 71–2, 93–4
  and group learning 35–6
  immigration status 20
  languages 15–16, 16*f*
  literacy 17, 18, 32
  migrant experience 20, 27
  needs and attitudes 33–5
Sunderland, H. 94–5, 98, 114
'survival English' 51, 55, 64
Swain, M. 47, 67
Swan, M. 51

taboo subjects 60–1
Tarone, E. 95
task-based language teaching (TBLT) 42, 43
Taylor, P. 142, 153
teacher education and development 133–54
  initial teacher training 133, 136, 147–8
  observation of teaching 135–42, 153
  policy 46, 134, 153
  professional vision 39–41, 46, 134–5, 152–3
  reflective practice 134–5, 147–8, 153–4
  research 142–52, 153–4
  teaching qualifications 134
teachers
  administration and bureaucracy 38–9
  backgrounds 30–2
  contingency 75
  professional identity 39–41, 46
  roles 29
  see also practice challenges
Teachers of English to Speakers of Other
  Languages (TESOL) 165
teaching methods 41–5, 47–8
testing oral communication 82–8, 90

communicative stress 87
constructs 83
conversations 83
failure to perform 87
interviews 84–5
power relations 84, 87
test-taking training 88
under-elaboration 85–7
Thornbury, S. 89
Tiezzi, L. J. 147
Tollefson, J. 51
Truss, L. 99
Tsui, A. B. M. 46, 89
'Turning Talk into Learning' project 149–51

United States 9, 94, 97, 102, 164–5

Van Leeuwen, T. 116, 132
Van Lier, L. 83
Vertovec, S. 2, 20, 27
Viney, P. 51
Vygotsky, L. S. 36–7, 47

Wajnryb, R. 140, 141, 153
Wales *see* England, Wales, and N. Ireland
Wallace, C. 43, 53, 61, 76
Wallerstein, N. 111, 113, 114
Walsh, S. 89
Walter, C. 51
Warschauer, M. 120, 124–5, 128, 132
web literacy 118–19
Wedell, M. 140, 141, 153, 154
Wei, L. 19
White, G. 90
Widdowson, H. G. 48
Wrigley, H. S. 114
writing *see* literacy

Yule, G. 87

Zetter, R. *et al.* 27
Zeuli, J. S. 147
zone of proximal development (ZPD)
  35–6, 67